DIRTY COMBAT

DIRTY COMBAT

SECRET WARS AND SERIOUS MISADVENTURES

DAVID TOMKINS

MAINSTREAM
PUBLISHING

EDINBURGH AND LONDON

First published in Great Britain in 2008 by
MAINSTREAM PUBLISHING COMPANY
(EDINBURGH) LTD
7 Albany Street
Edinburgh EH1 3UG

ISBN 9781845963897

A catalogue record for this book is available
from the British Library

Typeset in Caslon and Gill Sans

Printed and bound in the UK by
CPI Mackays, Chatham ME5 8TD

CONTENTS

ACKNOWLEDGEMENTS

IN THE WRITING OF THIS BOOK, I OWE MUCH TO MY WIFE, Mary, for her patience, advice and encouragement, to my daughters, Jay and Kelly, and to my son, Billy, for all his efforts in filling the gap during my enforced absence. Special thanks to Roger and Claire Peach and Mike Douglas for showing what great friends are all about. Thanks to Mike for letting me close the circle in Iraq. To Vanessa, Dan Showalter, Frank Garrison, Lev, Steve Osborne, Meli and Soni and all the crew down there, you can be assured you are not forgotten. Thanks to the people named (and the many not named) in this book who played their parts in making the tapestry of my life a colourful one. To all those in harm's way, stay safe.

David Tomkins
July 2008

CHAPTER I

IN THE BEGINNING

I WAS BORN ON 31 JULY 1940 IN ST GEORGE'S HOSPITAL IN Victoria, London. My parents lived in a basement flat nearby. As Nazi bombs rained down, my mother hid with me in a coal bunker while my father, an air-raid warden, retrieved corpses from collapsed buildings. My mother, Alice, was as hard as stone, an old-fashioned cockney from East Ham who worked in kitchens throughout her life. She met my father, Jimmy Tomkins, who was Irish, when she was a cook at Bullock's Café in Wilton Road. I cannot remember any affection from her towards him or me and when she shouted my name I heard her from a quarter of a mile away. I made excuses for her because we lived in such a grotty place and because my father was an alcoholic who would pawn the bed-sheets to buy a drink. To my mother's dismay, he introduced me to the pub and the greyhound track. She neither drank nor smoked and their constant fighting left me traumatised. As a child, I watched her put a pillow in the oven, put her head on it and turn the gas on.

The first time I ran away, a stranger took me to Rochester Row police station. The officers bent down to ask my name and where I lived. As would become my custom, I refused to assist them with their inquiries. When they locked me in a cell, I threw the tea and biscuits they offered me against the wall. I was just seven years old. I suffered from terrible nightmares and my parents put wire mesh up over my bedroom window to prevent me smashing my way out. This must have alarmed our neighbours, as the National Society for the Prevention of Cruelty to Children knocked on the door. I was taken to the children's ward at Maudsley psychiatric hospital. I was there for 18 months, during which time I made many escape attempts and staged several rooftop protests, climbing the drainpipes and waiting until the fire brigade were called to bring me down. After a while, I was made to sleep in a converted bed like a cage in an attempt to stop me absconding.

While I was in the hospital, my parents separated and, on my release, I went to live with my mother, younger sister and new stepfather in Croydon. When I was ten, we moved to Romford, an Essex market town bursting at the seams with refugees from the inner city. At lunchtime on my first day at Straight Road Junior School, the other boys flicked their peas at me, using their spoons as catapults. I threw tables and chairs back at them. My mother was summoned to a crisis meeting, where she was told that my expulsion had been ruled out solely on the grounds that I had been a pupil for only four hours. As an alternative punishment, I was beaten by the head teacher. It was a very public thrashing, watched by the whole school at morning assembly. My eyes watered and my skin reddened but I refused to cry. It was worth it. I had piss-marked my territory and after that everybody gave me a wide berth.

At weekends, I ran over the fields surrounding my home to scrump apples and pinch eggs from chicken sheds and played the trumpet with the British Legion Boys Band. I always seemed to finish my assignments before my classmates but idle hands were the Devil's tools and I tended to get into trouble. When I was 13, I was expelled from my first secondary school for hitting the headmaster when he caned me excessively hard. My family moved to Camberley, a town in Surrey near the Royal Military Academy Sandhurst. I was still being monitored by the NSPCC and social services, and when we moved to Camberley, I received a visit from a probation officer, who had been appointed to oversee my behaviour. He laid down the law as to how my life was going to be under his supervision and gave me a clip round the ear, which really rankled with me.

The kids I hung out with were all into hunting and we spent a lot of time in the woods and fields. Restrictions on the ownership of firearms were less strict in those days and I was able to buy a shotgun licence from the post office for ten shillings. I made the money back selling squirrel and fox tails to the council's pest control department. I'd cycle through the woods and along the riverbanks on my 'dirt-tracker' – a bike rescued from a refuse tip. I straightened its forks and bent the handlebars into the shape of a cow's horns.

I left school shortly before my 15th birthday, with the headmaster's endorsement ringing in my ears: 'You have caused more trouble than any boy I have ever known.' My first job was as a paint sprayer. I spent my wages on motorcycle parts and chasing girls, in which department the young US military personnel at Blackbushe airfield provided stiff competition. In this era of early rock 'n' roll, the Yanks cut a dash on their Harley-Davidsons, and cheap booze from the base PX ensured plenty of parties, which most of the local girls would go to. If I wasn't fighting a Yank, I was fighting a British squaddie and I would often return home in the early hours to find my mother had locked me out of the house. I'd sleep on the flat roof beneath the bathroom window and if I was lucky, I'd wake to find a cup of tea beside me, which my mother had leant over the windowsill to put there. She would lie awake all night worrying if I was cold outside but she was too hardnosed to open the door.

Before long, my wild behaviour came to the attention of the police and I had another visit from the probation officer. I told him, 'You're welcome to clip me around the ear again if you like, but you won't get out of this house alive.' Then I took a large carving knife and invited him to watch as I went outside and stabbed all his car tyres. He instituted proceedings against me and I was brought before a local youth court. I was officially deemed 'beyond parental control' and joined 100 other disruptive youths at a reform school near Redhill. It was set in the countryside and, as half-empty freight wagons rumbled along the adjacent railway track, I mucked out the school pigsty. I thought of these trains as an alternative method of escape should my appeal against sentence be dismissed. In advance of my hearing, I was evaluated by psychiatrists and psychologists, who concluded I was disturbed. But, as I had no criminal record, the court looked favourably upon me. The judge accepted my uncle Fred's offer to have me come to live with him in Brighton. I found work as a driver's mate, delivering Canada Dry mixers to pubs and clubs along the south coast and moved to my grandmother's house in the centre of town, which was more convenient for work. I grew accustomed to my own company and spent my free time beachcombing or, when I could afford it, going to the cinema.

My father visited me only once while I was in Brighton and I couldn't help but question his motives. He insisted we attend a greyhound race meeting at Hove and he seemed more interested in the dogs than in me. On the walk back to my grandmother's that cold evening, we passed a group of homeless men lurking in a shadowy doorway. One shouted, 'Hey, Jimmy, is that you?' My father continued walking and insisted I did likewise. When I asked who they were and how they knew him, he said they slept in the toilets he cleaned as the attendant at Hyde Park public conveniences. They were winos who spent half the year in London, the other in Brighton. He was supposed to stop them taking refuge but he was soft-hearted.

My father and I had very little in common and fought over what I was going to do for a living. He found my refusal to apply for a job similar to his own incomprehensible. I felt likewise about his suggestion that I should do so. He considered being a toilet attendant the best job in the world. He liked having his own little office with a radio and a mop. Before that, he had been a road sweeper for London County Council, so he'd graduated from the gutter to the public urinal. I, on the other hand, saw no future for myself in Britain and wanted to escape my family. But, because I was still only 15, my application to emigrate required a reference from my old head teacher. He said that his conscience prevented him from imposing my presence upon Australia, a country that had done nothing to deserve me. His rebuttal rendered my request null and void.

My mother's signature allowed me to join the Merchant Navy. The National Sea Training School was aboard the *Vindicatrix*, a former three-mast 'Cape Horner' berthed in the Old Arm at Sharpness on the Severn Estuary. When I arrived in 1956, its spacious old cabins and decks had given way to classrooms, where for three months I was taught basic seaman's duties: compass skills, navigation, the rules of the sea and cargo handling. I had much in common with my fellow 'Vindi Boys'. For as long as we cared to remember, many of us had been written off by teachers and others in authority. Together, we made our own entertainment and a popular initiation ceremony was to climb along the bowsprit and grab a breast of the ship's ornamental figurehead. It was an awkward climb onto the bowsprit, one that would result in a fall into the water if a boy lost his grip. I passed my final exams with good marks and prepared for the final ritual: the fight for the pool table. The pool table was not one associated with balls and a cue stick. It was named after the place where seamen registered and applied for ships and was an ordinary, large oak table that stood against the ship's bulkhead in the 'tween deck. Punches and kicks were banned in this fight but a spirited battle ensued between the two sides, those passing out and those with time to complete. I said my goodbyes and hoped to meet my classmates one day in exotic foreign ports.

I travelled to London by train and reported to the King George V docks, better known to seamen as KG5. The docks were a dark, exciting place, full of strange faces and voices. With my bag slung over my shoulder and carrying my sea boots and oilskins, I climbed aboard the 15,000-ton *Athenic*, bound for New Zealand. Of the 100 passengers, many hoped to start new lives there. The *Athenic* offered a cheap but slow passage to the land of the long white cloud. As we cast off our mooring ropes and ghosted along the Thames Estuary, I felt like a man, not a boy. I, too, was starting a new life.

The sea was choppy as we crossed the English Channel and entered the Bay of Biscay. I was horribly seasick and much to my shipmates' amusement spent an interminable time leant over the stern rail. Having seen and heard it all before, they offered little sympathy: 'When you chuck up again, if you feel something round and soft in your mouth, swallow hard – it'll be your arsehole.'

I was at the bottom of the pecking order; I'd have been lower than the ship's cat if she had had one. I knew my place and was eager to learn. I took my 'steering ticket' – a course of ten accumulated hours at the wheel in the Atlantic Ocean and another ten in the Pacific. Corrections to the course of the *Athenic* were measured by marginal degrees. It was good to feel that the ship was in my hands and that I was maintaining its course. I also acted as lookout in the crow's nest and painted winches and bulkheads on the ship's super-structure. This was done repeatedly to combat the corrosive ravages of seawater.

Our first port of call was the Dutch Antilles island of Curaçao. It was colourful and bustling, full of sunshine, noise and music, and I wished we could have stayed longer but the *Athenic* stopped only to take on fuel. Our next stopover was at the Panama Canal, a masterpiece of modern engineering. As we waited our turn to pass through the narrow waterway, my crewmates joked that I should save some rations to feed the mules that were going to pull us through the locks. The 'mules' turned out to be mechanical. I headed for the city of Colón to buy Levi's and Wrangler jeans and jackets in styles unseen at home. James Dean was every boy's hero, and my young shipmates and I attached our jeans to a heaving line and tossed them over the side of the ship to let the salt water fade the denim. We would haul them up to dry on deck before repeating the process. Colón reminded me of the Wild West; there was even a big old train with a cowcatcher front running through the town, taking freight to the docks. Sleazy bars on Bottle Alley sold cheap booze and cheap women. A sign above one bar read, 'Some of Our Best Customers Pass Out Through This Door', with a photograph beneath of a drunken customer draped over the saloon doors. Each bar had its own gimmick. I remember one gave away 'Peter Meters', paper rulers for measuring the size of your penis.

We departed through the Panama City end of the canal into the Pacific Ocean, sailing on to Pitcairn Island in the South Pacific. There was no harbour there, as the waters were too deep to set anchor, so the ship's engines were turned off and we sat a mile offshore waiting for the descendants of the HMS *Bounty* mutineers to board. They rowed out in ships' lifeboats, dashing my hopes that they would use canoes, which would have been far more in keeping with the idyllic setting. They offered carvings of flying fish, models of the *Bounty*, blood oranges and grass skirts for sale. I gave them a letter to put on the first ship bound for home.

I found I could smell land ahoy long before I saw it, and several days before we reached Wellington, albatross glided effortlessly alongside us, awaiting scraps of food. As I watched transfixed, shoals of flying fish leapt from the water and porpoise raced along our bow wave, criss-crossing like pairs of synchronised swimmers. We reached harbour a month after setting sail on our 12,000-mile journey. My shipmates' sense of anticipation was palpable. They had girlfriends in many ports, Wellington included. I would sail on the *Athenic* again but that first journey was the most memorable. I was exhilarated and felt that, now I had my seaman's ticket, I could go anywhere in the world that ships sailed.

Later that year, when I was 17, I joined another ship, a cruise liner called the *Braemar Castle*, and was promoted from deck boy to junior ordinary seaman. On our journey around Africa, we visited, among other places, Durban, Dar es Salaam, Mombasa and Cape Town. On our return voyage, we docked at Antwerp. In Danny's, a famous transvestite bar, the men looked like Hollywood actresses and the women like unshaven dockers. Many of the caterers aboard ship were homosexual. Cruise ship captains preferred gay stewards, rather than rough and horny seamen, to serve and chat to female passengers.

I had a fantastic time at sea and I knew that, because I wasn't spending money, I would have hundreds of pounds to come home to, as well as a great tan to impress girls. For a pleasant but all too brief time, I forged a rewarding career as a seaman. This came to an abrupt end one evening in 1957, when, at home in Camberley, I took my girlfriend Liz to the cinema. With fights between locals, squaddies and US servicemen commonplace, it was customary to see US Navy Shore Patrol cars on the streets of Camberley. Because the Americans had no powers of arrest, local policemen rode with them. As Liz and I waited at a bus stop, a Chevy cruised by with a local copper, Sergeant Phillips, in the back. Camberley was a small town; the local thugs and local police knew each other well. Phillips and I had locked horns in the past. We stared at each other. The vehicle turned around and pulled up.

'What are you doing?' he said.

Naturally, my reply was sarcastic. 'Well, if I'm not mistaken, this is a bus stop. And unless me and the other people standing here are mistaken, a bus will appear shortly to take us home.'

'Don't be lippy,' he snapped.

Phillips and I had a captive audience. Everyone at the bus stop watched to see who would flinch.

'Why don't you fuck off back to your big car and leave me alone?' I said.

I had given him the opportunity he had been waiting for.

'I am arresting you for using abusive language,' he replied, trying to twist my arm behind my back.

'Get your hands off me.'

I hit Phillips with my free hand, my punches propelling him backwards. A Shore Patrol cop leapt to his defence. The American was a huge man and, as Phillips cried out, he threw me onto the pavement and dragged me like a rag doll to the Chevy. My temper raged. As they tried to push me inside, I lunged at Phillips and shoved his head backwards over the rear door, which had swung ajar. I tried to break his neck over the door but the hinge gave way beneath our weight. I was conscious of my actions. I knew I was going down for this and that nothing would ever be the same. As we wrestled, I felt I was falling into a dark hole. I wanted Phillips to fall into that hole with me so I could kill him.

I was charged with assaulting a police officer. The magistrate granted me bail but prevented me going to sea until my case was resolved. While I awaited trial, I and four others gatecrashed a party at a bungalow in Yateley, a few miles away. It was hosted by some US military personnel, who objected to our presence. It did not take us long to cause trouble. I threw a television through a window and sat on it in the garden. Another fight ensued. I was charged with wounding with intent to cause grievous bodily harm.

When I returned to court, I received two six-month sentences, one for each incident. This ended my Merchant Navy career. I was convinced that the conviction would disbar me from serving. Some proof of reason for absence would be required when I got out and I was too naive to lie. I was gutted. I had only ever wanted to sail and, by the age of 18, I had been halfway around the world. Liz and I separated but I was stuck with a tattoo of her name on my thumb. I consoled myself with the fact that when I turned my hand upside down it read 'Z17'.

During 1958, I served time in three prisons and found Wormwood Scrubs, Winchester and Lewes fascinating. Every inmate was learning something, scheming, rehearsing and studying crimes past. There were hierarchies and cliques within the criminal community. Jewel thieves and cat burglars who stole from the wealthy and famous were held in the highest esteem. The prisoners spoke their own tongue. Safes were 'peters' or 'boxes', jewellery was 'tom' (derived from the cockney rhyming slang 'tomfoolery') and keys were 'twirls'. A burglary was a 'drumming' and someone who robbed people's homes while they were in was a 'creeper'. Inmates had little to do but talk and I was a willing listener. Every villain had a sad story to tell about how he had ended up inside. They often blamed grasses for passing on word of their jobs. I knew little better at the time but, looking back, it was their ignorance of the techniques employed by the police to apprehend and convict them that really did for them.

The Scrubs had a uniquely horrible smell, which no inmate could forget. It was at its most potent during the morning slop out, when every prisoner's piss and shit flowed into one giant sink. I felt vulnerable when I went to the toilet, or 'recess', as it was also known. This was where scores were settled and there was nothing you could do to fend off an attack if your trousers were around your ankles. Such beatings were brutal. Sometimes prisoners were smashed over the head with heavy stoneware salt pots wrapped inside socks. I hated the grey uniforms, the strict discipline and the food. At night, we were served cocoa with a cob of bread so hard I'd kick it around my cell.

I was transferred to Winchester and then to Lewes, where I worked in the kitchen. This had its advantages: a single-occupancy cell, as much food as I could eat and the time to bake cakes. One day, the prison governor called me into his office. He was a former army

15

officer who had fought in the Second World War; he loved the sound of his own clipped voice.

'Tomkins, I have a letter here from your mother. You don't write home, do you?'

'No.'

'Why not? Your mother thinks we keep you in shackles and chains. Kindly drop her a line and let her know this isn't the case.'

I read books on salvage diving – the recovery of metals from sunken ships – and on my release I applied to a diving school at Dartmouth run by a Captain A.J. Hampton. He told me his course was full but sent me a book he had written and encouraged me to reapply. I studied the theory avidly, reciting the Haldane depth tables and memorising chapters on underwater demolition, steel cutting and the use of oxyacetylene. I found it difficult to imagine how the flames survived underwater. I came to realise that explosives were not only destructive weapons but also sophisticated engineering tools.

I was without gainful employment and could only spend so many hours reading. I didn't want to overstay my welcome with the friends who were putting me up in Camberley, so I hitch-hiked to London to find work. A dumper truck dropped me at Marble Arch, from where I walked to the Norwegian Embassy. The shipping desk was located in the basement. I pushed my seaman's discharge book across the counter. A man flicked through it before asking, 'How quickly can you sail?'

'As quickly as you can get me a ship.'

'Good. Go upstairs to the medical room at the top of the building.'

I was pronounced fit after the briefest of examinations and returned to the shipping desk clutching my medical slip.

'You're sailing tonight,' he said, shuffling my paperwork. I was surprised to learn I would be paid three times my Merchant Navy wages. 'Your rank is *lettmatros*, which is ordinary seaman,' he continued. 'You're joining the oil tanker *Norfoss*, berthed at Queen's Dock, Swansea.'

'I don't have any money to get there, I'm afraid.'

'Not to worry, Mr Tomkins, I will issue you with a travel voucher for you and your sea gear.'

I thought I should see my mother, who was living nearby, before such a sudden departure. She told me that my father had terminal cancer and asked that I visit him in hospital. I found him slumped drowsily in his bed after an operation to remove growths in his bowels and stomach. He muttered incoherently, saying women were to blame for his troubles. I told him I would visit him again when I returned from sea. We both knew this was a lie. I left after a short time.

Before the *Norfoss* could sail, she had to ballast water to reduce the level of her freeboard. When I arrived, her 52-strong crew were ashore making the most of a last seamy night in Swansea. As I crossed the long, sharply angled gangplank, my sea bag was taken from my shoulder. Having struggled beneath its weight, I was amazed how easily it was lifted from me, as if hoisted by a crane. The giant who relieved me of my kitbag was the deck boy; I thought that if he was a mere deck boy, I wouldn't want to fight the bosun. I could not translate a word of Norwegian, so I was glad he spoke English. The giant directed me towards my dingy two-man cabin. My roommate was absent, ashore, I presumed, trawling for women. My eyes were drawn to a switchblade knife on the dressing table.

'Who's my cabin mate?' I asked my giant friend.

'Italian bastard, all hairy.'

Maybe joining the *Norfoss* was not such a good idea.

'There's no bedding.'

'Amidships. Go to one of the officers' cabins.'

I followed his instruction and knocked on a door.

'Hello, I'm the new lettmatros. I've got no bedding in my cabin.'

'Fuck off, English,' came the reply.

With 15 nationalities aboard, this became a common refrain. I spent my first night without bedding and awoke at dawn to cast off.

Giuseppe Murdaca was as hairy as the giant had intimated. He shaved twice daily and his arm hair protruded in tufts below his cuffs and spilled over his collar. As he confided, his condition was a cause of great distress.

'Will you write me a letter?' he asked.

'Sure.'

'I need a note for, how do you say, er, *farmacia*?'

'Chemist?'

'I need a cream, for the hair.'

'You need Immac cream.' I knew this request would raise a smile in Boots. This depilatory product was more often sold to women.

The food was better aboard the *Norfoss* than it had been on the *Athenic* and a large fridge containing tinned crab and *fiskeboller* (egg-shaped fish balls) catered for snacks. In bad weather, the cooks served 'storm soup', which was everything thrown into one big pot. I drank the strongest coffee of my life. The Norwegian sailors poured ground coffee to a third of the way up the pot and never added milk. Rather than stirring in sugar, they placed a lump in their mouths as they drank.

As a merchant seaman, I had signed on for the duration of the voyage but the captain of the *Norfoss* only guaranteed his sailors seven days' notice of work. This rule made all the members of the crew jumpy, except one. He was from the tiny island of St Helena and had sneaked aboard the five-hundred-foot-long ship two years earlier.

'When nobody was looking, I climbed into the anchor-chain locker,' he explained. 'They found me eventually but I pleaded to join the crew.'

Not having a passport, the stowaway never went ashore and hence never spent any of his earnings. I think he was saving up to buy St Helena.

I befriended Ari, or Aristide Panayotopoulos, after an accident that almost cost me my life. Ari knew nothing about ships or sailing and was too delicate to be at sea. He even wore gloves to protect his immaculately manicured hands. On runs ashore, he wore Italian suits, handmade shoes and tailored shirts, clothing beyond any regular seaman's means. My curiosity led me to question him.

'You must not tell anyone,' he said. 'This must be a secret between us.'

'OK, OK,' I replied.

'Come, look at this.' He pulled out a photograph album. 'You see me there?' He pointed to a picture of a dashing olive-skinned young man wearing a spotless white tuxedo and holding a champagne flute. 'That is me with beautiful women. Ah, those days!'

He remained a handsome man and was a dead ringer for Omar Sharif. Ari opened his wardrobe excitedly to reveal expensive clothes, watches and jewellery. 'I had to leave where I was before, and quickly. Something bad happened. This was all I could take with me.'

'Where are you going?' I asked.

'America, I hope. I have relatives there. When we reach America, I am going to jump ship and be with my family. But please, Dave, it is our secret.'

He was less forthcoming about the knife fight in Marseilles that had triggered his hasty departure. A man had died, or at least got seriously hurt. Ari had not hung around long enough to find out.

English was the international language of shipping. When we docked and when we transited the Suez Canal, a harbour pilot would come aboard to assist with navigation and liaise with the helmsman. Our captain's call at such times was always, 'Get the Englishman.'

I enjoyed steering the 15,000-ton *Norfoss* through rough seas. Like an iceberg, a fully laden oil tanker is much bigger below the surface than above. At top weight, the *Norfoss*'s freeboard stood a mere 8 ft high, which made for interesting sailing into 20-ft-high crests. The *Norfoss* would be awash from stem to stern. I got to know her every twitch and prided myself on keeping her course with the minimum fluctuation in heading. To anticipate the waves and make corrections was a contest against nature – fun for me but less so for the crew, especially at meal times. In a playful mood one day, I looked out for a particularly nasty-looking wave and sailed so it struck us where the anchor was hanging. The slightest slack in the chain meant the anchor was sent smashing against the side. I chuckled inwardly as the ship shuddered from bow to stern and I knew my name was being cursed in the mess hall. The bosun's punishment was to give me a job known as '*marlin flek per bow*'. This was to paint the rust spots on the bow, in a cradle lowered to just a few feet above the water. A stint painting the ship's mast was not for the faint-hearted, either.

When we berthed at an oil terminal off the port of Baniyas, in Syria, I received a message from my mother. I was sad to hear of my father's death, sadder to think his life had amounted to a perpetual struggle against hardship, never having more than the minimum required to get by. I wanted more than to inhabit a single room and use a public bathhouse to wash as I grew old. His dying days were spent at a Catholic hospice and at my mother's house. He regularly absconded from the nuns and, dressed only in his pyjamas, jumped on the first bus he saw. He never had any money or an idea where he was going. The sisters pleaded with my mother to take him in, telling her she was the only person he knew. My father passed away in 'my room' – kept for me in case I ever came to stay.

When the *Norfoss* ran aground in a snowstorm off the Swedish coast, we changed course for Hamburg. The strip joints, live sex shows and prostitutes of St Pauli were magnets for seamen. I got very drunk one night and pulled a positively horrible female. I couldn't remember how she'd ended up in my bunk; it wasn't even as though she'd appeared attractive the previous evening. She had walked into the bar with a rough old sailor who was unshaven and wearing a greasy peaked cap. He looked as if he'd just walked off the deck as he was still wearing thigh-high sea boots. The following morning, I dragged her down to the engine room and exchanged her for two cartons of cigarettes. The engine-room boys rarely saw a woman and were less picky.

While she was undergoing repairs in dry dock, the *Norfoss* changed hands. She was renamed *Regina* and her crew were told to set sail for the United States. This was good for Ari but not for me. I had already been on the *Norfoss* for six months and I knew that, because of immigration restrictions, I would not have been able to pay off as we sailed up and down the American coast, which would have meant another year without home leave. I disembarked at the Isle of Grain, Kent.

I returned to Camberley, briefly, before travelling to Jersey, where I worked alongside an explosives shotfirer. His job was to blast wells in the Rozel Bay area. I also learned to use a hazel divining rod. Though I was sceptical at first, eventually I found I could track the source of underground water, finding a point where we could blast down through the rocky overburden.

In Jersey, I met two chancers called Billy and Smudge in a nightclub.

They bragged about the crooks they hung around with in London, faces whose names I recalled from the Scrubs. Billy's mother ran a pub in Notting Hill. He was an old-fashioned thief 30 years my senior. He and Smudge recognised the prison artwork on my arms and hands. 'Which nick, son?' they asked. One night, they suggested, 'We're going to do a bit of work later. Do you fancy it?' I joined them on a 'job' at a local factory, watching as they hacked clumsily at a safe until the door opened. The reward was meagre and I was on the smallest cut.

On my return to Camberley, I felt inclined to accept offers of illegal employment – out of boredom as much as anything else – and did a few jobs with Baz, a charismatic local criminal with a cavalier attitude to life and a dry sense of humour. Neither he nor I was interested in breaking into people's homes. I had never wanted to whack old ladies over the head and knew the average working person kept little of value at home. Baz and I were driven by cold cash and were on the lookout for more lucrative opportunities.

CHAPTER 2

PANDORA'S BOX

IN THE 1950S AND '60S, CRIMINAL GANGS IN LONDON PULLED OFF spectacular robberies, pocketing hundreds of thousands of pounds in cash, stones and gold. Rather than 'peeling' safes – breaking them open by force – they used oxyacetylene cutting gear and an ice-lolly stick to feed an explosive charge through the key-way into the lock mechanism. As a result, it became recognised in law that if one was carrying an ice-lolly stick, one could be said to be 'going equipped'. In response to this wave of robberies, insurers demanded that banks and jewellery stores up their security, and safe manufacturers developed new models, which, while not impregnable, required thieves to expend more time. Design improvements included thick copper sheets and composite materials built into safe doors, which dissipated the heat produced by oxyacetylene torches.

While there were no manuals for apprentice safe-blowers to study, manufacturers' brochures detailed the specifications of their latest products and I also attended trade fairs. At one of these, I was invited to watch a promotional film for a new safe, which featured slow-motion close-ups of gelignite detonation. Just when I thought the door was about to burst open, it sprang back into place. The manufacturers knew about gelignite's limited detonation velocity and brisance (the shattering effect of the sudden release of energy in an explosion) and had begun to use up-to-the minute, highly tensile materials. Many safe-breakers relied upon gelignite, as it was easy to obtain because of its use in the mining industry. The type most often used was a commercially produced variety called Polar Ammon. For less technically proficient robbers, there were hundreds of the old-style Victorian safes still around, especially outside London. These were fabricated from mild-steel plates, with the outer shell and back plates manufactured separately. There was usually an exposed seam, a rivet or an overlapping lip vulnerable to a crowbar or sharpened chisel, so these safes could be broken into using brute force.

I did not belong to a gang as such but to a loose association of freelance thieves. I favoured working as one of a pair, in tandem with either Baz or a guy called Don. Baz and I were the principal movers within the group. Seeking an explosive more potent than gelignite, we approached a chemist who worked at the Atomic Weapons Research Establishment at Aldermaston, Berkshire. We watched him produce picric acid, or trinitrophenol, in his back yard. The process produced yellow fumes and by the time he was finished, his hands and face were yellow, as if he had jaundice. The finished product looked like mustard powder and stained everything it touched. It had a high detonation velocity, approximately 7,400 metres per second, far in excess of Polar Ammon, and had a shattering, shock-wave effect rather than the slow rending action of gelignite. I was cautious in my own trials with picric acid and followed the advice of the shotfirer I had worked beside in Jersey: he had always said that less was more when using explosives.

We also required industrially produced explosives and detonators. In order to get hold of these, we targeted the West Country, where many quarries were to be found. The further the mine from an area of human habitation, the larger the quantity of explosives to be found. Smaller companies were more complacent about their security than bigger ones and I was never required to break into an explosives safe. Not that to have done so would have posed any great difficulty: these safes were simply cabinets welded together from metal sheets, with the detonators kept in a separate chamber. On our first raid, however,

I found cartridges of explosives and a dozen detonators standing unguarded in a bucket.

When choosing targets for safe-blowing operations, we favoured remote factory plants and professional premises offering entry and escape routes across countryside or woodland. As so many thieves got caught on the road, we avoided highways. I never saw a police car on a riverbank or railway track. We stole based on our own intelligence and homework, ignoring tips about possible scores supplied by third parties. My thinking was, if a venue was so wide open and the bounty so precious, why would someone tell us about it?

To break open older models, a small explosive charge was introduced into the lock mechanism with a flat ice-lolly stick. When the charge detonated, the lock disintegrated without causing any other major internal damage. The handle withdrew the bolts and the door opened. Or at least that was what was supposed to happen. Not all safes were as straightforward. Manufacturers began to restrict unnecessary space inside the lock casing, leaving little room for explosives. They also built safes that responded to various types of attack by activation of a secondary locking mechanism.

For a safe that required a larger explosive charge to remove the door than the lock would take, even after the charge was compressed using a knitting needle, a small charge would initially be detonated to remove the lock mechanism. When this charge had destroyed the obstructing lock, a condom would be introduced into the key-way until the collar was flush with the door plate. Using an ice-lolly stick, a greater quantity of explosive would then be introduced, a detonator placed in contact with the explosive-filled key-way and a fistful of plasticine moulded over the key-way, detonator and charge to tamp the blast.

If our first job had been a failure, perhaps I would have drifted away from crime. But like a successful first-time gambler, I inevitably returned to the table. The laundry company had a reasonable sum in the safe and plenty of sheets and pillowcases to reduce the sound of the explosion. Having studied the safe on a reconnaissance mission to the premises, I knew it would be straightforward to blow. I removed the escutcheon plate from the keyhole, introduced a thin roll of plasticine into the key-way to bridge any gaps between steel plates, folded a piece of card into a V shape and poured picric acid down into the key-way. I used an artist's paintbrush to push the powdery substance along and into the lock mechanism. I set it off using a commercially produced explosives detonator from a quarry. The office filled with smoke and I feared the blast had been too loud. Picric acid was a violent explosive and the quantity required to get the job done was far less than the amount of Polar Ammon that would have been needed. When we removed the bedding, the door was hanging open before us and the safe's contents were intact.

Our anonymity in the criminal community was advantageous; our names were absent from police lists of the usual suspects for such crimes. It was satisfying to be skilled operators rather than petty thieves. We hid our explosives deep in the woods and kept changes of clothes in dustbins buried in the ground at a separate location, choosing places that were familiar to us and could easily be reached on foot. We weren't earning fortunes but our incomes were well in excess of what we might have earned in wages. Our lifestyles changed. We owned cars, bought clothes at Cecil Gee, wore Italian shoes and ate in exclusive local restaurants such as Skindles in Maidenhead. We didn't often make a huge amount from one score but we accumulated a fair amount of money from smaller robberies.

One night, I was doing a job with Don at a factory that produced arc-welding rods. The office looked onto a main road and the gate to the premises was left open at night to allow the police to check around the building. I was working on the box when Don, who had been on lookout, suddenly rushed up to me. I thought it was about to 'come on top' (thieves' slang for when the police arrive or when the job has to be aborted).

'You've got to see this,' he said, as he stood panting before me.

'What?' I replied.

He pointed towards the main road, where two girls wearing miniskirts had squatted down to pee. Their bottoms smiled up at us.

On another evening, Baz and I worked a safe at a haulage company. The box was six feet tall and had huge double doors. Its owners had obliged by leaving oxyacetylene cutting equipment in a workshop. We wheeled the gear into the office and draped a large tarpaulin over the safe to block out the light from the oxyacetylene. Within seconds, it was as a hot as an oven beneath the material and the air was filled with smoke. The paint on the safe started to burn while drops of molten metal set the linoleum flooring alight. I pushed back the tarpaulin to allow the fumes to dissipate and myself to breathe.

'Are you sure you can't see anything from the outside, Baz?' I shouted over.

'No, you're fine, Dave,' said Baz, who was keeping watch in the open air beyond the office door. 'Just carry on,' he said, keeping a straight face. 'I can't see anything.'

I continued until, finally, the doors opened. As we left the site, which was close to a residential area, Baz started laughing.

'What is it?' I asked.

'You should see your face. You're as black as a coalminer.'

'I can't believe there was no light showing outside.'

'Well, there was. But you were doing so well under there I didn't want to put you off. The sky was lit up like a war zone. It must have been visible for miles.'

About two years into my safe-breaking career, a breach of our own rules brought us crashing back down to earth. We had frowned upon cars, and for good reason, feeling able to justify their use only when our target was a considerable distance from our homes. Even then, we only moved when the traffic was at its heaviest. We were convinced that this would stop us getting caught. In fact, we were convinced that even if the police did pull us in, as long as we never left fingerprints or other forensic evidence and refused to provide statements when questioned, we would always get away with it.

Then we had a job to do that was so far off our patch we had no choice but to drive. But, rather than waiting for the morning rush hour, as we would usually have done, we headed home straight away and found ourselves driving alone on open roads. We were halfway home and about to join a dual carriageway when we saw a cop car sitting by the side of the road. We could see them looking at us as we passed by and instinct told us we would get pulled. We were reasonably clean as far as tools were concerned, but we were carrying a linen bank bag from the safe that contained the cash and cheques we'd taken from the box. There was a hedge separating the two lanes of the carriageway, so we put a little distance between ourselves and the police car, and, at a point where the road curved, we pulled in tight to the hedge and threw the bag into it. We caught the traffic lights at the end of the carriageway on the red; the police car came into view and the officers pulled us over. As our car was clean and had not been reported stolen, they allowed us to drive on.

Later that day, we returned to look for the cash bag but had no luck. The money in the bag was only a secondary concern. We had to recover it because in time it would be discovered and put us in the frame for the robbery. We were already too late. A woman taking a walk along the pathway at the edge of the road had spotted the bag a short while after we had dumped it. She had recognised it as a bank cash bag and handed it in to the police. Within 24 hours, we were arrested and taken to a station in the area where the robbery had been committed for questioning.

We stayed mute but were charged with conspiracy to commit robbery, as well as all the frilly bits like causing explosions. A bit of 'naughties' from the police, such as the false suggestion that we had been overheard discussing the crime in the cells, spiced up our trial at Winchester Assizes. We had little to say in our defence and relied upon the prosecution's evidence being circumstantial. Taken in isolation, none of it was sufficient to gain a conviction but together it painted a picture. We were convicted and the judge handed down three-year sentences to give us time to mull over our mistakes. I was only twenty-one years old and if I kept my nose clean, I would be out in two years.

At Winchester Prison, I met Harry Houghton, a member of the infamous Portland spy ring. My favourite joke at his expense was to ask him if he could keep a secret. As a civil servant based at the British Embassy in Warsaw in 1952, Houghton had passed top-secret naval documents to the KGB. Later, while working at the Underwater Weapons Research Establishment at Portland, Dorset, he supplied the Russians with information about the Royal Navy's first nuclear submarine, *Dreadnought*, and the recently developed Asdic sonar system, which was to be used to find and trace Soviet submarines. Houghton and four others were exposed by MI5. They were jailed, some later to be exchanged for British spies held in Moscow. Harry and I sat together stitching up mailbags, eight stitches to the inch and three to four mailbags per week, earning enough credit at the canteen to buy half an ounce of tobacco and some rolling papers.

A short time into my sentence, I fell seriously ill, coughing a lot, losing weight and getting flushed in the face whenever I made an effort to do anything. At first, my complaints were brushed aside and aspirin was the strongest drug I was prescribed. Eventually, though, they put me in a wheelchair and took me across the road to the local hospital to be X-rayed and examined. The wheelchair was a cosmetic affectation on the authorities' part: inside the prison, I was made to walk. The doctor at Winchester Hospital diagnosed tuberculosis and said I had deep cavities in my lungs. I would die unless I received emergency treatment. I couldn't be certain how I had contracted TB. I had smoked since I was ten years old but TB was an infection rather than being caused by smoking. My money was on the hookah I had smoked on the *Norfoss* as we sailed through the Suez Canal. It was the most basic hubble-bubble pipe I had ever seen, made of bamboo and a jam jar and handed to me by an old man who must have been in his 80s. I watched in fascination as he sucked and sucked, his cheeks caving into a toothless mouth. I was amazed by the amount of smoke he produced: huge clouds emerged from his mouth; he was like a snorting dragon.

The prison hospital had bar doors like those in American prisons. I made friends with the most unlikely of armed robbers in the cell opposite, a former public schoolboy who had blown away a bank teller with a shotgun.

'So why did you do it?' I asked.

'Same as you. I wanted the money. But it was to save my family business. The chicken farm was about to go bankrupt. I had to save the family name. We would have been in disgrace if we'd gone under.'

'You weren't much of an armed robber, though, were you?'

'I guess not. I didn't even bother to saw the barrels off my 12-gauge.'

His candour surprised me, not to mention his sanguinity. The case against him was overwhelming and the death penalty was yet to be repealed.

'I pointed the shotgun over the counter but I didn't want it to go off. Because the barrels were so long, he was able to grab them. We wrestled over them for a second or two and then the barrels got lined up with his chest. He pulled the gun towards him and it went off at point-blank range.'

I couldn't resist asking him, 'Look, how come you're so relaxed? You're going to end up on the end of a rope.'

'No,' he smiled, 'not a chance of that happening, my friend.'

'How can you be so sure? You know the death-cell screws are here from Wandsworth waiting to carry out your sentence?'

'I'm a Freemason at one of the lodges near the court. So are my defence counsel and the judge. They've got a responsibility to protect me. I'll be found guilty of manslaughter not murder. I'll get a ten-year sentence.'

I guess the funny-handshake brigade really do look after each other: as it turned out, he was spot on about his conviction and sentence, and the hangman had to put his rope away for another day.

To aid my recovery, I was moved to the Mount Sanatorium near Eastleigh. It was set in manicured grounds and surrounded by rolling fields. Badgers came out at night and scratched at the windows in search of food. A male badger was always the first to arrive. When he considered it safe, he signalled for his family to join him at our door. I fed them by hand. The matron assured me that while she and her staff knew I was a convicted criminal, none of the patients did and she would withhold this information. For the next two months, I was to take total, compulsory bed rest, known as a 'bed splint'. This drastic sentence of inactivity, with continued doses of streptomycin, was required for my lungs to recover. I was not allowed up for any reason whatsoever, and bedpans and bed-baths became the norm.

I was very well treated and, being so much younger than my fellow patients, I was well in with the younger nurses. I was 21 years old and thought I was going to live forever. The cancer ward was next door to mine. As I recovered, I spent more time with those whose lives were almost at an end. I ran the hospital radio station and delivered the patients their newspapers. You could tell a patient was about to pass away when he cancelled his order: as his eyesight faded, he could no longer read the print. He would also complain that the lighting was too bright. Three or four days later, I would hear that he had died.

I struck up a rapport with the patient in the next bed to mine. When the staff invited him to move to a vacant chalet, he suggested I apply to join him. My application was refused. A nurse who had been unfriendly towards me since I arrived had lodged an objection to my transfer. He said that if I were removed from an area that was monitored permanently, I would abscond. Since recovering the ability to walk, I could have escaped at any time. However, I lacked the inclination to do so.

I stormed into the matron's office, determined to make an issue of it. 'When I first arrived, you told me I would be treated the same as the other patients. If you have an issue of trust with me, you should call the prison and have them come and collect me, because that is the appropriate place for mistrust, not here.' Her attempts to becalm me were in vain. 'If the screws from the nick are not on their way in an hour, I will leave of my own accord. But not before I've given the bastard who objected something to remember for a long time to come.'

I was dispatched back to Winchester but only for an overnight stay. At the crack of dawn, I found myself in handcuffs in the back of a van. The guards told me I was being transferred to Verne Prison on the Isle of Portland off the Dorset coast. Such a sudden move without advance notice was known as being 'ghost-trained'. Usually, it was for security reasons or because the governor considered you a problem prisoner. In my case, it was because my lungs still needed as much fresh air as possible. At Verne, there was dormitory accommodation and no restrictions on access to the yard until lights out. Only as we approached the prison did I recall why Portland rang bells with me – Harry Houghton, the spy who couldn't keep a secret.

In good weather, access to the island was across Chesil Beach. The island was made of limestone and the prison occupied a former army citadel and prisoner-of-war camp. The dry moat and parade ground remained. Unlike any other prison I knew, there were no cells. Prisoners shared long dormitories cut from Portland stone and sunk into the rock. I knew I was not going to like it here and demanded to see the governor, who by chance had also been my governor at Lewes.

A senior screw marched me into his office. He was lying back in a comfortable chair with his feet on the desk, smoking a pipe.

'I know this one,' said the governor, glancing at my file. 'Keep your eye on him. He could be trouble.'

We eyed each other coldly. He cultivated the same tough image as he had done at Lewes. He liked to claim that he had been bitten by a poisonous snake in India and that the snake had died.

'I want a transfer,' I said.

'Why?'

'Because I know I'm not going to like it here.'

'No transfers from here,' he scoffed. 'The only quick way out is to hit the tins.'

This was Verne slang for an attempt to escape – the prison walls were made of corrugated steel.

'I'll bear that in mind,' I said.

Verne bore the full force of the wind and rain that whipped across Portland. Being dressed in the full canvas waterproofs and heavy boots issued to us reminded me of my seafaring days, the most fulfilling period of my life. The sounds of the seagulls and foghorns sharpened my memories. The strange thing about Verne was that its inmates were surrounded by water but could not see any. It was sickening, under these circumstances, to be so near and yet so far from the sea.

After two months, I was ghost-trained to Maidstone, where I remained until my time was up. By this time, I spoke like a prisoner, using all the slang phrases that had sounded so alien at first. Jailhouse tattoos adorned my body – I had crude versions of the stick figure with a halo, the symbol on the calling card of Simon Templar's alter ego, 'The Saint' in the crime thrillers by Leslie Charteris, and of the featureless face wearing a top hat, bow tie and monocle, with smoke rising from a cigarette holder that was the sign of 'The Toff', another fictional character, this one created by John Creasey.

I had been through the mill of indoctrination into criminal society and on my release I vowed to renew my career with increased vigour. Yet, at the same time, I found the thought of being classed as a criminal repugnant. The hypocrisy of this was not lost on me. I hooked up with my former associates, none of whom had gone straight. We just upped the ante and went for broke, deciding to take down bigger scores. Unfortunately, these were inevitably also more high profile and this gave the police a bigger incentive to catch us. I was looking for opportunities to use Hydrobel, an explosive I had liberated from a 'mining source'. It was used in coalmines that were prone to firedamp, or methane gas. Hydrobel was used on the coalface in a method called 'pulsed infusion shotfiring', a technique that could be adapted for use in safe-blowing. Unlike gelignite, Hydrobel had two speeds of detonation, which would allow me to control the amount of energy released by the explosion.

On a wet, blustery night, Baz and I trekked through the woodland surrounding the Royal Military Academy Sandhurst to recover tools buried on a previous visit. Our target was the CEPO, the pay office for civilian personnel, a collection of single-storey administration buildings linked by covered walkways. Thick woodland bordered the road leading to this complex. On reconnaissance missions, we had tried but failed to record reliable timings of Royal Military Police patrols and, as we made our final approach, I hoped the heavy rain would convince the RMPs to remain indoors.

With Baz keeping watch, I entered through a window and located the safe, which, in a bid to prevent anyone carrying it away, was surrounded by brickwork and cement. At first glance, it looked as if it should have been a straightforward box to blow but the slim key-way that was visible when I crouched down proved a nightmare. Using an ice-lolly stick, I fed an ounce of explosives into the hole before the flow stopped. I resorted to working the lock with a knitting needle, to compress the explosives. The quantity of explosives in the key-way was well short of what was required to remove the door but I rejected the option of blowing the first charge and loading again with a condom. I knew the blast, while insufficient to blow the door open, would be too great to simply clear the lock. This would cause the door to jam and the steel plates to buckle, resulting in gaps through which the second charge would vent. Baz appeared at the window, wet through, to enquire what the fuck I was doing. For some reason, he had dressed most inappropriately for the evening's little adventure, in a brown mohair suit. His knowledge of safe-blowing made him a handy partner on such a night, however. As we discussed the problem, the thunder rumbled and the lightning cracked above us. Luckily, there was still no sign of the RMPs. The storm must have kept them away.

It took me three hours to insert a satisfactory quantity of explosives. I pushed a desk up against the safe door and joined Baz outside. There is no such thing as a quiet explosion but, with no mattresses or laundry to hand to muffle the sound, this was truly a big bang. It never ceased to amaze me how those in earshot of our explosions mistook the sound for something else. They would tell police they had heard a car backfire or fireworks going off rather than a safe being blown. Their senses lacked a frame of reference and they assumed that the noise had been caused by something familiar. It also worked the opposite way. An insomniac pub owner once testified that, as he was sitting in bed reading a book in the dead of night, he had heard two safes being blown in the same premises within a few seconds of each other. Of course, it was quite possible that he had imagined that he had heard an unusual sound when in fact he had heard a familiar one: the dull thud of empty wooden beer barrels falling in his cellar.

The blast was followed by a shattering of glass. The force of the post-blast shock wave shot coins clean through the window of the CEPO like bullets. I climbed back inside the smoke-filled office to find the door completely off the safe and files from inside it sitting neatly in a pile on the floor. We bagged the night's reward and departed the scene unhindered.

The *Daily Mirror* reported an altogether different version of events. I read how the robbers had 'silently' crept past armed guards and blown the safe, only to find it empty. Frustrated, they had apparently looted the NAAFI canteen and store instead, leaving with thousands of pounds worth of electrical items, watches and cigarettes. I scratched my head. 'Did we do the NAAFI the other night, Baz?'

'No, Dave. Are you going mad?'

Several years later, I read about a military policeman caught thieving from a post office, who, when invited to declare previous crimes, admitted he and a colleague had robbed the Sandhurst

Martin,

Thanks for taking care of the kitties :)

Here is your mail + interesting book. Help yourself to any food /coffee etc. If you could put bin (black — I think) out on tuesday am,

for sure

thats great — if you forget, no worries. Wet cat food: 1 box should feed them for 3 days (i.e. 6 servings). If you fancy trying do put them outside for a bit, the harnesses are in the same cabinet as food. Downstairs shower was being an arsehole to me Saturday, but I hope it behaves for you! Don't forget to put coffee ground in Right hand (Big) sink only! My hotel has wifi so I should be contactable via facebook. If you need to reach Mateus his office number is 028 70124009, home is 028 70328337. He's arriving back late weds night, so kitties will be taken care of thursday onward. Thanks again!

Meow   —Scarlett

35.   Koradi, R., Billeter, M. and Wuthrich, K. (1996) MOLMOL: A program for display and analysis of macromolecular structures. *Journal of Molecular Graphics*, **14**, 51.

26. Cang, X., Sponer, J. and Cheatham, T.E., III. (2011) Insight into G-DNA Structural Polymorphism and Folding from Sequence and Loop Connectivity through Free Energy Analysis. *Journal Of The American Chemical Society*, **133**, 14270-14279.

27. Guedin, A., Alberti, P. and Mergny, J.L. (2009) Stability of intramolecular quadruplexes: sequence effects in the central loop. *Nucleic Acids Research*, **37**, 5559-5567.

28. Karsisiotis, A.I. and da Silva, M.W. (2012) Structural Probes in Quadruplex Nucleic Acid Structure Determination by NMR. *Molecules*, **17**, 13073-13086.

29. Mergny, J.L., Li, J., Lacroix, L., Amrane, S. and Chaires, J.B. (2005) Thermal difference spectra: a specific signature for nucleic acid structures. *Nucleic Acids Research*, **33**.

30. Webba da Silva, M. (2007) NMR methods for studying quadruplex nucleic acids. *Methods*, **43**, 264-277.

31. Webba da Silva, M. (2005) Experimental demonstration of T : (G : G : G : G): T hexad and T : A : A : T tetrad alignments within a DNA quadruplex stem. *Biochemistry*, **44**, 3754-3764.

32. Goddard T.D., K.D.G. University of California, San Francisco.

33. Schwieters, C.D., Kuszewski, J.J., Tjandra, N. and Clore, G.M. (2003) The Xplor-NIH NMR molecular structure determination package.*Journal Of Magnetic Resonance*, **160**, 65-73.

34. Webba da Silva, M. (2003) Association of DNA quadruplexes through G : C : G : C tetrads.

NAAFI. I checked the dates and it was the night Baz and I had blown the safe.

Because of the lack of sound-insulation materials, the CEPO safe made more noise than almost any other I blew. One box we opened in a factory, on the other hand, barely made a peep. Two guards sitting in a little office at ground level did not even move from behind their television set when it went off. Their behaviour in the hours before the raid was so routine that we simply worked around them. Every hour, one of them punched time clocks strategically situated around the premises. We worked undisturbed between rounds. At 'clock time', we simply left the building by a window and climbed onto an adjacent roof.

As we were suspected of having blown so many safes in our area, the police put me and the people I worked with under surveillance. But, by night, we slipped our nooses and met up at pre-arranged off-road locations, walking for several hours to reach the rendezvous. We received a hot reception whenever we travelled to counties policed by other constabularies; the message was 'Don't even think about operating on our turf'. When the police were not watching our houses, they staked out factories and offices they reckoned we might hit. Late one night, or early one morning, we very nearly walked into one of their traps.

The generating station was on our to-do list and I had been inside on a scouting mission. It was so tempting to take down; the staff always left the windows open and there was no burglar alarm. The bosses must have assumed that, as the building was permanently manned, such a system was unnecessary.

Baz and I were returning from other premises and we had been disappointed to find the safe was a 'combo'. At this stage, we were not attempting to break boxes with combination locks. It was around 4 a.m. when we saw the officers and their vehicles hidden in the treeline near the generating station and several heart-stopping minutes before we convinced ourselves it was the score they were onto, not us. We knew that if we were arrested in proximity to such a building, we would be likely to face conspiracy charges. We opted to sit in our hide and wait for the surveillance operation to conclude. When the police pulled out about an hour later, we had the opportunity to take the score down right then, when we knew it was clean. This carried the added incentive of really sickening the police. What a choker to discover the target they had watched all night had been robbed minutes after their departure!

We made our entry via the rear of the big old Victorian building. The safe was positioned directly opposite a set of double doors providing access to a large open-plan office. Hearing voices and passing traffic added to my sense of urgency. I asked Baz to fetch materials to muffle the sound of the explosion. He returned carrying a mattress from the first-aid room. As I inserted the detonator and looped the flying leads around the safe door handle, I heard a strange noise, which grew louder. Peering through the office doors, I spied Baz pulling a carpet behind him as he ran towards me. The noise was the popping of carpet studs along the corridor.

By the time we had wrapped the carpet around the mattresses and placed a desk up against the muffled safe door, it was light. Then I heard workers swapping banter as they arrived to begin the morning shift. As rain was in the air, they were hunched beneath a portico. Either we blew the safe immediately and risked the workers hearing the explosion, or we made a run for it and, if necessary, battled our way out past them. When the detonator leads touched the battery, there was a thump. The desk slid across the office floor and smashed into the double doors. Baz was standing in the corridor with his back to them. Much to my amusement, he was thrown off his feet. The noise aroused the workers' curiosity. One emerged from beneath the portico and looked up at the now brightening sky. He held his hand outstretched, as if expecting rain to follow the thunderclap.

Eventually, the police gathered sufficient circumstantial evidence relating to several scores to arrest us. Our behaviour patterns were simply not those of law-abiding citizens. Officers also found my collection of safe brochures and arrested a known associate of ours who moved and purchased equipment on our behalf. Finding an ice-lolly stick in his wallet, detectives charged him with possession of an explosive implement and misprision of a felony – failure to report a crime about which he had knowledge.

We were charged with conspiracy to cause explosions and steal from safes and strongrooms, which was a very difficult charge to beat. Aided by a clever barrister, the police and Crown Prosecution Service presented a sufficiently convincing case for Baz and me to be found guilty at Kingston Crown Court and sentenced to another three years' imprisonment.

CHAPTER 3

DOING TIME

THE ONLY SOURCE OF HEAT IN MY ONE-MAN CELL IN WANDSWORTH
Prison was provided by a pipe that ran along the wall at floor level.
The tiny room was particularly cold because the previous occupant
had smashed the postcard-sized windowpanes. The authorities did
not bother to repair the windows, as they knew inmates would only
smash them again the following summer. The newspapers I had
stuffed into the iron frames offered little insulation and got soggy
when it rained.

One day, as I lay on my bed with a blanket wrapped around me, an
icy draught blew the papers away. The gust was followed by a pigeon,
which landed on my wooden table, answered a call of nature and stared
at me. It showed no fear or disorientation and seemed accustomed to
human beings. I stretched across to inspect the identity tag on its
leg. The ring was cut from an old can and had been engraved with a
mailbag needle. It read, 'Scruffy, Wormwood Scrubs'. My bedraggled
visitor evidently belonged to another con. Scruffy must have mistaken
Wandsworth for the Scrubs. Over the following weeks, Scruffy sat
happily on my hand as I fed him pieces of bread. He had a large
appetite, consuming half my daily ration when he wasn't flying laps of

my cell and making annoying pigeon noises. There was only so much cooing I could tolerate and I evicted Scruffy before my transfer.

After classification, I was transferred with two of the guys convicted alongside me to HMP Chelmsford. As is often the case, we were not separated, and we ended up in a three-man cell together. Our friend with the ice-lolly stick had no prior convictions; he received nine months and was sent to an open facility. I worked as a welder in the 'tin shop', a light-engineering factory that produced dustpans, metal coat hangers and other crap for outside contractors.

We had no intention of curtailing our criminal careers in the future and we used the facility as a centre of learning. I applied myself to studying more advanced methods of opening safes, receiving magazines each month on industrial welding and cutting techniques, which didn't seem to create any suspicion on the part of the prison authorities. Educational books were available from an outside library and I ordered books on quarrying, mining and metallurgy for over a year. Then it came to a full stop when I was called to the governor's office. A sharp-eyed librarian had contacted the prison about my reading habits, wanting to know if they were aware that the subject of my studies was basically explosive techniques. My external-library privileges were revoked.

At Chelmsford, I was friendly with a Gypsy boy called Trigger. He would come to me and ask a variety of questions related to safe-blowing. Now, Trigger was not the brightest bulb on the Christmas tree and at first I responded to his questions without thought. However, he came back on a daily basis asking just one or two salient questions. Follow-up queries or requests for clarification that I would have expected him to make straight away would not be forthcoming until the following day. It dawned on me that he was just the proxy in this question-and-answer session. On Trigger's next quest for knowledge, I told him to tell the person who wanted to know to come and ask himself. Trigger was a little put out and would not immediately admit there was another party involved. I told him jokingly that the only thing he was capable of blowing was his nose.

The recipient of Trigger's information was Canadian but all referred to him as 'the Yank'. Larry Duncan was his name and we finally got to meet him after Trigger advised him that his espionage game had been foiled.

'So, you're a safe-breaker, too?'

'Yes, Larry,' I replied. 'What brings you to our shores?'

'Advanced safe technology making work almost impossible,' he responded.

That remark had a familiar ring to it and it made him of interest to us. Larry was a dead ringer for Sid James, the actor best known for his roles in the *Carry On* movies. He was loud and opinionated. He had spent most of his life in New York and spoke with a Brooklyn gangster accent. Larry was a safe-blower, doing time for being captured on the premises of a supermarket after shopping hours were over. He was serving a two-year sentence.

'I thought you were originally from Canada,' I said. 'You can't work there?'

'Nope. Jumped bail a while back. I'd be off the street a long time if they caught me for that one. I'll probably go back to the States for a while when my sentence is up, then come back here. Maybe you'd like to work together?'

I hesitated. Beyond curiosity about the extent of his knowledge, I had no reason to work with a stranger. Anyway, the best-laid schemes of future alliances usually went no further than the prison gates. 'Maybe,' I replied, keeping my options open. 'What do you use?'

'Liquid explosive, nitroglycerine. Mainly in seam shots; we have no other choice in the States, as they're all combination locks.'

I had seen a number of Western movies depicting the use of nitroglycerine and its dangers, and there was a classic French film, *The Wages of Fear*, about truck drivers transporting a cargo of the volatile explosive across treacherous South American roads to an oil-well fire.

Most of Larry's criminal career had been spent in Canada and the USA. Older than us by some years, he had been told that safes in England were predominantly opened and closed by key and had visited these shores to investigate this phenomenon. Historically, safes in America and Canada have always been manufactured with combination locks, which poses a major problem for a safe-blower, whose principal aim is to get explosives into the lock mechanism. Without a hole to introduce them through, he is up the creek without a paddle.

We swapped crime stories and compared technical notes on the methodologies used in our different parts of the world. Larry was brash and could easily get up your nose. I could overlook all his abrasive ways when it came to the subject of crime, however. He had obviously been a criminal for many years. The most interesting part of Larry's conversation revolved around the use of nitroglycerine for the purpose of blowing safes. The problem was that, as in England, safes in America were being manufactured to such high standards and tolerances that older methods used to get explosive inside the door were becoming obsolete. We listened to the stories and debated methods over the months. Technically, Larry was pretty accurate, which gave some credibility to his words.

Contrary to the impression you might get from old movies, a stethoscope is of no use when it comes to cracking a combination safe. In reality, you cannot hear the tumblers falling into place. You'd have more chance of hearing Elvis Presley singing. Now, if you could see into the door and view the combination tumblers, that would let you successfully open it. The tumblers are a set of discs revolving around a spindle attached to the safe's external dial, with a drive cam fixed to the spindle end. Each disc has a wheel fly and a slot known as a 'gate' cut into it. The gate's correct position internally corresponds to a number dialled. These discs are close together, each with enough tolerance to allow it to move independently to its gate position when the correct turns of the dial (both number and direction must be right) are made. This process has to be repeated until each slot on each disc lines up with the one next to it. At the correct combination, a bar, or 'fence', as it is called, drops into the gate channel. Of course, if one number or letter is wrong, the fence cannot pass through the gate and the safe will remain closed.

Methods such as seam shots (whereby a small amount of liquid explosive, carefully placed, can be used to blow a safe that has only a combination lock) were unheard of over here, as they were not possible with solid explosive. In our past night-time forays, we had on occasion come across combination-lock safes. A lot of models in

Britain had two-stage locking: that is, with key and combination. As long as we had a key-way entrance, the combination lock didn't matter, as it would be coming off with the door. If our target had only a combination lock, we would simply abort and go home. The production of nitroglycerine was now high on our 'to try' list.

I had studied it enough to know how it was produced commercially and, while Alfred Nobel is often credited with it, Ascanio Sobrero in fact discovered nitroglycerine before Nobel used it to create dynamite. Only a few chemicals are required to create it, arguably one of the most powerful non-nuclear explosives in the world, but making one's own nitro sounded like a very risky procedure. My explosive of choice was plaster, or blasting, gelatine. The most powerful commercial explosive available, it already contained 92 per cent nitroglycerine (mixed with nitrocellulose) so I could see no logical reason for using pure nitro when I first met Larry.

Two years after we were sentenced, we were on the street again. I had to take stock of my life and it did not amount to a hill of beans. With no trade behind me, my prospects for the future did not look rosy. Nitroglycerine was still an issue that aroused burning curiosity in us and, not long after our release, we purchased highly concentrated nitric and sulphuric acids in one-gallon Winchester bottles ordered from a chemist's shop. Glycerine and bicarbonate of soda were also required. The chemicals had to be cold if an explosion was to be prevented and, to avoid buying a large block of ice, we used a freezing stream in a wooded copse at Blackbushe for our laboratory. The process was more nerve-racking than technically demanding. Wearing rubber gloves, I poured strictly measured quantities of the acids into a large Pyrex bowl embedded in the shallows of the stream. As the acids are incompatible, they had to be introduced gradually. I stirred the mixture using a floating dairy thermometer. I knew that when I added the glycerine, the temperature would shoot up. I continued to stir, dissipating the rapidly rising heat. One rash addition of too much glycerine would result in the production of brown smoke – a very urgent warning sign that an explosion was imminent.

Eventually, when all the glycerine was added, the explosive appeared as an oily substance floating on the surface of the acid admixture.

We separated it out by flooding the bowl with cold water. The nitroglycerine then sunk to the bottom of the bowl. Any remaining acidity was removed by 'washing' it with bicarbonate of soda. The finished product was snowy white, unlike commercially produced nitroglycerine, which is yellow. I could not believe how long it took: ten hours, one hour for each fluid ounce produced. The nitroglycerine was decanted into two-fluid-ounce containers with snap-on lids, the lids pierced with a pin to allow the substance to breathe.

When I wasn't playing mad scientist in the woods, I made some straight money at the 47 Club in Camberley. After a visit to the late-night drinking club, I was offered the job of doorman. The place was licensed only during normal pub drinking hours but was frequented mostly after hours, when all the other bars had shut for the night. My job was to vet the clientele who wished to gain access. Only known faces and people not pissed out of their brains were allowed in. I made my own door rules and introduced a sliding scale of financial penalties: in by 10.30, admission free; after 11 p.m. the charge increased incrementally every 15 minutes until midnight, when the door was closed to everyone. This did not go down well, of course. The door charge wasn't ideal but we didn't want the customers drinking elsewhere all evening and using the club to nurse a beer for hours because they couldn't drink any more. I had several fights and two broken noses over the new rules before it sunk in that they weren't going to change. A small casino was opened on the ground floor (this was a few years before stricter gambling regulations would be introduced). It was mainly cards – blackjack, brag and poker. I dealt five-card stud poker and charged a session fee. After a while, I became club manager and was offered free accommodation there.

I found that the Surrey Police followed me and my associates everywhere we went. Yet, when we spoke to them, the same officers seemed to take a perverse pleasure in our successes on other constabularies' patches. Larry returned from New York and we agreed to work together. We carried nitroglycerine 'on the person', usually stuffed into a rolled-up sock and tucked into a breast pocket. If it had exploded, I wouldn't have heard the bang that killed me. When using conventional explosive, I set it in the lock via the key-way, positioned the detonator then withdrew to a safe distance before pressing the wires against the battery at the opportune moment. Introducing nitroglycerine was a little more complicated. Another myth perpetuated by films was that you needed only an eyedropper's quantity of the stuff to blow a door off. I used nitroglycerine to attack the safe at its weakest point. Generally, this, by virtue of its purpose to provide access to goods stored within, was the door. Manufacturers cast their safes in extremely strong, monolithic bodies without seams or apparent structural weaknesses, while only internal hinges and locking bars prevented the door opening. Explosives took the path of least resistance, which in most safes was the area of least metallic mass. To open safes of equal size and weight did not necessarily require equal amounts of explosives. It was determined by the internal door design, the number of bolts and their positioning.

For one job, Larry, Baz and I worked on a new-generation Chubb vault at the headquarters of a large business chain. Given its weight, the door required six ounces of nitroglycerine, more than we had used previously or did subsequently. We packed three tons of peat against the door to prevent it flying onto the nearby motorway. When using explosives in a confined space, there is a fine line between just enough and too much. After the explosion, we found the door still closed in its outer frame but lying several feet from the vault wall, buckled and lying on top of the peat. It was a testament to how good the door was that the path of least resistance was the wall that held it.

The game was almost over again. I was fed up of seeing a police car parked near my house and wanted to work abroad. We should have stopped, because the next one went badly wrong and prompted an even more determined effort to get us off the streets. The police got lucky, as they received a 999 call from a man who heard or saw a disturbance at a factory. We were ready to enter the premises via a long, dark alleyway when police cars pulled up and officers jumped out, torches in hand. My colleagues and I were trapped. Any lingering hope that this was just a routine check vanished when the two policemen shouted, 'Come out. We know you're there. We've got dogs with us.'

What happened next was every British policeman's worst nightmare. Clad in black, Larry emerged from the darkness and pointed the twin barrels of a sawn-off shotgun at them. He fired above the officers' heads, the blasts illuminating the alleyway. I watched as the policemen dropped their torches and ran – the most sensible option, I thought. Knowing the local roads would be blocked, we ignored the escape vehicle we had parked nearby. As we made off on foot, we heard emergency sirens wailing. We kept our heads down as we made our separate ways out of the area. The police scoured the roads and when daylight broke, a local flying club surveyed the countryside looking for an abandoned getaway car. From the reports in the papers, it seemed that the first police officers on the scene had given an inaccurate account of proceedings. Had they not done so, we might not have made it home. Rather than admitting that they ran off when Larry fired the shotgun, they claimed to have been confronted by several armed robbers, whom they chased but who eventually managed to escape in a fast car. As a result, the police put most of their resources into manning roadblocks and searching for an escape vehicle they would never find.

The detectives eventually knocked on our doors because there was a shortage of suspects. As we had left nothing behind and had not even entered the premises, they had little on us. As a rule, we were unarmed robbers; I figured, wrongly, that this would be enough to keep us out of the frame. Again, I put my case to my colleagues that it was time for us to flee these shores. While we would not remain anonymous to Interpol for long, we would have the advantage of international borders and extradition requirements, which would hamper investigations into our activities. This advice again fell on deaf ears. Criminals tended to be parochial. Foreign shores were not on the agenda for the majority; they wanted to swim in the pond they knew best. This applied to my associates as well and it would be our downfall.

The newly constructed prison at Bisley had its safe blown. A security guard was tied up in this raid. His photo appeared in the local paper under a headline that read: 'Ex-Army Desert Rat Fights Six Masked Bandits'. The guard claimed he was a former army wrestling champion, who, after initially beating the crap out of the raiders, was only overpowered by sheer numbers. We got arrested.

With no marks or injuries to indicate we had been in a fight, we were released, although, in fact, there were no marks on the guard either, which would seem to indicate that his ordeal had been somewhat exaggerated. This arrest elevated us into another category: we were now considered armed and dangerous.

I seriously considered calling it a day; my future looked like being 'life on the instalment plan' if I went to prison again. The police had plans for us, however, and a concerted effort to put us behind bars was under way. The 47 Club was raided early one morning in a synchronised operation that targeted all our homes. There was no evidence of safe-blowing to be found but there was a revolver on the premises and I was charged with its possession without a firearms licence. A charge of conspiracy to cause explosions and to steal from safes and strongrooms soon followed. Larry, Baz and Don were accused of being my co-conspirators. The prosecution evidence given at Kingston Assizes was the usual ambiguous stuff; surveillance teams whom we had shaken off didn't exactly present us as law-abiding citizens.

We probably would not have been convicted on the circumstantial evidence the police had of our involvement in the many scores we were accused of being behind; but they had a very big ace in their hand. Larry was living with a woman and her two children. The police had threatened her with being an accessory and the removal of her children to social services. She went Queen's evidence against us. Her testimony was that Larry's pillow talk was about his exploits and who was on what job. She claimed that we had visited her home once and that she had brought coffee into a meeting, stating that she had overheard us discussing safe-blowing. It was suggested that the revolver was the weapon that had been fired at the police officers. This was disproved, as a large wall was directly behind the police, with no strike marks and no bullets found. But evidence such as this paints the picture the prosecution wishes to portray – even if the picture is out of focus. The bottom line was 'guilty'. The aggregate sentences imposed on us totalled over 90 years; fortunately, most of these were concurrent.

I was back in Wandsworth Prison as a long-termer, with a five-stretch on my back. My associates and I were caged in separate cell blocks and put on the A list. The A list was for high-risk prisoners considered to be potential escapers. I was allocated a maximum-security cell, with an armoured outer wall and special anti-cut bars. I had to wear 'patches' on my clothes: a bright-yellow stripe ran down the front and rear of my trouser legs, while big yellow patches adorned the front and back of my jacket. The guard dogs were trained to go for the yellow. I was not allowed to associate with general-population inmates. I went to work for a couple of hours each day in the mailbag shop, where A men sat separately from others. We had our own toilet with a large 'A' painted on it. I was taken to and from anywhere I was going accompanied by my own screw, who carried a passport-type book on him with my picture and other details. At 8 p.m. every evening, my cell furniture and clothes would be removed, leaving me only a shirt, my bed and a piss-pot. At lights out, my light was switched off but an orange night light came on. Even darkness was denied. Every 15 minutes, there was inspection through the peephole; head and face had to be visible above the blanket or the bolt would rattle.

My allocation was the 'special wing' at Chelmsford Prison but notorious armed robber John McVicar was next in line. McVicar was doing time in the chokey block, or punishment cells, considered too dangerous to be let out. I got to Chelmsford eventually, but it took two years. The patches were removed and I went into the long-term block. Parole had been on the Government's agenda for some time and for years prisons had been awash with rumours. Finally, the first releases began; I became eligible and applied. One day, I was called to the governor's office, where he told me, to my surprise, that parole was approved; I could pack my kit, as I was going home early.

One of the conditions of my release was that I had to find work. A construction site subcontractor took me on as casual labour, cladding the steel-frame beams for fire protection. Two weeks after I started, I returned to work after the weekend to find the subbie and his mates had abandoned the site. The site agent gave me the number of the main contractor for the steelwork. I phoned D.H. Charndley Ltd and asked if they were sending a replacement gang. They asked me if I could find my own crew and carry on and I said yes. I was paid by the square foot completed against the site drawings; I submitted the figures verbally every week and payment was made into the local post office to enable me to pay wages. It was six months before I met any of the people I worked for but I had done a good job and they offered me more contracts. I registered Pyroclad Ltd and was on my way to a legal fortune.

With contracts across the country and a workforce of over 50, crime was a fading memory, although the opportunities for criminal ventures were many: I had the drawings for all the sites I worked on, including banks, supermarkets and post offices. On one site, I kept my equipment in the newly installed vault. More than a year after my release, the rest of the crew were out of jail. Baz and Don located me working away from home in Middlesbrough. This contract, on the Teesside Law Courts, was not without a touch of irony. It made a change to walk in and out daily without any worries. I declined the opportunity to go at it again. I would never blow another safe in the UK again. Baz and Don would be arrested a few weeks later after a robbery that involved a shotgun. Don would turn Queen's evidence against Baz, who was sentenced to an extended term of 12 years. Don would get 8 years in a Rule 43 prison for informers and sex offenders requiring protection.

I was awarded a contract on a huge new site in Nottingham. Several weeks after it began, I was asked to attend a site meeting attended by union officials. Local tradesmen on site had lodged a protest at the high wages my crews were earning. Pyroclad was not a union-registered company; my crews worked all hours possible for a fixed price per square foot. The unions wanted my pay scale to come in line with union rates. After much discussion, in the end I refused to comply and Pyroclad Ltd was blacklisted from every union site in England. I was barred from entering the Nottingham site and almost all others. When I was allowed in to recover bench saws and equipment, they had been trashed. I paid all my guys a basic wage while my main contractor tried to resolve it. It was to no avail: four months later and nearly broke, my crews were laid off. I got the non-union jobs but these were small sites and Pyroclad became a one-man band instead of an orchestra.

Larry and a guy called Gerry found me. Like me, Gerry was a former merchant seaman. He had also served with the British Army in Korea. They were rather amused that I was working and said it didn't suit me.

DIRTY COMBAT

I said no to the same question Baz and Don had asked. I put forward the same argument as before: blowing boxes in England was suicidal. The game was history. There were no others to look for if a safe was blown; we might as well leave our driving licences on top of the safe. I knew I wouldn't keep my one-man business going for long, though, and I told them, 'If you decide to go abroad to work, give me a call.'

The call came. We hoped to find a high-value target we could retire on. The downside of working on the Continent was the fact that the police were armed and we, for the most part, were not. We agreed to continue as such and to be cautious in our target selection. Another potential problem was that I was unfamiliar with foreign security systems.

Having entrusted our work tools and explosives to a courier friend, we travelled separately across the English Channel. Scouring a new country for targets, we got a taste for the rich pickings on a visit to an ice-cream company. We blew the strongroom to find canvas bags with brass fittings that resembled Wild West stagecoach bags. They were empty but the banking documents from the previous day showed that the strongroom had contained £100,000 in local currency. We cursed our misfortune and headed towards the coast. We found accommodation in an inconspicuous motel and behaved like tourists, joining guided tours of what was a famous region. We passed a supermarket that met our criteria: remote, accessible only by a narrow country road with no street lights and with no residential properties in its immediate vicinity. We visited it again the following day and left a man there overnight. He observed police armed with sub-machine guns who visited every two hours, while a private security team staggered its inspections so that the supermarket was attended every 60 minutes. There was no nightwatchman but burglar alarms guarded against any attempt to enter through doors or windows.

The weak link in the security chain was found on the roof. Box-shaped ventilation stacks were spread at intervals along the steeply sloped terracotta-tiled surface. A few wiggles and off they came. Gerry, as lookout, lay on the roof, peering over the apex to get a commanding view. We lowered ourselves down onto the roof beams. Stairs below led to the office door but I favoured gaining entry via the suspended tiled ceiling. An impending police inspection meant we had to hide for 15 minutes. Once my colleague on roof detail gave me the all-clear, I removed some tiles. After checking for any hidden alarm systems, Larry lowered me down. The safe was a real beauty, six feet tall with a single door, a wheel-bolt retractor and a handle. Judging by the length of the key shank hanging on the rack, the door was very thick. It was too much to ask that the key would be complete. The notched blade had been removed from the end of the shank.

I lined the inner key-way with plasticine and removed the container of nitroglycerine from my pocket. I poured in multiple fluid ounces and laid the detonator in a pool of the liquid explosive that was draining into the key-way from the small plasticine moulded bowl around its entrance. The detonator's flying leads were looped around the handle on the safe door to prevent the detonator pulling out of the nitroglycerine. As I was going to blow the safe from the roof beams, extension cables were attached to the ends of the leads. The cables ran from the safe, up through the office, into the maze of beams and cantilevers in the roof. Given the remote rural setting, there was no need for materials to pack around the safe to deaden the noise. My concern was a plate-glass window overlooking the shop floor. The police or security guards would notice any shattered glass on their next inspection. A hit on the battery terminals was followed by a healthy-sounding blast. The beauty of such a sturdy modern safe was that it absorbed a lot of the energy of the explosion. The door came clean off, its bottom half having corrugated as it was ripped away from the monolithic body. The shop-floor window remained intact. Beneath clouds of smoke and fumes, cash-boxes and bundles of currency had spilled out across the floor. I was aware that there might be a silent alarm system and, besides, we would have to carry everything on an exhausting cross-country hike back to the nearest town, so we allowed just two minutes to stuff as much of the loot as we could into a bag.

The return journey, along an untried route, was a catalogue of painful errors and false alarms. Every farm seemed to be home to a pack of dogs that sounded our arrival and departure. We lost considerable time zigzagging across the rough terrain to avoid more farms. 'Fuck it,' I said eventually. 'Let's make for the road we came in on.'

Larry, Gerry and I marched in single file, keeping at least 50 metres apart so the point man and tail-end Charlie could sound the alarm. It was a cold, moonless night and the sky was as black as coal. Headlights lit up the bend ahead and we dived for cover. Gerry, whose turn it was to carry the swag, jumped over a wall, not knowing what was on the other side. Larry and I emerged unscathed from the bushes. No sign of Gerry. We peered over the wall. Larry spotted him soaking wet and crawling up the bank of a stream.

'Have you still got the bag?' asked Larry, his tone less than sympathetic. Gerry cursed him through chattering teeth.

'Well done for not letting go of it, Gerry,' I chuckled.

'Fuck off, Dave.'

We remained on schedule to reach the outskirts of the town by dawn. As locals made their way to work, we would merge into the pedestrian traffic. We climbed a big hill and I caught a glimpse of flickering street lights. Just then, there was another shout warning of an approaching car and I dived for cover. I burst through the roadside bushes; beyond was only fresh air. My head-first descent lasted long enough for me to contemplate my fate. In all probability, I was going to die. I had fallen over the edge of what had once been a quarry, now reclaimed by nature. My fall was broken by a tree, which I met head-on, before I crashed through its branches from top to bottom. My right foot got trapped in a branch, leaving me hanging a few feet from the ground in teeth-grinding pain. It was a couple of minutes before I heard familiar voices.

'Dave?'

'Dave, are you all right?'

'Help me.'

Larry and Gerry pulled me from the tree and I fell the last few feet to earth. I hobbled back up to the roadside, anxious to make up for lost time, but my every move brought pain. I was furious, knowing that the sight of three strangers, one of whom could barely walk, was going to attract attention. I feared I was now a burden to Larry and Gerry. Having done some thinking through the waves of pain, I came to a halt.

'Look,' I said, 'we can't go on like this. You two go on. I'll wait here.

Everyone's going to be staring at us, especially since I need help to walk.' I don't think Larry and Gerry knew what to say. I continued, 'I'll get myself to that bus stop over there. You go for the car and come back for me. I'll sit there and wait for the pair of you.'

'But what if there's a problem at the motel or you have to move before we make it back here?' asked Larry.

'You guys can leave a signal marker in the window at the hotel. If I get back without you and it's not there, I'll know something's gone wrong and I'll be on my own. We can't plan for everything. We'll just have to be lucky.'

I felt sick as I watched Larry and Gerry depart. The town was awake. Shopkeepers lowered awnings and buses passed by. I felt so conspicuous, hobbling and sweating profusely. I watched a butcher fill his window display, arranging cuts of meat to maximise their desirability. He glanced at me. I smiled, hoping he had not seen me limp to my seat at the bus stop. I didn't want him to offer me any assistance. With passengers boarding and alighting every few minutes, my sitting there looked peculiar. When my friendly butcher shuffled outside to lower his awning, I thought it was time to move. I hobbled to the nearest café, stopping occasionally to peer through shop windows. The pain was such that vomit flooded the inside of my mouth. I swallowed repeatedly to get rid of it. I composed myself before entering the café and propped myself on a stool.

'A large coffee and a cognac, please.' The barman nodded. Lowering my eyes, I saw business cards advertising a local taxi company. I downed my cognac, ordered another and requested the barman to ring me a cab. I heard the wail of sirens and craned my neck to see a cavalcade of police vehicles speeding along the main street, their lights flashing. Patrons and staff rushed to the front window for a better view. Only I knew what had prompted such a response from the usually underworked constabulary. The cab pulled up outside the bar and I shuffled towards it. The driver dropped me off at a hypermarket close to the motel, from where I could see the marker indicating that it was safe to return. As agreed, a towel was draped out of the window as though drying. I hobbled to my room, showered, shaved and put on clean clothes. My right leg was discoloured up to the thigh with bruising. Larry and Gerry arrived half an hour later. I had left before they'd arrived at my bus-stop resting place, the police convoy having passed them en route.

'I think we should head to the airport immediately,' I said. 'I'm not going to be fully mobile again for a long time and it's likely to get very hot around here.'

'OK,' said Larry. 'We'll clear up anything that could have forensics on it and check out.'

We returned the hire car and booked ourselves onto the first flight to London. It was an indirect flight via another European city. We deliberately kept apart at the airport, as we guessed that the police would be searching for a gang rather than an individual. I sat in a bar downing brandies and swallowing painkillers, hoping the pain in my ankle would subside. Eventually, I took a seat in the terminal. I was drowsy and woozy from the alcohol and pills. I woke up soaked in sweat to discover I had missed my flight. The assistants at the check-in desk told me they had called for me over the loudspeaker system. I booked myself onto the next London-bound flight. It was a direct service; I would reach London before the others. I passed through customs without any difficulties and met up with Larry and Gerry at Heathrow.

I visited a hospital the next day, explaining to the nurses that I had fallen from a moving car while drunk and my foot had caught beneath the seat. From the colouration of the bruising, it was obvious that I hadn't sought treatment immediately. They didn't ask too many questions, however. They just plastered me up and gave me painkillers.

CHAPTER 4

TIPPING THE SCALES

MY ANKLE WAS BROKEN AND I WAS OUT OF THE LOOP AS FAR AS safe-blowing was concerned. This would turn out to be my retirement from the game. I got stopped by local detectives shortly after my return across the English Channel. They had paid a visit to the scene of a robbery somewhere on the Mediterranean coast, during which a large safe had been blown open with nitroglycerine. They laughingly advised against taking a trip back there for a while, as the cops there were very pissed off. I, of course, denied all knowledge, even though it was far from their jurisdiction. They had enjoyed their trip, apparently, and asked me if I would consider having my next overseas venture somewhere even more exotic, like the Caribbean, so they could have some fun in the sun at some other country's expense.

I'd pushed my luck far enough, at least for the time being. My mate Baz was still doing time and he was the only one I really trusted. Larry had become a liability. When he'd had a drink, he was loud and full of gangster talk. Thankfully, he was living in London's East End with a drinking pal, an Irishman in his 60s called Leo Carroll. It wasn't long before Larry was arrested again, for a robbery in Kent that went pear-shaped. He eventually stood trial at Canterbury Crown

Court, where he was acquitted. The police had gilded the forensic lily just a bit too much for an astute jury to trust the evidence and the jurors returned a unanimous not-guilty verdict. Financially, I was up and down like a yo-yo, betting on racing and playing poker. At least my gambling wasn't going to put me in jail. I took the odd contract in the fire-protection game to keep the wolf from the door if my horses ran slowly or everyone else got the aces.

Then I was arrested along with Gerry, Larry and Leo. In a raid on Larry and Leo's flat, they had found nitro. One of the robberies we were suspected of was of a school somewhere in Sussex. I said to them, 'What the fuck were you thinking about? Were you so broke you went after the kids' dinner money?' There was no way they were going to plead guilty and get me out of their shit, so I stood trial for conspiracy to cause explosions and steal from safes and strongrooms at the Old Bailey alongside Larry, Gerry and Leo. The prosecution QC told the jury, 'Ladies and gentlemen, we cannot prove that any one of these individuals committed any one of these specific crimes. What we intend to prove by the end of this trial is that they conspired to do so.'

I accepted the advice of my legal team and remained silent throughout the two-week trial. This was my legal right and it was the customary procedure in cases of this nature. The QC was clever enough to make the most innocuous items and events sound incriminating. I found it frustrating not being able to rebut the flimsy evidence against me. The jury listened intently to an introduction to safe-breaking, the tools, the methodology and the techniques. As the main explosive used in the alleged crimes was nitro, the prosecution stated that, historically, it had not been used before in England and that all safes and vaults known to have been blown using nitro bore the signature of the same criminal gang: us.

The jury retired to consider their verdict of guilty – or so we assumed. After a stipulated period of consideration, the judge recalled them. 'I must advise you in law that if you are having difficulty finding unanimous verdicts, I will accept majority verdicts of ten to two. I will now send you back.'

A few hours later, the judge recalled them again. He must have wanted to know whether they required hotel rooms that night. Then the foreman stood up and took everyone by surprise, saying, 'Your Honour, we have now reached unanimous verdicts on two defendants.'

This appeared to please the judge. 'I will allow you to give those verdicts.'

'On the charges against Duncan and Carroll, we find them unanimously not guilty.'

I don't know who was most dumbfounded: Larry and Leo, the chief counsels or the old judge. The colour drained from his face. I was absolutely convinced I would be acquitted.

'We haven't reached verdicts on the other two,' the foreman said.

There was no way the judge was going to let a favourable jury acquit Gerry and me. He said, 'Well, obviously you're having some difficulty. We'll call it a day here. Record this as a hung jury on Lane and Tomkins. It will have to go to a second trial.'

His intervention angered me. But what choice did he have? It was accepted in the legal profession that there were more acquittals in trials of this nature in London than elsewhere. Most professional criminals then would prefer to be tried at the Old Bailey than anywhere else. If we had stood trial in Somerset, we would have been found guilty before a word of evidence was heard.

Sureties of £10,000 were stood against Gerry and me, and we were free on bail again. It left us hanging. At the second trial, the prosecution would have had the opportunity to refine its case, combing through the evidence and arranging its presentation in a style more suited to convincing the jury of our guilt. The lead QC was becoming an expert on explosives. He and I had a little previous, too. He had prosecuted me at an earlier trial and won. By the look of him, he relished the chance to do so again and put me away for a longer stretch.

At our initial arrest, to ensure that all of us would receive bail, I did a deal that very nearly backfired. Against my better judgement, I agreed to hand over to the police a quantity of explosives stolen from a quarry in the French Alps.

'We wouldn't want anybody else getting hold of it,' said the policeman as he began his gambit.

'Well, I don't know what you're talking about. I'm as pure as the driven snow. But I might be able to get hold of some explosives, if you give me a little time.'

'Good.'

'But to reiterate, they wouldn't be my explosives and this exchange between us couldn't be used against me in any future legal proceedings.'

'Agreed.'

'And you can take the credit for finding it.'

'OK.'

The same policeman rang me every week. Eventually, I told him that a criminal contact of mine had located some explosives and I could arrange transfer into police hands. 'I've just had a bit of a result. Where do you want it?'

'I'll meet you.'

'Where?'

'Bagshot.'

'Down the A30? Whereabouts?'

'Opposite Pennyhill Park Country Club. There's a Little Chef and a car park.'

When he arrived, a friend of mine was waiting in the bushes with a camera. He captured the event for posterity and my peace of mind. I never knew when a policeman might rat on me.

'I've got the explosives and detonators with me.'

'Sit down. We'll have a cup of coffee,' he replied nervously.

Afterwards, we went back outside and I put the package in his hand. Yes, I thought, I've got him on film receiving explosives from me.

Suddenly, as he was holding the parcel, he must have realised his mistake.

'Hold on. How am I going to explain this?'

'I'm merely honouring my obligation to you.' I was angry. But we had come this far. 'Look, we'll pick a place we both know and you can come and collect it. I'll hide it. This is the last I ever want to hear about it.'

I put the explosives behind an agreed boulder and he 'found' them.

Near the date of the second trial, I was arrested for possession of explosives. My solicitor looked at me like I was mad when she found out about it. I explained the circumstances. She knew me very well and was aware that I wouldn't try to spin her a line, but nonetheless, it must have sounded far-fetched. Special Branch had requested, via an intermediary, that I supply them with a quantity of explosives, which they would then use in a sting operation against the IRA, enticing the terrorists to purchase it on the street. My motive was not to defeat Irish republicanism but to help Larry, who, having been found not guilty at the first trial, was already back behind bars. His case required some bargaining.

It was a very hush-hush deal, not least because the last thing I wanted was for word to spread that I had got into bed with the enemy. Prior to this occasion, I had always done everything possible to obstruct the course of justice. What was required was a monitored sale of stolen explosives that would eventually lead to a terrorist bomb factory. 'If they get it from you, it'll be coming from a credible criminal source and they won't be onto the fact that it's a set-up,' explained the Special Branch detective. My concern was palpable. 'Look, there'll be no comeback for you. You won't even know who you're supplying to.'

'Fucking hell!' I replied, 'If it goes boss-eyed, I'm going to have the Paddies after me.'

'No, no, you'll be fine. It won't be the bombers who turn up for it. It'll be a courier. But we need to see the transaction take place, wherever. After you hand it over, we'll never lose track of it. We want to follow it until it arrives at the actual place where the bombers are going to build their device. It will be very far removed from you, Mr Tomkins. Nobody will have any idea how instrumental you were.'

I told him I'd try to get hold of the explosives and he asked me to bring the material to a police station in Marylebone. On the day, I went upstairs and into a boardroom. He and I were discussing the operation when a senior station officer burst in. He had the broadest of Irish accents, which I considered ironic, given the set-up.

'I am arresting you for possession of explosives.'

I assumed the Special Branch officer would have the cuffs taken off. He only put up minimal protest as I was led downstairs, searched and had my property booked into the log. I signed a sheet for my wallet, cigarettes, a cigar box full of explosives and some detonators.

'Where did you get this?' said the woodentop behind the desk, pointing at the explosives. What did he expect me to say?

'Funnily enough, I was at a bus stop when I looked down and there it was. I picked it up and thought, fuck me, I'd better do my job as a good citizen and bring it to the local police station.'

I was surprised and confused when my property was handed back minus the explosives and I was granted police bail. I walked down the steps, furious that I had been set up. The Special Branch officer was standing outside. 'Mate, I'm sorry about that. It wasn't supposed to happen. We hadn't briefed the crime squad about what's going on.'

'Mate? Don't "mate" me. Fuck off. You promised me you were going to protect me from the IRA and you can't even protect me from your own police. I came here by your appointment and I only got hold of those explosives in order to give them to you.'

Sitting in her office, I told my solicitor the story. When I'd finished, she said, 'Good God, how are we going to get out of this? How are we going to prove your version of events?'

'I don't know, but on my life, I was there with the explosives by appointment. All I've got is the phone number of my controller at Special Branch. I memorised it.'

She reached for her telephone and put in a call on speaker. Her staff gathered around so that they could be called as witnesses in court.

She asked for my contact but was told he wasn't available and was put through to another officer.

'Hello, I am speaking on behalf of Mr David Tomkins, whom I represent. I am concerned about an incident this morning at a London police station that allegedly involved him, regarding the transfer of a quantity of explosives.'

There was silence at the other end of the telephone. We glanced at each other, wondering what was going to happen next.

'Yes,' the male voice stuttered, 'I have Mr Tomkins' file in front of me. I am informed of the circumstances to which you refer. But I am afraid I am not at liberty to discuss them. The control officer you mentioned is temporarily absent. Any further discussion about this matter will require the approval of his and my superiors.'

'We've got them,' she said when she hung up.

The policeman's tacit acknowledgement of my relationship with Special Branch supported my defence. I felt vindicated.

Knowing that the outcome of the second trial was going to shape my life, I was extremely nervous. By this time, it wasn't just my own life that would be affected if I was put away. I had a wife and daughter, and a son about to be born, as Mary was heavily pregnant. Only somebody who has sat in the dock as a defendant can empathise with my frustration at listening to the version of events as presented by the prosecution. As they put their case to the jury at the Old Bailey once again, I felt helpless and angry listening to the police officers giving evidence as if they were angels and to so-called explosives experts giving ambiguous answers to leading questions about how safes were blown and how evidentiary exhibits might be applied as tools. I could not take another few weeks listening to all that, followed by the almost inevitable guilty verdict. I would be taken down from the dock never to see the light of day again, or at least not for a decade.

I experienced a moment of epiphany at Waterloo railway station. 'I'm going to fight. I'm going to give evidence. I'm not just going to sit there and listen to all the conjecture and half-truths.'

My legal team advised against it but I was immovable. I was sworn in on the opening day of defence evidence and asked by my counsel, 'Mr Tomkins, what is it you do for a living?'

'I am a professional safe-breaker.'

Everyone in court was stunned. The prosecution team must have been inwardly elated, thinking I was three-quarters of the way to admitting I had done everything of which I was accused.

The judge banged his gavel for order and silence fell over the courtroom. 'Mr Tomkins, is your statement accurate? Is it an admission of your guilt?'

'Your Honour, I am well known to the police for my exploits. But I no longer operate in the United Kingdom. My work is now confined to overseas.'

'Oh, I see,' the judge replied caustically. 'You admit to being a safe-blower but it's the geographical area that is in dispute?'

'Yes, that is correct.'

I hoped this all-guns-blazing start would win over the jury. It also gave me licence to challenge all the so-called expert prosecution witnesses on the technical aspects of their testimony. For the benefit of the jury, I gave a lengthy address on how to blow a safe and what implements and materials were required for the task. The prosecution had claimed that nitroglycerine was introduced to the lock mechanism through the inside of a ballpoint pen with its cartridge removed. I disputed this and openly described my own method of inserting nitro without a ballpoint pen. I challenged the prosecution on other supposedly incriminating items such as knitting needles, ice-lolly sticks, condoms, plasticine and modelling clay, 'These are generic items that have historically made up a conventional safe-blowing kit. My alleged offences involve the use of nitro, for which different methods and pieces of equipment are used.'

The prosecution claimed to have found a baby doll's toy bottle in the garden at my home, one that I had supposedly used to store nitro and feed it into a lock mechanism. My defence counsel put it to the jury, 'If Mr Tomkins is careful enough to enter the crime scene undetected, blow the safe without leaving behind any incriminating evidence, leave the crime scene undetected and deposit no forensic evidence on his clothing or at home, it is highly unlikely that he would idly discard the baby's bottle on his lawn.'

There were moments of theatre. One involved a home-made key, or picklock, a device the prosecution claimed I could use to turn off burglar alarms fitted with a tubular lock. Again, this was in any case gilding the lily, as none of the robbery sites under discussion were fitted with such lock-equipped alarms. The moving parts of the picklock were modified hairpins, with an elastic band wrapped around the main shaft. Two seemingly identical tubular locks mounted on a wooden board were brought into court. The unseen difference was internal: the second of these locks was used to enable or disable burglar alarms. In front of the jury, and against the clock, I opened and closed the first lock but had no luck with the second, and I explained why.

The prosecution's locksmith, who had made unjustifiable claims for the picklock, was recalled. My counsel asked him to use the device to open the lock I had had no success with. With a stopwatch ticking and the courtroom silent, he set to work. He failed, even after several attempts.

The prosecution called for a recess. As we filed out of the courtroom, I saw the members of the jury looking at me. Several gave me a nod or a wink and one whispered to me from the corner of his mouth, 'I would love one of those.' When we resumed, the prosecution came off worse again. Mary was called to give evidence about items removed from our house. She explained that the police had removed her riding crop. 'Do they think he whips the safes open?' she added.

The prosecution decided to play dirty. Counsel asked the judge if he would allow an additional charge of possession of explosives – explosives I had signed for as 'in my possession' on an official police property sheet at the time of an arrest.

My barrister and I were furious. The jury was requested to leave while legal arguments were put. When these failed, my story was explained to the judge. The judge summoned my Special Branch handler to the Old Bailey. For security reasons, his testimony was heard in camera. The judge said, 'We're not interested in hearing your name or what you were doing. But was Mr Tomkins on the morning in question at the police station attending a previously arranged appointment with you and were you aware that he would be bringing explosives with him?'

'Yes.'

'Thank you very much. That is all you need to say.'

The judge tore into the police and told the jury to ignore what they had not heard and not to assume any guilt on my part in connection to it. This, and the time the jury spent out of court during the legal arguments, harmed the prosecution.

Then they tried a similar trick with the explosives I had handed the police officer outside the Little Chef restaurant. The prosecution requested permission to introduce new evidence relating to the 'discovery' of a quantity of explosives. A statement was offered as evidence of the recovery of this explosive material, which incriminated me. The court was adjourned for 30 minutes and the jury sent back to their room. The statement did not match the facts. I called out, 'How would you like the truth? Do you want it in full colour?' The prosecution looked startled. I explained the photographic evidence I could produce to my counsel. Prosecution and defence went into a huddle. The statement was withdrawn. The jury returned looking even more puzzled at what they were not about to hear.

During the judge's summing up, I received another hint of what the outcome might be. Some of the jurors had their arms cradled, mimicking the carrying of a baby as a reference to Mary's pregnancy. When I mouthed the word 'boy', they gave me thumbs-up signs. I was taken down to the cells as they retired to consider their verdict. Time passed slowly. After a few hours, the jurors were recalled and briefed on the option of passing a majority verdict. It was nearly 7 p.m., and court staff were waiting with their keys to close the Old Bailey when the jurors were recalled again. The judge offered them a hotel for the evening and suggested they could continue their deliberations tomorrow. The foreman told the judge that this was unnecessary. I looked at them; from previous experience, I knew that jurors avoided eye contact with you when they had reached a guilty verdict, as if ashamed of their decision. One juror looked straight at me and, with a half-smile, shook his head.

'Your Honour,' said the foreman, 'we are completely divided. We are unable to reach even a majority verdict.'

The judge looked crestfallen.

'Are you sure you don't want to come back tomorrow?'

'We could sit for another three months and we would not reach a verdict.'

This left the very unhappy judge with no option but to discharge the jury. He took the rare step of excusing them from future jury service, an implicit reprimand. The chief counsel for the prosecution threw down his papers and marched out. The police officers who had worked for so long on my case looked equally disgruntled. The judge then sought to remand me in custody for three weeks. He could not legally do this but he was so angry I think he lost the plot. My team raised objections and he withdrew his order. With a look of disgust, he read me the law pertaining to my situation: 'Tomkins and Lane, as you have twice been tried by a jury of your peers and no verdict has been reached, the law states you should be formally acquitted on all charges. I pronounce you not guilty.'

With that, he slammed his books closed and left the court.

'London juries,' I chuckled to myself. The jurors had seen me for what I was: a right villain. But some had also taken a shine to me.

Gerry, who hadn't said a word throughout the case, was amazed. I felt so relieved that when we bumped into the cops outside the court, I said, 'I have now retired.' The senior officer replied, 'I'm glad to hear it.'

Gerry moved out of the area and got married. He started a construction company and some years later he died of cancer. For my part, I was unaware, when I walked out of court that day, that a new adventure was just around the corner.

CHAPTER 5

FOOL'S GOLD

WHILE THE OLD BAILEY TRIALS WERE GOING ON, I REACHED another crossroads in life when I had the dubious privilege of meeting John Banks. It was 1972 and Mary, our daughter and I were living in Camberley in a maisonette above a shopping precinct, a few hundred yards from the Royal Military Academy. The apartment shared with three others a communal patio overlooking fields to the back of the building. Having been in residence only a few days, I awoke on a Sunday morning and followed my nose to the kitchen where Mary was making coffee. Mug in hand, I stood idly staring out the window over the fields. Our next-door neighbour's door opened and into view came an incongruous figure. Everything he was wearing was black, from head to toe; black jumpsuit, boots, gloves, helmet and visor. The apparition had a parachute on its back.

Mary told me it was John Banks, our neighbour. She said he'd been in all kinds of secret-squirrel military outfits. I glanced at the fields again to make sure I hadn't missed a plane; I hadn't. This had to be investigated. With my coffee, I went out and sat on the step to our front door. Banks was a showman if nothing else; looking skyward, he waited until he was good and ready before he acknowledged my presence. With an upward flip of the visor, in a clipped army officer's voice, he spoke: 'Morning! Good ceiling – 22 thou, my guess.'

I responded politely, observing that he was probably going parachuting. I figured this would impress him with my powers of deduction.

'Do you jump?'

'Not unless it's absolutely necessary . . . but it's always looked interesting. There's still time.'

As I watched, he removed his pack and explained its inner workings. He unfolded the silken chute and laid elastic bands, lengths of paracord and pins on the ground. He was trying, but failing, to impress me. I had met my share of bullshitters already; John Banks was just another name on a long list. My instinct told me that he was a plonker, but an interesting plonker. If he jumped out of planes and trekked to faraway countries in his job as a long-haul truck driver, as he said he did, he was certainly more interesting than most of the people who lived around here.

Inside Banks' flat, which was spotlessly clean, I was drawn to his military memorabilia. A shield emblazoned with a winged dagger and the 'Who Dares Wins' motto implied a connection to the Special Air Service Regiment. Other mementos recalled covert operations in Radfan and Borneo. Nonetheless, I made allowances for any inflation of his military prowess.

Over coffee, we swapped life stories, embellishing certain aspects and skipping over less noble episodes, as men do. I hinted at my safe-blowing expertise while mentioning on the legitimate side the fire-protection company I ran and my construction enterprises. He hinted that I might be useful to him. Likewise, he might be useful to me.

Banks looked more like a second-hand car salesman than a soldier but nevertheless he had served with the Parachute Regiment's elite Pathfinder unit. I gave little credence to his claims to have been wounded in action. He said he had been shot in the stomach in Borneo and grazed across the face by shrapnel in Aden but he didn't have any scars. His British Army career had ended acrimoniously in 1968. He had used a bouncing cheque to buy a Jaguar car, which he proceeded to drive without insurance and while disqualified for previous driving offences: a triple whammy. He had been given a one-year prison sentence and discharged.

For more than a year, Banks and I were neighbours but our paths rarely crossed; our jobs took both of us away from home. On one of the rare occasions when we bumped into each other, he asked, 'Is it possible to open a bank account with an overdraft?'

'No, not unless you're related to the bank manager . . . Why?'

'Because I'm thinking of starting a transport company, trucking goods to the Middle East. You might want to get involved.'

'Perhaps.'

Banks was better placed than me to borrow money. As a rule, I'd visited my local branch to blow the safe and by this time I had spent eight of my thirty-four years behind bars. He explained his business proposal. A driver who owned his tractor unit or rig could demand 75 per cent of the fee up front to deliver freight to far-off destinations such as Afghanistan. The first serious obstacle to this venture was that he didn't have a lorry but bluffing came easily to both of us and we persuaded Ipswich Transit Express over the phone to subcontract the delivery of oil-drilling equipment to Iraq. For one pound, we registered the company name Trans-Asian Express and with ten pounds we opened a bank account. A call to Rentco Ltd secured a 40-foot trailer, the fee payable 24 hours after our load pick-up. Basingstoke Haulage obliged on the same terms. We parked our truckless trailer in a nearby lay-by. In four days, we turned £10 into £1,800, less rental and collection costs. The balance of funds was used to repeat the exercise and for £600 we purchased a lorry from Wall's Ice Cream, which we painted red and called 'the Baghdad Flyer'. We purchased a second truck the following week and rented a third after the necessary transit permits were obtained, or forged.

The world of long-haul road freight was embryonic; many firms of owner-drivers like ours were trying their luck to make a buck but there was a lot that could go wrong. The journeys were long and frustrating, with corrupt border guards to be bribed and bandits to be avoided in isolated areas. However, we stood as good a chance of success as the next bunch of cowboys and to begin with everything went swimmingly. Banks drove one of the trucks and we hired two drivers for the others, Mick and Andy. My role was to oversee operations from our office at the Banks' kitchen table. Then Mick's vehicle jack-knifed in the Tarsus Mountains of Turkey, leaving his load hanging over a cliff edge. The only way to save his Volvo F88 rig was to pull the pin and let the trailer drop. His insurance papers for the trailer load were my forgeries. Banks and Andy, meanwhile, were having a hair-raising time in Iraq, finding themselves in the midst of a gun battle between Kurdish separatists and the Iraqi army.

Butcher's load, now languishing in a ravine, had been subcontracted to Trans-Asian Express without the knowledge of the main contractor, a large European outfit. The company were major players, moving freight across several continents. Its bosses were unlikely to be blasé about the loss. I thought it better to make contact and admit what had gone wrong. The same day, two executives from the company knocked on Banks' front door. His wife looked ashen-faced as she ushered the pair into the lounge, from where they could hardly miss the 'office' in the kitchen. She made coffee while I explained what had happened. They listened and then chatted among themselves.

The younger of the two said, 'Mr Tomkins, you are the first honest Englishman I've met in this business. Many of our cargoes go missing, are abandoned in remote places, sold on, stolen or confiscated at borders. You are the first person who has voluntarily brought this to our attention. We recognise that accidents of this nature will occur. Your driver did the right thing. Our insurance will cover it. We just need your driver's telephone number so we can arrange for a wrecking crew from Istanbul to visit the site.'

To my surprise, he made me an offer. 'Mr Tomkins, we've got freight contracts piling up faster than we can move them on. In order to shift them, we'd prefer to work with a single company we can trust.'

'How much freight are we talking about?'

'Around 2,000 trailer movements for the first year.'

On Banks' return from Iraq, we agreed terms and Trans-Asian Express was incorporated as a limited company. Its shares were divided between Banks and his wife, who took a controlling stake of 60 per cent, and me. We rented out a neighbouring maisonette and turned the lounge into an international operations room, equipped with multiple telephone lines, telexes and radios. Maps and clocks for various time zones adorned the walls.

During 1974, we squandered a golden opportunity. The pace was frenetic and the days long; we struggled to cope with the schedules imposed by the main contractor, loading up to 13 movements a day and trying to get them on the road with all the correct documents. The pool of owner-drivers was depleted as demand exceeded supply. The average trip turnaround time was six weeks and trucks were out of the loop in ever-increasing numbers. The trailer companies we used were running out of trailers and we began importing them from Holland. Having accepted too many orders, we were forced to rent an airfield and park the freight awaiting transportation – more than 100 trailers and goods worth millions of pounds.

We asked the Europeans to reduce our workload but they dismissed our request, explaining that they too had overcommitted themselves. I was working my nuts off on paperwork to get trucks through many different borders, with typists who could barely spell Istanbul or Baghdad and didn't know enough geography to realise that Germany preceded Iraq on the drivers' route documents. Banks seemed to employ these girls on the basis that they looked like they might shag him. At one point, there was a sudden influx of new staff. When I asked what this was about I was advised that we were diversifying: the strangers were ex-rear gunners from Borneo or some other old war zone and we were starting up a craneless crane-hire company.

Money was flooding in daily but there were many arguments over the appalling wastage of company funds. The crane-hire division had company cars; even Banks' mother had a company car. One day, Banks went to TAE's London office in a brand-new Jaguar and came back in a Range Rover towing a caravan. When he was questioned about this, his response was that the caravan would *save* the company money on hotel bills on trips abroad to resolve breakdowns! Sensing trouble, given the lack of freight movements, I hired an accountant to conduct a forensic audit. After ten days, he emerged from the office where he'd been working to say, 'You're all mad and you're going to end up in jail.' Prophetic words.

It became obvious to the European company that they were killing our operation with overload. We were invited to attend a meeting at their London office. They brought in Lombard Finance and a senior sales rep from Mercedes-Benz. We were offered a million-pound credit line with a blanket guarantee by them for the purchase of 100 Mercedes-Benz tractor units at £10,000 each. I requested time to consider it. I had to advise them that we had a shortfall of over £150,000, required to clear the trailers parked at the airfield, this caused a mini-panic. They had no idea about the crazy spending spree of our MD, who had taken half the staff on a business trip to Beirut.

The cash-flow problem was resolved at a meeting with their lawyers several days later. They drew up a legal agreement between the bigger firm and us. The sum we owed them was to be repaid by a deduction of £100 per trailer loaded and they were prepared to give us over £3,000,000 worth of business to balance the books.

At this point, I thought that common sense would prevail, that this diamond-studded lifebelt would be the turning point for us, from disaster to success. But it was not to be. When Banks returned from Beirut, major rows developed over how the company was going to operate in future. He saw the lifeline we'd been thrown as the key to the sweet shop. I learned he was purchasing a £200,000 house from some ex-army officer he knew; he paid a £20,000 cash deposit without getting a receipt. The seller sold the house to another party and flew to South Africa, leaving TAE in an even bigger hole. At a very loud board meeting, demanded by me, with minutes taken, the details of John's commercially unsound approach to the company's financial well-being were discussed. The result was that I resigned. Six weeks later, the company was declared insolvent when the European company pulled the plug. In due course, TAE was taken before a bankruptcy tribunal; Banks' lack of cooperation was duly noted in case of any future application to have his bankruptcy discharged.

For the time being, I was not interested in going into business with Banks again, at least not on his terms. As far as I was concerned, I couldn't trust him – not because he was deceitful (he never disguised his exorbitant expenditure of company money and indeed I don't think he would have minded had I treated myself to a Jaguar) but because he was plain irresponsible. On the other hand, there was always an outside chance that he would bullshit into existence a scheme that I could benefit from.

By May 1975, I had moved my family to a house in the same area. I still paid the occasional visit to the defunct TAE offices, out of curiosity. The phones and telexes were still in place and a few of the ex-military staff were still hanging around. Over a few beers, outrageous suggestions for a new company were bandied about. Rent-a-Thug and Rent-a-Stud were suggested. Then, someone suggested that, with all the former soldiers they knew, a mercenary army could be raised for hire. Banks was not slow to see the potential. Within minutes, he was on the phone to the *Daily Mirror* and the *Daily Mail*. The advertisement read: 'Ex-commandos, paratroopers and SAS wanted for interesting work abroad. Ring Camberley 33456.' Within 48 hours, the response was overwhelming. The phone rang off the hook, CVs were requested and details filed on Rolodex. Transport movement wallboards were transformed into lists of battle groups as hundreds applied. This next venture would be funded by the sale of TAE assets. Banks was in his element: from a transport company MD without a truck to commander-in-chief of a cardboard army. Another one-pound registration fee bought the name International Security Organisation (ISO). All that was required now was a war.

Fantasist and bullshitter that he was, Banks was also a pioneer of the modern mercenary industry and saw an opportunity to provide former British soldiers to fight in private wars overseas. He could not resist a bit of embellishment, claiming that a very famous ex-SAS officer had agreed to bankroll his private force. To my mind, Banks' trips to meet retired colonels in Herefordshire were figments of his vivid imagination.

Banks wanted to send ISO soldiers to Rhodesia, where Ian Smith's government was engaged in a guerrilla war against groups such as the Zimbabwe African National Union (ZANU). Many recruits must have assumed that Banks intended them to fight on Smith's side but at a recruitment meeting at a London hotel, Banks said, 'Any person present not prepared to fight against white soldiers on behalf of a black army should leave now.'

A few South African and Rhodesian soldiers got up and left,

mumbling profanities. Banks briefed the remainder on the itinerary. Interviews and selection in the UK would be followed by a period of intensive training across the border from Zimbabwe in Zambia. The unit would divide into four-man teams, or 'sticks', for infiltration and sabotage operations on the railway system, bridges, roads and military instillations.

Banks continued, 'A rank system and strict codes of discipline will be in operation at all times. Any person found guilty of rape will be summarily executed by firing squad. Anyone wounded too badly to return to base unassisted will be left to die or be captured by the enemy.' Banks was stony-faced. I couldn't hide my disdain. To me, this ran contrary to the natural instincts and camaraderie of men fighting alongside each other.

'Our weapons,' Banks went on, 'will be from Warsaw Pact countries and China. Most, if not all, of you will be familiar with AK-47s. The pay will be generous. Ordinary troopers will get £150 per week, officers as much as £500. A sum of £2 million to finance the assignment has already been deposited in a Swiss bank account. There will be no difficulty getting you your wages and I will be staying here in the UK as paymaster, so if there are any problems, I will sort them out.

'There are forms being distributed for you to fill in, regarding life insurance. Put down your names and addresses, followed by the names and addresses of your next of kin or other beneficiaries. I also require you to sign a form declaring yourselves to be in good health and not suffering from any physical infirmities. We can arrange life-insurance cover at a rate of £25,000 in the event of your death. Those chosen for this mission will be notified in a fortnight and departure for Africa will be at very short notice.'

While Banks did not mention Rhodesia by name at this event, the media were certain of the destination. There was a great deal of negative publicity and ISO was bombarded with hate mail. Supporters of Smith's regime called radio stations to protest about the coup being planned in London. Two RAF officers wrote to tell us they would drop their payloads on our offices. The news didn't even please ZANU. A representative of the organisation wrote to Banks:

Comrade,

It was with great anger that I read the article in the *Daily Telegraph* of the 2nd of June which was entitled 'Paratroopers join anti-Smith mercenaries'.

Who the bloody hell do you think you are? What makes you think we require you and your bunch of cut-throats to liberate Zimbabwe? We in ZANU are proud to be our own liberators. We fight our own battles and do not require the assistance of a pack of wild white dogs. In Zimbabwe, it is essentially a war between black and white.

My comrades and I believe your so-called 'International Security Organisation' is really a cover to recruit not anti-Smith mercenaries but pro-Smith mercenaries. Because of this, I warn you here and now that unless you discontinue your treacherous activities forthwith, steps will be taken to eliminate you and your friend Tomkins. You have said you don't want your head blown off. That is exactly what will happen to you if you don't heed this serious warning.

It seemed that we could safely rule ZANU out as the mystery recipient of ISO's services. I was a bit pissed off at having been mentioned in this communication – not so much because of the threat, more because I thought I'd kept a reasonably low profile.

Banks was undeterred: the Rhodesia operation would go ahead. He signed up 12 officers, 68 sergeants and 90 troopers, to be divided into 2 squadrons, A and B. Former French Foreign Legion warrant officer Mike Johnson would command A Squadron. His sergeant major was ex-Para Raymond 'Sammy' Copeland. A Squadron would deploy first to Africa. An advance party of 12 soldiers – accompanied by members of the press who had been leaked the information – gathered at the Skyline Hotel near Heathrow Airport. Banks told them they would be en route in 24 hours. But 48 hours later, they were still on the ground and drinking the hotel dry. Inevitably, tempers flared. Hotel rooms were damaged. The management ordered Banks to remove his men or the police would be called. He readily agreed. His planned coup of Rhodesia was going nowhere; now his men had given him the opportunity to sack them for poor discipline. This way, he wouldn't have to pay them compensation or expenses. He stormed down to the hotel and dismissed everyone, claiming their behaviour and the bad publicity it had generated had caused the mission's sponsors to pull out at the last moment.

I never bought Banks' explanation as to why the Rhodesian operation never got off the ground. He claimed to have been a pawn in a political game. 'I've realised that my mercenary army was never intended to leave the UK. The object of the exercise was to show Ian Smith that an army of white, Western soldiers could be raised against him. Once he saw that, he agreed to talks with the black nationalist leaders. We did our job in Zimbabwe without leaving Heathrow. We applied the pressure and pushed Smith to negotiate. But there'll be other jobs.' Banks was not going to let this setback deter him: 'My belief in this is unshakeable.'

'Come on, John,' I replied gently. 'This has been a complete fiasco. You've lost any credibility the ISO had. You stood the men up then had to stand them down again. Maybe you can start afresh with a new company and a new name.'

The glint returned to Banks' eye. 'You think of a new name, Dave. Or write some suggestions on a piece of paper and I'll choose one.'

Banks opted for Security Advisory Services. In all likelihood, he picked the name because of the appeal of the acronym. 'We'll focus on anti-terrorism and bomb protection,' he said, adding, 'We'll offer executive bodyguard services and threat analysis.' I didn't have the heart to tell him that the 'we' should be used very loosely. As far as I was concerned, Banks' schemes were his alone.

For a while, it looked like SAS was going to get off the ground. Banks talked animatedly about his new company and crowed that he had signed up Peter McAleese, saying that he was a law unto himself but also a phenomenal soldier. McAleese could offer the skills and experience of which Banks' sales literature boasted. A squat, pugnacious Scot (the word on some people's lips might have been 'fat' but it would have been very unwise to have said so), he had reached the rank of sergeant in the real SAS and it seemed that his appetite for warfare was insatiable.

'And where do I fit in?' I asked.

'Building security procedures,' he replied. 'You're there to tell people how to build strongrooms and where to hide the safe.'

For reasons beyond Banks' control, SAS failed to take off. Major companies attended SAS seminars on bomb search-and-detection procedures and evasive/defensive driving techniques but before they could part with any real money, Special Branch tipped them off about Banks' past and they withdrew their interest.

However, Banks' notoriety had evidently spread, because in December 1975 he was invited to Zurich to meet a man with whom he had been in contact. John and I, accompanied by a friend, drove to Switzerland to meet this guy, who was supposedly an agent for an American oil company. The story was that he was recruiting for people to go into East Germany and smuggle VIP refugees over or through the Berlin Wall. We arrived in Zurich on the afternoon of 15 December and checked into separate rooms in a hotel on the Banhofplatz. After a cruise around and an evening meal, I lay down for a good night's sleep. A few hours later, I was awakened by a persistent knocking at my door. I turned the knob to be confronted by four plain-clothed men armed with Walther pistols. They spreadeagled me against the wall and searched my room and luggage. I was ordered to dress and escorted to a waiting police car. This was the first time in my life that I had considered the sight of a squad car a blessed relief.

At the police station, I told them, 'I want an interpreter and to see a representative from the British Consul,' I demanded. The Swiss officer ignored my request and walked out of the room. I pressed the panic alarm. A squad of policemen descended, assuming that one of their colleagues was receiving a battering.

'I want to go to the toilet.'

On my return, they sat me back down.

'You are a terrorist.'

'A nuisance, maybe, but never a terrorist,' I replied.

'No tourist, terrorist!'

'I am not a terrorist,' I repeated.

Not even a giant, snarling Alsatian dog could convince me to agree with them. I smashed a chair and pressed the panic button again.

DIRTY COMBAT

They threw me into an underground cell. I ripped off the paper sheets on the bed and used them to cover the video camera. When they shouted at me through the speaker mounted on the wall, I swore back at them and removed the paper from the camera so they could see my Nazi salute.

The Swiss transferred me to a higher security facility, where I was photographed, fingerprinted and accused again of being a terrorist. I was transferred to a windowless cell, where I spent the next 28 hours with little sleep and no food. I was then escorted upstairs to a room where I found Banks smiling and looking much better than I felt. He gleefully informed me that they had kept him happy with meals and cigarettes.

'I had the sense to talk to them politely,' he told me sickeningly. 'Do you know why we're here?' he chirped.

'How the hell would I know that, John?'

'Well, we're notorious, it seems. Special Branch monitored our exit from the UK and informed Interpol who tracked us across France and Germany.'

I scowled at him.

'They told the Swiss police we were terrorists and likely to be armed. They're willing to let us go, though, as we haven't committed any offence, so just let me do the talking from now on, yeah?'

I nodded.

'They searched our vehicle and it's clean, so they've got nothing on us. So long as we agree never to return to their country, they'll escort us to the German border and that will be that.'

CHAPTER 6

A WOLF IN WOLF'S CLOTHING

THERE WERE NO ANSWERS TO BE FOUND AT THE BOTTOM OF MY beer glass. Sitting in Ragamuffins in Camberley, I had 56 pence in my pocket and not a farthing more. After handling hundreds of thousands of pounds with Trans-Asian Express, this was a depressing state of affairs. It was January 1976 and my prospects for the new year didn't look good. I felt I had no chance of making a living in this country, honest or otherwise. I felt bored and trapped; I was under constant police surveillance. Any criminal job in the UK involving explosives, I was first on their list of suspects.

The bouncer lifted my chin off the bar. 'John Banks is in the club and he wants to see you.'

Banks was wearing a full-length black leather coat, a bit of a fashion faux pas given that he was only 5 ft 6 in. tall. He looked like a vertically challenged highwayman in search of a coach to rob. He was grinning from ear to ear. 'We've got a contract,' he said.

In my experience, when uttered by Banks the word 'we' meant one of three things: he couldn't handle the job on his own; he didn't know what to do next; or the job might result in one of us – probably me – going back to prison. Having recently avoided a conviction, I was least keen on option three. I was intrigued only because I was skint and Mary needed housekeeping money.

'Have you seen any money?'

Banks pulled a wedge of ten-pound notes from his pocket.

'Count me in.'

When we were sitting in his Range Rover, Banks continued, 'Nick Hall, a former private in the Paras, has promoted himself to the rank of major and is fighting with a guerrilla army in Africa. He's looking for twenty-five volunteers to travel to Angola, within three days if possible.'

I had not heard of Nick Hall. I just hoped he was less of a bullshitter than Banks.

'The men must be experienced,' he continued, 'and with specialist skills, like yours. He needs to turn his men into a formidable fighting force. We're on £200 a man to find volunteers now and he's given me £1,000 in cash to cover initial expenses.'

'Where are we going, by the way?'

'To the Tower Hotel, London. You remember Frank Perren? Ex-commando? Former officer in ISO?'

'I'm trying to forget ISO but yes, the name's familiar.'

'He's staying in Room 323, with Leslie Aspin. They've signed up.'

Les was another guy we'd met during recruitment for ISO.

At the hotel, we met Nick Hall. Aged 24, he was too young even for a self-promoted major. But his bearing and confidence belied his years. Hall was one of four former British Army soldiers already actively involved with the National Front for the Liberation of Angola (FNLA). The other three were Cyprus-born Charles Christodoulou and Costas Georgiou and Michael Wainhouse. All four had served together in 1st Battalion The Parachute Regiment on the troubled streets of Northern Ireland. Only Charlie Christodoulou had received an honourable discharge. Wainhouse and Georgiou were convicted of an armed robbery on a post office using army-issue weapons and were sentenced to five years' imprisonment. Nick Hall was sentenced by court martial to two years' imprisonment for supplying guns to the

Ulster Volunteer Force. In due course, they all met again to renew their old friendship and Saturday nights in London clubs and pubs became standard practice for four very bored ex-soldiers. In a remark reminiscent of the throwaway comments that started ISO, someone observed, 'What we need is another war.' Those words might have faded away in the smoke-filled atmosphere of the bar, if it hadn't been for Nick Hall.

In a short space of time, Hall found a cause. He made contact with the British arm of the FNLA, which was purely a humanitarian operation, supplying medical support and assistance to a country in need. It was based in Leeds and run by Donald 'Doc' Belford. Belford was a former British Army medic and volunteer worker who had become the UK emissary for FNLA leader Holden Roberto. In the wake of Angola's achievement of independence from Portugal in 1975, the country's rebirth had been stifled by in-fighting between the nationalist groups that had opposed colonial rule. The Russians and Cubans backed the left-wing MPLA, the United States the anti-Communist FNLA. Nick Hall volunteered his three companions and himself to fight for the FNLA against the Soviet-sponsored, Cuban-supported army of the People's Movement for the Liberation of Angola (MPLA). Don Belford told him that if a trip could be arranged, it would be for the purpose of helping the sick and injured, not to create more.

When the call came, it was Georgiou who went to Leeds to meet Belford. The FNLA would supply a ticket for one person; Georgiou made sure that would be him. In November, in company with Colin Taylor, a self-styled 'security officer' for the FNLA, he flew to Kinshasa, the capital of neighbouring Zaire. Much to the amusement of the three friends who were waiting back in London, Georgiou had told them he was going to change his name to Callan, which resulted in some piss-taking, as this was the name of a seedy private detective played by Edward Woodward in a popular TV series of the same name. As Callan, Georgiou became an ambulance driver and medical orderly for the FNLA. Working in desperate conditions with meagre medical supplies, he proved tireless, not to mention fearless when driving his ambulance to 'casevac' the injured from front-line fighting.

As each town fell to the enemy's relentless advance, Callan and his comrades fell back to the next hospital. At Negage, next in line for the MPLA forces' attack, Callan decided to stop retreating without firing a shot in anger. With several Portuguese commandos, Callan sneaked up close to a unit of the 9th FAPLA (the military wing of the MPLA) awaiting orders to advance on the town. They were not prepared for Callan's hit-and-run tactics. His small group fired on them with machine guns and shoulder-fired 66-mm rockets. The results were devastating: dozens of the unsuspecting troops were killed or wounded as their own Katyusha rocket launchers exploded among them. When Negage finally fell to the advancing enemy, Callan and some of the Portuguese soldiers hitched a flight to Zaire, shortly to be joined by Hall, Christodoulou and Wainhouse, who had received tickets and instructions to report to Kinshasa.

News of the Negage incident filtered back to Zaire, reaching the ears of 'Jean-Pierre' the CIA station chief in Kinshasa. The United States supported Holden Roberto and had given financial assistance to the FNLA for over a decade. It was obvious to all that the FNLA were losing the war. Many of the troops were deserting and those who remained were under poor leadership and without the arsenal of weapons supplied to the enemy by the Soviets. The CIA convinced Roberto that what the FNLA needed was Callan – and a thousand more like him.

Nick Hall was given funds and issued with instructions to recruit a battalion of ex-soldiers to fight under the command of Costas Georgiou, now known as Colonel Tony Callan, who had been promoted to field commander of all FNLA forces in Northern Angola. In 1970, at his trial for armed robbery, a psychiatrist had examined Georgiou and in his report described him as 'a textbook example of an aggressive psychopath'. He concluded that Callan possessed 'very ambitious leadership qualities' and was in his opinion 'a wild dog on a leash'. That leash would be slipped on the battlefields of Angola.

Despite Hall's reassurances ('The FNLA troops – that's our side – have plenty of equipment, weapons, vehicles and so on. They just need to be taught how to use them.') the recruitment mission was in fact a desperate last attempt to stave off defeat. Not that I cared; I needed the money and my appetite for adventure had been whetted. We were all broke or leaving behind some scene of domestic devastation. I met bricklayers, labourers and factory workers, all tired of their dead-end jobs, all wanting the bounty and tax-free wages, charmed by Hall and Banks. I was excited but if I had a nagging worry, it was that my lack of military experience would count against me. I felt I would have to find something extra to compensate, particularly as all drill would have to be learned from scratch. I knew I was fit for the adventures ahead and my survival instincts were well honed. If I had to kill, so be it; so long as I acted in self-defence, I wouldn't have any moral qualms about it. I was there for as long as the war lasted or until I got killed. Mary, inevitably, was concerned for my welfare but she would be grateful for my pay of $300 per week.

It all happened so quickly. The time that elapsed between Banks approaching me in the nightclub and our being in transit to Angola could not have been more than 72 hours. None of us had time to memorise the initials of the groups we were fighting for and against. We even forgot Holden Roberto's name occasionally, referring to him as Roberto Holden. Around 20 of us, including Peter McAleese, began our journey to Angola from London Heathrow Airport on a cold day in January 1976. The first leg was a flight to Brussels, Belgium. After the Switzerland experience the previous month, I was worried we might be intercepted by Special Branch or MI6. From there, we flew to Athens and then on to Kinshasa. En route, I listened to the conversations around me. From my prison days, I could tell who would go the distance and who could only talk a good fight.

At Kinshasa airport, we were the last to deplane. A grubby-looking coach waited for us on the runway, enabling us to avoid customs and immigration. We were driven through the gloomy streets, past roadblocks manned by surly-looking paramilitary police and soldiers brandishing automatic weapons. At each of these checkpoints a fire burned in a 50-gallon drum, which in the gloom and smoke created a menacing atmosphere. The police and soldiers, who, we would find, were always aggressive and usually drunk, brandished their weapons as if they were about to use them at any minute. These roadblocks were as much for the purpose of extortion as for the sake of security and there were always demands for a *matabish* – a small bribe of money or cigarettes. We soon learned that it was easier to give them a little something, especially if you were not mob-handed. The soldiers never showed any thanks and would bang on the vehicle as it departed, in what seemed to be an attempt at intimidation.

We met Roberto and Jean-Pierre at the Palace Hotel, which was in need of a facelift. The FNLA leader, dressed in a grey suit, hid behind dark glasses. He was a man of few words that evening. From the hotel, we drove through well-lit avenues, beyond which tin-shack slums could be glimpsed, to Roberto's safe house, a large white villa called Kirkuzi, at which sentries were on guard. I was exhausted but reassured by my surroundings. As soon as we had changed into camouflage gear, however, we continued our journey to Angola. There were already clear warning signs that this might turn out to be something of a misadventure: my boots were ill-fitting, my water bottle was attached to my belt using a bootlace and there were only three spare magazines for my M2 carbine. I'd had no sleep for three days. A mixture of British mercenaries and black Angolan FNLA troops, we were travelling in a battered old single-deck bus, the aisle blocked by stinking diesel drums and 66-mm LAW (light anti-tank weapon) rockets. I found not knowing where we were in relation to our destination disconcerting.

It was 350 km from Kinshasa to our crossing point into Angola, a further 100 clicks to our destination, São Salvador. The roads were potholed, sometimes impassable, so that the bus had to divert through the bush. The sight of an upturned jeep prompted a sudden burst of shouting and the bus came to a sliding halt. We jumped off and took up defensive positions in anticipation of our first enemy contact. I was struck by our vulnerability. Our bus had no armour. If we'd driven over a mine, our visit to Angola would have been short. Mercifully, the jeep had overturned as a result of bad driving rather than an enemy mine or ambush. I was beginning to think that this mercenary game wasn't all it was cracked up to be.

As night became day, we could see the hills and savannah stretching into the distance, the road littered in places with wrecked vehicles and rusting bulldozers that had been ambushed by FNLA soldiers when they drove out the Portuguese. Their skeletal remains were all that was left as a reminder of a colonial power in defeat. We passed through many FNLA military checkpoints as we drove through small towns and villages. Their wary populations watched us pass without any show of welcome.

My first impression of São Salvador was that it would make a good film set for a spaghetti Western. It was a worn-out town of empty shops with broken windows and faded whitewashed buildings daubed with slogans supporting the FNLA. The FNLA's HQ was a large two-storey mansion. Referred to as 'the Palace', it was the former residence of a colonial governor, painted in washed-out pale blue with a red-tile roof and surrounded by high whitewashed walls. When we arrived, there were Portuguese mercenaries already *in situ*, ELNA commandos, according to the letters emblazoned on their T-shirts. They stood smoking cigarettes and staring at us as we stepped off the rusty bus. Jeeps, Land Rovers, and Panhard armoured cars were parked on the faded lawns. We debussed to the accompaniment of a trumpeter on the steps to the building. At the sound of the trumpet, dozens of troops ran to form up on the parade ground in some semblance of order. The place fell silent and then we had our first sight of Callan.

A short, olive-skinned man in his 20s, wearing a US pilot's vest over his camouflage shirt, he emerged from the doors at the top of the steps. I had assumed Callan would be taller, perhaps simply because he was in charge. Despite his short stature, he was physically impressive. His made-to-measure uniform was tailored to accentuate his lean, muscular physique and he wore his thick black hair combed straight back. His jowls were blue. I guessed he shaved twice a day. His eyes were as cold and bereft of humanity as a shark's. With his swarthy complexion, he resembled the Maltese pimps I had met in a previous life, handsome but extremely conscious of their appearance. Callan looked over the assembled parade with sheer contempt. The Angolan troops were in torn and tattered uniforms and I guess we didn't look much better, after days of travelling. In contrast, Callan was clean and smart. Another man joined him, also smart in appearance, with a moustache and carrying a swagger stick. This was Callan's second in command, Michael Wainhouse. Some instruction was given and the trumpeter started playing the FNLA anthem as the red, yellow and white flag was slowly run up the flagpole. The trumpeter was awful and the notes were out of tune; he wasn't helped by Wainhouse, who cracked him on the shoulder with his stick.

Peter McAleese had us formed up in ranks in advance of Callan's arrival. He marched briskly towards Callan and saluted, reporting us for duty. Callan walked along the line-up of recruits, his footsteps getting louder as he approached me. He stopped and stared at me. His eyes had landed on a leather thong I wore around my neck. Its African mojo motif was a good-luck charm I had relied upon for years. Without speaking, Callan leaned towards me and grasped it as if to rip it off. My whole body tensed. I would have exploded with anger had he done so. I would go as far as to say I would have killed him at the first opportunity. However, he released his hand from around the charm and moved along the line. He concluded his inspection then addressed us. 'Thank you for coming to our aid. My men and I have been in need of reinforcements for some time.'

McAleese dismissed us from parade and we headed to the dining room. Wainhouse demanded that we had our hair cut. He had been a private in the Paras but was now a captain. There were few rules in this guerrilla conflict and rank came in a cornflakes box, with all the ex-Para corporals and privates reinventing themselves as majors and colonels. Wainhouse seemed suited to being an officer, though; if I had met him on the street in Camberley, I would have assumed he had attended Sandhurst.

We were allocated bunks with no mattresses or bed-linen. On a recce, I discovered that Callan's room was conspicuously comfortable, with a double bed, sheets and pillows. There were knee-high stacks of pornographic magazines on the floor and AK-47s and an M79 grenade launcher were scattered across the carpet like children's toys. There were wooden cases stuffed full of unused Angolan escudos and bottles of whisky.

Nick Hall had promised me a full range of explosives and anti-personnel mines to rig to my specifications. I should not have swallowed the sales pitch. Dilapidated, with its door hanging off, the demolitions store looked more like a cowboys' bunkhouse. The place filled me with dismay. The first thing I lifted up was a bag of gelignite. Three of an original batch of twenty-four sticks remained in a labelled plastic bag. These were exuding nitroglycerine. The explosives fuses were 40 years out of date, having been manufactured in 1936. There was some TNT, a jumbled ball of detonating cord and one shotfiring generator, minus its winding key and firing cable. 'If there are bridges to blow, they'd better be small ones,' I muttered to myself.

During the weeks that followed, sleeping on mattress-free beds and eating rancid meat and rice with our hands – not to mention the absence of medical facilities, field dressings and antibiotics – sent morale plummeting. While some spoke of overthrowing Callan, he controlled us with ease and nobody else there had his strength of character or charisma. On days when I shared his Land Rover, it occurred to me that I might want to 'put one in that bastard's head' but most of the time we coexisted with a minimum of fuss. He indulged my military ignorance and habit of forgetting to add 'sir' to the end of sentences directed towards him. His nickname for me was 'Explosive'. Callan gave nothing away about his past life as Costas Georgiou or his personal life during our conversations. He had no problem with me being an ex-con and I was older than him and posed no threat to his leadership, all of which was advantageous. When he probed me about John Banks, I replied, 'I know him quite well. I'm not exactly in love with him, though.' Later, I discovered that Callan hated Banks for rejecting his application to join ISO.

Callan's mate 'Shotgun' Charlie Christodoulou had got his nickname in Angola. Charlie had sawn off the barrels of a shotgun he'd found in a local village. When he and fellow Brit Chris Dempster were returning from patrol one day, Dempster had spotted a mango hanging on a tree and started throwing stones at the fruit in a bid to dislodge it. Suddenly, there was a thunderous noise and the mango burst into tiny pieces. A furious Dempster shouted, 'That's fucking clever! You just killed my mango!'

Shotgun Charlie was never the best shot. However, he boasted that he and his old Para mates were responsible for the deaths of 167.5 captured enemy and FNLA deserters. He had regaled Dempster with this boast when they were together in Quiende, a neighbouring town in the FNLA-controlled area.

'Why point five?' Dempster asked.

Christodoulou replied, 'One of the prisoners brought for execution at Quiende Bridge the other night had a lucky escape. He was bound hand and foot and had a pistol put to his head. But the weapon didn't fire. The gun was re-cocked but it jammed again. The poor bastard was terrified. He jumped off the bridge. We sprayed bullets into the water but since it was unconfirmed whether he was hit, and just in case he could swim with his hands and feet tied, we decided it was only fair to classify him as "half dead".'

Chris Dempster had been put in charge of the vehicle pool. He was a former soldier who had also worked as a disc jockey under the stage name Oliver Plunkett. He had also taken his mobile sound system out on the road as a support act for stars such as Gary Glitter, The Sweet and Hot Chocolate. I'd first met Dempster when we were both labourers, digging roadside ditches. It was exhausting work, which I'd been determined to make easier. I knew it would be faster to blast out a ditch than to dig one, so I made an explosive mixture from garden weedkiller and sugar. The explosion blew the ditch – and the street's drainage system. Dempster and I were sacked but we became good friends.

He confided to me that there were no spare parts for the vehicles and that it had required the cannibalisation of several Land Rovers to render a few roadworthy. Then, some of the vehicles were sabotaged by our own side. Our Angolan soldiers were reluctant to go on patrol against thousands of Cubans equipped with tanks and missiles. To get out of Callan's death-or-glory missions, they poured sugar into the fuel tanks and jammed live ammunition rounds into the engines, where they were likely to explode when the vehicles warmed up. Callan threatened to execute every black soldier on our side. Self-preservation led most of the Angolan soldiers to flee into the bush. I didn't blame them. Callan was more of a danger to their lives than our enemies were. 'Fucking black bastards deserting my command!' Callan screamed as he chased them down the street firing at their heads with an AK-47.

Several days after this incident, we received word from the garrison at Quiende that the Angolan troops there were in a state of revolt. We were dispatched to reinforce Sammy Copeland (one of the former Paras who had signed up for Banks' abortive mission to Rhodesia) and his men. We descended on the town in a heavily armed sweep line. The mutinous troops, including many of those whom Callan had driven away from São Salvador, were eventually rounded up with minimal casualties.

In the blistering heat, they were disarmed, stripped to their underwear and made to sit in two separate groups, one on the parade ground and the other on the town football pitch, guarded by soldiers with machine guns, while Callan and Copeland decided their fate. They were exhausted, dehydrated and bereft of the will to fight. I risked a bollocking by allowing them a drink of water. I thought it was the least they were entitled to. I watched as about 20 men were dragged behind the town's church and executed.

We returned to São Salvador after searching every dwelling in Quiende for weapons and deserters. We confiscated everything in the garrison armoury; some of the guns were reissued to troops who volunteered to soldier on under Sammy Copeland's command. The armoury yielded more mines and some detonating cord but little in the way of explosives. The mood among the men was beginning to show signs of strain. They had left England only a short time ago but it seemed like a lifetime. One night at São Salvador, I stayed up late chatting to 'Fuzz' Hussey, our radio operator. When we left the main room to go to bed, we found a local guy lying tied up at the side of the staircase. His face was swollen, bloody and misshapen. He was bound hand and foot, gagged and barely conscious. I knew that in the morning he would be taken to the bridge and shot. As I went upstairs, I felt anger and remorse.

The tension wasn't helped by lack of sleep. We seemed to be on the go all hours of the day and night, and when we did get a chance to rest, we were so uncomfortable we were lucky if we got any sleep. Most had given up on the hard bed bases and found the floor more appealing. There were no sleeping bags and it was very cold at night. By day, we were permanently wet either with sweat or rain. There were no ponchos. Our health was not improved by the lack of decent food, either. Pedro, the cook, was as bad as he looked, in his dirty, greasy shirt. In fairness, though, he couldn't fuck up what he didn't have. We had no cutlery and I disliked eating with my hands. If I had known in advance, I would have brought a knife and fork with me.

As morale deteriorated and the strain began to show, Jamie McCandless and Mike Johnson, ex-SAS and French Foreign Legion respectively, both of whom had initially been recruited for Banks' Rhodesian mission, had a row that nearly developed into a shooting war. McCandless died a few weeks later in an enemy ambush. Perhaps he foresaw his own death, as he became increasingly paranoid, ranting, 'We're all going to fucking die out here!'

Several of the men, in particular Sammy Copeland, were adopting the aggressive attitudes and behaviour patterns of Callan and Wainhouse. Meanwhile, others found quiet corners where like-minded individuals could discuss the options available to them, options ranging from desertion to a full-scale attack on Callan and his sidekicks. Callan was without doubt an extreme psychopath but, while his military acumen could be somewhat lacking when it came to strategy and tactics, he was not entirely stupid and could sense the growing hostility his actions were creating among the men.

Not long after our return from Quiende, Callan instructed Peter McAleese to select six Britons (all to be ex-Parachute Regiment or Special Air Service) and be ready to leave for Santo Antonio, a small coastal town on the banks of the Zaire River. The seven-man detachment consisted of McAleese, 'Brummie' Barker, Dougie Saunders, Mike Johnson, Mick Rennie, Stuart McPherson and John Tilsey. This group was to train the remaining FNLA troops in preparation for an expected attack by a Cuban/FAPLA brigade that had taken the town of Ambrizette, further down the coast. Not long after McAleese's group had departed, a telegram arrived from Holden Roberto informing us that enemy tanks had been seen at Damba airport and that the town had fallen to the 9th FAPLA Brigade. He ordered that reinforcements be sent to Maquela, the town between Damba and São Salvador. We were the last stopgap preventing the complete closure of the Angolan border with Zaire. There was non-stop activity for the next 24 hours as we got all available vehicles in order and loaded with stores. Sammy Copeland's garrison from Quiende joined the convoy, with every available FNLA soldier in the region, which was not very many. We were so heavily outnumbered that we needed support from the civilian population but Callan and Copeland's 'hearts and minds' tactics were based on brutality and fear. We never gave a neutral member of the indigenous population an incentive to join us, only a threat.

Given the lack of opportunities to do what I did best, not to mention the dearth of resources, I was beginning to wonder why Hall had recruited me. A rare chance to demonstrate my prowess with explosives came at Maquela, where Callan asked me to destroy a bridge spanning the Zardi River. I listened to his pre-operation briefing: 'Our forces will split into two groups. Most of the Angolan soldiers will deploy with Explosive [pointing at me] at the bridge to the rear of Maquela. This will be demolished using explosives in the event that we are unable to prevent the convoy of enemy vehicles reaching this location. The second group, mainly Portuguese and British combatants, will lie in wait on the road between Damba and Maquela, using anti-tank rockets and machine guns. Stop groups will wait in position to kill any escapees from the initial ambush position. Any black soldiers on our side seen running away are to be shot.'

Dempster asked Callan, 'What's the estimated strength of the enemy convoy?'

'About seven tanks, four to five truckloads of troops, some Scout armoured cars and a few hundred troops.'

This sounded like the longest linear ambush in the history of warfare.

CHAPTER 7

A MESSY LITTLE WAR

PRIOR TO OUR NIGHT-TIME DEPARTURE FROM THE PALACE FOR Maquela, Callan ordered the headlights on all our vehicles to be smashed. He did not trust his men to drive without lights as he had ordered them to do. I took it as an indication of the importance of blowing up the bridge that I was ordered to ride in the back of his vehicle. As the Land Rover bounced over rain-filled potholes, he urged his Portuguese driver Uzio to accelerate, shouting, 'Rapido, rapido!' Callan's interpreter Joe Akoo and I were thrown up and down as Uzio responded to Callan's command. Joe, born in Ghana and educated in the USA, told me that he had been an FNLA commandant in Maquela before falling out with his commanding officer, who had ordered him to be imprisoned for 40 days. Callan had had him released and, impressed with his grasp of English, had appointed him his personal interpreter.

The rain was relentless. We frequently had to get out and push when the vehicle got stuck. Joe, Callan and I looked like mud wrestlers, covered in sticky dark-red clay. I was grateful for Joe's strength. He was huge, born to play American football. In a week's time Joe would be missing, presumed dead, in the aftermath of an ambush. At first light, an emergency message crackled through on Callan's walkie-talkie. To his chagrin, one of the vehicles in our convoy had overturned and rolled down a steep muddy bank. Explosives, mines and rockets had sunk into the mud and a number of local soldiers had been hurt. Two of them later died but their fate was of secondary concern to Callan. With some reluctance, he ordered Uzio to turn back and head for the place where the Bedford had crashed.

With Callan barking instructions, we salvaged what we could from the wreckage. I loaded some of the TNT blocks onto our Land Rover. Not waiting for the rest of the convoy, Callan ordered Uzio to Maquela 'rapido'. Some miles before we reached our destination, again driving through torrential rain, we came across a small thatched hut just off the roadway. I think that even Callan's resolve was now taking a beating and he ordered Uzio to pull up in front of the tiny dwelling. There were no other homes nearby that we could see but, isolated as it was, at that moment the hut looked to me, soaked to the skin and caked in mud, like a warm and comforting haven. A very frail old woman came to the entrance as we ground to a halt; she had no shoes on and was wearing a faded dress. She must have been afraid to see armed and mud-splattered men emerging from the vehicle but her lined and wrinkled face showed no fear. Joe Akoo spoke to her in the local language and she ushered us in out of the rain.

The hut was small, just one room for living and sleeping, a bit larger than a single-car garage. It was gloomy. A small fire provided heat and the air was heavy with woodsmoke. The furnishings were a table and a crude wooden workplace on which cooking utensils and a bowl rested. There were two single bunk beds made from branches, with thin mattresses and grubby blankets. One of the bunks contained an old man, who was obviously alarmed and was calling to his wife. She went and reassured him, helping him to sit up. Then we could see that his eyes were just pale orbs staring sightlessly. The man was about 80 years old and the tendons on his arms and throat were prominent on his emaciated frame. The woman spoke to him again and then to Joe, who told us that the old man wanted to shake our hands. We each went to him in turn and he clutched our hands and said something. I guessed that he was blessing us with good fortune.

The old lady made us a hot drink; it might have been tea of some kind but whatever it was, it was black and hot and greatly appreciated. Callan sat on a chair; we sat on the floor. While we waited, I looked around at just what little these two poor sods had in life apart from each other. If ever I felt that anything I was attempting to do in Angola was worthwhile – other than try to make money – it was at that moment in time. I thought it was sad that they had nothing but what little they did have they offered us. I don't think it was through fear. They had a look of resignation about them that seemed to indicate that nothing could frighten them any more. I would like to have left them something but had nothing to give. We thanked them for their hospitality and returned to the vehicle. Callan said very little during this interlude and showed no hostility towards them; maybe even he was moved by the experience – for a moment, anyway.

In Maquela itself, buildings not occupied by those mad enough to stay or too old or infirm to leave had been looted. As we drove on towards the Zardi River, I asked Callan to describe the bridge. His replies were so vague that I figured he had neither seen it himself nor had its features described to him in any detail. When we arrived, the size of the bridge surprised me. It was about 180 ft across and divided into three separate spans, each supported by concrete piers jutting upwards from the fast-flowing river.

Callan wanted the bridge flattened beyond repair, which was beyond my meagre resources. The best I could manage was to make one span impassable, at least for heavy vehicles. With luck, the 40 kg of TNT rescued from the Bedford would cause the span to fall into the water. Callan was in a great hurry and accepted this course of action. I was grateful he knew nothing about demolitions. I decided to drop the far span – tactically not ideal, as it was the enemy's side; however, I figured I might get another crack at it later. We had no sandbags, so Joe Akoo was dispatched to the village close by to organise the remaining population to bring earth in whatever receptacles they could find. We would use it to tamp the charge, directing the explosive force downwards.

'Explosives,' said Callan, 'tell me what you're doing.'

'I'm using a hollow-centre charge. This will result in a massive overpressure of force downwards, exceeding the load-bearing capacity of the span. The charge will be initiated by det-cord ring main, from the top. It needs to detonate evenly to produce the optimum result.' This explanation meant little to Callan; he just liked the sound of it.

I created the pressure charge, using flattened cardboard boxes to cover the centre cavity, with more TNT layered over the hollow. The villagers came in a steady stream, carrying earth in old buckets, tins and washing-up bowls, some women carrying loads in their aprons. In their innocence, the small children thought this was great fun, contributing cups and jam jars full of dirt to the pile and running off laughing to get more. Finally, I was satisfied with the mound of earth covering the charge but one major problem remained: how was I going to detonate the charge and not be on the bridge when it exploded? The remaining det-cord that constituted the firing train left me 100 ft short of the bridge end. I had no safety fuse or electric detonators, so I removed the detonator and spoon-trigger lever from a Chinese grenade. I got hold of a length of three-ply nylon clothes-line from an old woman, which I unravelled and tied back together to extend its length. Using this, I lashed the detonator to the detonating cord. Needless to say, Angola had a shortage of adhesive tape as well. This botch-up was tied to the guard rail and the remaining line was attached to the pull ring of the grenade for some stupid sod like me to pull. It was still short of getting me off the bridge, so I wasn't out of harm's way – not according to the recommended guidelines, anyway, but I figured Angola wasn't taken into account when those were written. I went ahead and pulled the line. The detonator went off but it parted company with the det-cord. The nylon line was shiny and slippery, and the whole delicate assembly came apart.

I was saved the embarrassment of another attempt and another potential fuck-up by the arrival of Jamie McCandless and Bryan Lewis, who announced that our convoy was approaching Maquela. Within minutes of their arrival at the bridge, small-arms fire was heard coming from the direction of Maquela. Callan was confused about his priorities for a moment and then it dawned on him that if the Cubans were in Maquela, this bridge was the only way out for our vehicles. He made the decision that I was not to demolish until I received orders to the contrary and headed off towards Maquela, leaving me, Bryan and Joe to stand guard, steam drying in our camouflage now that the rain had stopped.

Later in the afternoon, Callan returned and told us the gunfire was FNLA troops training. He reunited me with my full demolitions kit and I prepared to blow the bridge. I taped a detonator and length of safety fuse to the det-cord, which was then lit. I walked back towards a stone marker with 'Rio Zardi' carved on it, shaped, perhaps appropriately, like a gravestone. One minute later, the charge went off with a tremendous blast and a great column of smoke and dirt rose over 300 ft into the air, encircled by a perfect smoke ring. Callan, crouching next to me, said, 'Fucking hell.' Personally, I thought my effort deserved more than that. There was no debris, as the force had been downwards, but the column rising into the sky was full of the earth used to tamp the explosion. For several minutes, as the smoke dissipated, it fell like black rain. There was now a gaping hole some 16 ft across in the roadway, with massive reinforcing bars sheared through and hanging like tentacles. The side beams, which had not been charged due to lack of explosives, had shifted and now sat only a few inches from dropping into the river below. I was disappointed that the span itself had not fallen completely into the river. This would take a second, smaller explosion but I had used all our TNT. A resupply arrived as darkness fell but we had no torch, so it would have to be done in the morning. I settled down for the night in the shadow of the bridge, with only Bryan for company. My every muscle ached.

I ate a tin of pilchards from my French army ration pack and within a few hours I was struck down with dysentery. As fever set in, I sweated one minute and shivered the next. The cold and river mist did not allow sleep for long. What rest I did get was memorable for surreal dreams of naked deformed men and growling dogs approaching me. I snapped awake, ranting and cursing in my feverish state. I woke Bryan and must have disturbed half the village, too, because Joe, who had found a place to sleep up there, brought down a blanket and a reed mat to help keep the cold out.

When the sun rose, I summoned the strength to complete the job on the bridge. I used linked anti-tank mines. When the smoke cleared, the span was beneath the water, a twisted guard rail protruding skyward. Callan and Sammy Copeland proclaimed their satisfaction – we had secured our rear flank from enemy attack.

Unbeknown to us, however, the enemy had no intention of launching such an assault. It transpired that, having overflown our positions in light aircraft, they ignored the evidence of their eyes in favour of Russian intelligence reports, which insisted that we kept high numbers of troops in reserve. The Russians had got carried away with all the media attention devoted to Banks' and Hall's recruitment drive. Throughout our time in Angola, the enemy grossly overestimated our strength. As a result, the skirmishes we were involved in were rare and brief. FAPLA troops might fire rockets at us but we had none to fire back, so fighting was not prolonged. Or Callan would prepare an assault on an enemy position only to cancel it with as much haste as it was arranged.

We established a base camp at a cluster of huts at Quibocolo, where there was an old colonial house once occupied by the Portuguese owner of a banana plantation. Beyond this point, about ten clicks further down the road, was a crossroad where two dirt tracks that had once serviced the now abandoned plantation met. This we named 'Banana Junction' and we metaphorically drew a line in the sand: from this point to the Zaire border was ours; beyond it was FAPLA territory.

The house at Quibocolo contained a large safe, so, of course, I gave a lesson on how to blow the door off. Disappointingly enough, there were no riches inside, only a book on cryptography written in Portuguese, but the distraction lightened the mood.

There was a chapel next door to the house and I awoke one morning to the sound of automatic gunfire. I scrambled into a defensive position but I need not have concerned myself. Callan had walked into the chapel and killed some Angolan troops as they slept, having spotted a pile of civilian clothing, which was forbidden. (In his paranoid state, he considered possession of civvies as evidence of probable desertion.) He shot some more of the men as they ran for their lives.

Patrols left the camp, probing slowly up the Damba road to gather human intelligence. We were supposed to win over the populace by distributing tins of pilchards and money, in the hope that they would give us advance warning of enemy movements or ambush sites. This attempt at a hearts-and-minds campaign did not last long, however. One day, we arrived in a small village and as Callan's Land Rover drove past, a man greeted him loudly by calling out, 'Comrade!' Callan ordered us to 'grab the Commie bastard and ransack every mud hut in his village'. He asserted that the man must be a spy but all we found in his house was a cardboard suitcase full of biro pens. His wife and infant daughter pleaded desperately as the man was bundled into the back of the vehicle. On the return journey, I looked him in the eye. He gazed back at me, a look of terror in his eyes. Inside, I was screaming at him to jump over the tailgate and run into the tall elephant grass by the roadside. If he had done, the dilemma would have been whether I could allow him to get that far. If Callan was to realise that I hadn't attempted to shoot him, my own life would be at risk.

When we arrived at camp, I walked the man towards a mud hut, where I understood he was to be questioned. We had only covered about ten yards when Mick Wainhouse put a pistol to his temple and shot him. The muzzle flashed in front of my eyes. A chunk of his head blew off and blood spurted from his skull. I instinctively recoiled as the man dropped to the ground. Wainhouse fired two more rounds into him and told me to 'get him dumped around the back somewhere'. He walked off nonchalantly and left me to my task. Momentarily, I thought about the man's wife and child, who might never even learn of his fate. The only consolation I could find was that he had not been 'questioned' before being killed.

Soon afterwards, Wainhouse contracted dysentery and malaria. Good, I thought, as for days he lay on the floor drifting in and out of consciousness and sweating profusely. Eventually, he was flown to Kinshasa. When the pilot returned, he told us that he had seen enemy forces leaving Damba and heading for Maquela. He said the column of vehicles was proceeding with great caution to avoid mines. (As a defensive measure, I had laid mile after mile of anti-tank mines along this major road.) The enemy were using a bulldozer to skim the road surface and reveal the devices. Callan and I were both keen to blow up the bulldozer. By the light of a paraffin lamp, he pored over maps of the area before asking me if I could take it out with explosives. I said yes and he announced that we would set up an ambush position the following day.

We left Quibocolo base camp in three vehicles. Shotgun Charlie looked like a Mexican bandit, with twin bandoliers of 12-gauge ammunition across his chest. Callan's intended ambush site was a stretch of road flanked by steep hills covered in thick elephant grass. Sharp leaves sprouted from the long stems. These could easily cut open the palm of a man's hand. We needed a hole under the road sufficiently deep to house 30 kg of explosives way down beyond the reach of the bulldozer, with no metal for a mine detector to pick up. The explosives could be detonated from a concealed position and the dozer would be history. Without a camouflet set to create an underground chamber, I told Callan I needed a six-foot-deep hole dug into the road and he ordered the Angolan soldiers he'd brought with us to begin the work.

One thing we were not short of was mines: we had Russian, Chinese, Belgian and Italian varieties in all shapes and sizes. I laid anti-personnel mines off-road along the length of the linear ambush site, choosing positions where I imagined the enemy soldiers would run for cover when the ambush was initiated. This task would not have taken as long as it did were it not for Shotgun Charlie's attitude. He refused to help me. 'You must be mad,' he told me. 'You can get fucked.'

I was in the elephant grass, treading narrow pathways to lay the POMZ-2 anti-personnel mine and its tripwire. This Russian mine was about the size and shape of a tin of beans, with a percussion detonator switch screwed into the top. A round wooden stake was driven into the ground and the mine fitted to its base. A second stake was then pushed into the earth about 30 ft away and a tripwire strung between them. By the time I was nearly finished, I was exhausted and my hands were bleeding where the grass had cut them. I had only two mines left to set and had just connected one end of a tripwire to a stake when one of the set mines exploded. The force of the blast threw me into a gully and the wire wrapped around me from my waist to my ankles.

Shotgun Charlie screamed, 'What the fuck's happened? What the fuck's happened?'

Instinctively, I put my hand between my legs. My vital parts were intact. But where my left buttock met my thigh, there was now a hole. My fingers easily slid inside.

'Don't come through that way, Charlie,' I screamed back as the pain kicked in. 'You'll get blown up.'

'I'll go and get help then,' he replied.

'Let me guide you in. I need you to get me out of this wire. Come level with my voice.'

There was no reply. I lay there squinting beneath the sun, cursing my misfortune and wondering why I had agreed to join this ragtag army. When I attempted to stand, my legs buckled beneath me. They were riddled with shrapnel. I would later be told that a large metal fragment had entered through my butt cheek and embedded itself in my pelvic bone. I was carried from the minefield and, as we beat a hasty retreat by road, the plan to ambush the enemy was forgotten. As we crested every rise in the road and sunk into every pothole, the agony came in waves; I was adrift in a burning sea of pain.

That day, we lost Jamie McCandless and Joe Akoo. Jamie had become more and more anxious, frequently ranting about how none of us were getting home alive. We'd heard it all before and had given up taking any notice. I used to respond by saying, 'You speak for your fucking self. One thing's for certain, if everyone else in Angola gets killed, I'll be the last man still alive!' As we headed back to Maquela, Jamie took a Land Rover and, with Joe, went to check there were no stragglers. They picked up Bryan Lewis and two Angolan soldiers from an observation post and, instead of returning to base camp, they headed towards Damba. As we found out later, they got into a firefight with an enemy patrol; they survived that but got ambushed on the way back. Jamie had been right after all: he wouldn't make it home. He was riddled with bullets as he drove and the vehicle went out of control, crashing and throwing Bryan into the long grass. Joe and the other troopers were missing, presumed dead. Several days later, a battered Bryan returned. He'd lain low during the day and tabbed it towards camp by night.

At Maquela, on the morning after the accident in the minefield, Callan inspected my wounds and decided I should be airlifted to hospital. With him, I flew to São Salvador to await the Fokker Friendship plane to Kinshasa. Meanwhile, John Banks had arrived in Zaire. 'Major Banks', as he was now calling himself, and 96 would-be mercenaries had touched down on a Sabena flight from Brussels. To Holden Roberto's fury, Banks had defied his wishes. He wanted the new arrivals to join the fight immediately but Banks said he would agree to their transit only after he had seen detailed intelligence reports on the FNLA's progress. I figured the stand-off was really about Banks seeking to squeeze more money out of Roberto. A compromise of sorts was agreed. Banks and ten members of his new group travelled to São Salvador.

'Where are the rest of your soldiers?' Callan began, as the two men stood on the steps of the Palace.

Banks' men had their weapons pointed at Callan. They looked knackered after their journey from Zaire. The sight of them reminded me how I had felt after ten hours on the road to get here.

'The remainder of the men will not arrive until, or unless, I am satisfied,' explained Banks. 'I haven't seen any intelligence reports yet. I want to know what's happening here.'

Sammy Copeland marched to Callan's side and pointed his sub-machine gun directly at Banks. Copeland was intimidating enough even when unarmed. He had an enormous tattoo of a spider across his muscular chest. You only needed to see it once and you never forgot it.

'You shouldn't point weapons at me,' Callan told the new recruits. One of them was an old friend of Banks', Cecil 'Satch' Fortuin. He acted as Banks' minder and had been promised £300 and a return to the UK after a weekend in Angola. Satch would not see the UK again for another eight years.

'They work for me, not you,' Banks replied, 'so they will not listen to your orders or advice. And neither will I. They take orders from me, Major John Banks.'

'Let's continue this discussion inside,' said Callan.

Banks was taken aback to see me wrapped in bandages and propped up on a mattress. Having overheard the conversation outside, I ushered him towards me. 'John, I'm all right; just a little accident with a mine that exploded when it shouldn't have done.'

'OK, I'm pleased to hear it.'

'Look, John,' I said, lowering my voice, 'you've got to be very careful about what you say and do around here. I'd think twice before having confrontations like that with Callan. You may end up a casualty of this war yourself.'

Banks had not spent any time in Angola and had no idea what a psychopath Callan was. They must have reached an agreement in the end, as the remaining 86 mercenaries passed through São Salvador within 36 hours, stopping briefly for refreshments and fuel. Banks disappeared. He had no intention of getting his boots dirty or getting shot. He was sufficiently wise to keep his involvement in this mess limited to making money.

I was flown to Kinshasa, carried from the plane into an ambulance and driven to Mama Yemo Hospital. An angry mob waited outside, desperate for medical attention. Armed police and baton-wielding security guards dissuaded them from climbing the gates. While the stench of urine and sweat inside the accident and emergency ward made me nauseous, my discomfort was replaced with excruciating pain when the porters lifted me unceremoniously from my stretcher onto a metal gurney. I let out a burst of expletives when a bracket dug into my spine. Losing my temper did my chances of receiving favourable treatment no good. The medics ignored my repeated and increasingly aggressive demands for morphine. 'Wait your turn,' an American doctor insisted, reluctantly turning his head towards me. 'And don't frighten the orderlies. They'll be responsible for your care later.'

It was obvious that there were insufficient staff to cope with the patients, many of whom were worse off than me. I was in such pain that I was insensible to their suffering. Finally, I was X-rayed and carried to the intensive-care ward, where men, women and children with every conceivable illness or injury lay on and beneath beds. The people under the beds were not patients but relatives or friends staying with the sick to feed and wash them.

I was moved into an adjacent room that had only two beds. My roommate was unconscious and made gurgling sounds as he breathed. Suddenly, he sat bolt upright and coughed so violently that black blood shot from his mouth onto the wall. With that, he flopped back down again and lay motionless. The orderlies eventually arrived and pronounced him dead.

Having not had a drink since São Salvador, I was too dehydrated to sleep. Mama Yemo did not provide water, only a drink of tea if you had a cup. The best offer I got was an invitation to suck the spout of a battered aluminium kettle. In the early morning light, I saw a wet pink-coloured patch on my bed-linen. Evidently, I had stopped bleeding but now my bodily fluids were seeping through my wounds.

Later that day, the orderlies hooked me up to a saline drip and I began to feel a little better. Then my first visitor arrived. Douglas 'Canada' Newby had looked after me at Maquela and São Salvador in the days following my accident. He was a photojournalist first and a mercenary second, or so he claimed. He said he was going to write a bestseller about the war. He was either extremely confident or very naive. Why else would someone fight for the FNLA as an unpaid volunteer?

'You're still wearing your camouflage gear?' he asked me, sounding surprised.

'Yup. No pyjamas in this hospital. I'm so thirsty,' I added, seeing the three bottles of Coca-Cola in his hand.

'Drink these, and here are some escudos to bribe the orderlies to treat you well. I've spoken to one of the doctors. You'll get looked after better from now on.'

Canada glanced at the lizards scuttling across the walls to investigate the bloodstains.

'I'll be back later,' he said.

I drank the three Cokes then fell asleep, only to wake with a raging thirst and find that the money Canada had left for me was missing. I hurled my empty Coke bottles across the room. The breaking glass brought a pair of orderlies to the door, who eyed me with contempt and amusement. I lunged towards them, clinging to the drip stand for balance. They rushed away as I collapsed on the floor.

Canada returned and had me discharged. He and Wainhouse rushed me, unshaven and wearing bloody camouflage gear, through the lobby of the Intercontinental Hotel. Wainhouse still looked deathly pale from his bout of malaria. Canada changed my dressings using his field medical pack and gave me a dose of antibiotics. Canada had contacted Holden Roberto about the delay in receiving treatment and he in turn had telephoned President Mobutu to complain. I was operated on within an hour of returning to hospital the following day. The chatty American surgeon provided a running commentary. After a spinal anaesthetic was administered, he dug about inside me with forceps to remove the pieces of shrapnel, which I counted as they clinked into a kidney-shaped metal dish.

The largest piece was embedded in my pelvis. 'I'm going to have to cut you open to reach it,' he said, sounding enthused rather than deterred. He cut into me with surgical scissors. It took a second dose of anaesthetic to ease me through the clamping open of the folds of my flesh. One assistant poured a saline solution inside me while another removed it with a suction tube. A final tug removed the shrapnel from my pelvic bone. I could see little of what the doctor and his team were doing to me but the operation certainly made for uncomfortable listening.

Back in intensive care, my new roommate was Hugh Morrison, formerly of the French Foreign Legion and one of Banks' second wave of mercenaries. He was a victim not of the MPLA but of Uzio's driving. Their open-top vehicle had flipped over on a wet bend. The weight of the Land Rover would have crushed Morrison had it not pivoted on the machine-gun mount. The crash drove Morrison's femur through his pelvis and now he was in traction rather than action. Callan, of course, emerged unscathed from the wreckage. I could just hear Callan shouting, 'Rapido, rapido,' at the hapless Portuguese driver seconds before he lost control. My next two days passed in a sweat-soaked, hallucinatory haze, courtesy of Librium, penicillin and anti-tetanus injections.

CHAPTER 8

MASSACRE AT MAQUELA

WHEN I'D BEEN RECOVERING FROM MY OPERATION FOR A COUPLE of days, a dozen more injured mercenaries arrived at the hospital. One of them was Barry Freeman and the news he brought was not good. A few days later, Chris Dempster confirmed his version of the terrible events that had taken place back in Angola.

Callan had been led to expect that the fresh batch of recruits would be elite ex-SAS soldiers, paratroopers and marines. Instead, Banks delivered an eclectic bunch, including many who had no military training. The youngest was a 16-year-old boy who was supposed to be in council care, the oldest a 52-year-old Scotsman, Andrew 'Jock' McCartney, a committed anti-Communist and self-taught Russian linguist. Many had travelled on the understanding that they would be given non-combat roles. Another of Banks' lies had been that he would remain in Africa as their commanding officer. They soon realised he had left them to their fate.

Their first mistake was to arrive late, having got stuck on the mountain road. Only the advance party completed the journey to Maquela successfully. Dempster was ordered to go to the rescue of the main party and pull them out of the mud. The morale of those waiting by the roadside plummeted by the hour. They were unwilling to travel further. That journey had been a nightmare, the rain was lashing down and they had no waterproofs or food. With Dempster's assistance, the vehicles were righted and they made it to camp. The more vociferous among the party told Dempster how disappointed they were to be treated so badly and reminded him that they were only here to train the Angolan soldiers. Dempster promised to do his best to get them jobs that kept them out of the way but advised them against telling Callan of their pacifist stance.

Colonel Callan was far from impressed with what he saw and he began to question the new recruits about their backgrounds. He let out a snort when he discovered that two of the men were submariners, sneering, 'That cunt Banks, now he sends me men who fight underwater!' He was candid when he addressed them, admitting that his forces were outnumbered and outgunned. One of the recruits responded, 'How can we fight against thousands of heavily armed Cubans who have tanks and missiles? This is madness.'

'Those of you who don't want to fight,' Callan replied, 'stand over there to the one side. We'll see who we have left.'

He counted as at least a quarter of the new recruits shuffled out of line. Their numbers were bolstered by those Callan summarily rejected as not up to standard. This decision bemused many, because some of the men he turned down were willing to fight and had served in respected infantry regiments in the British Army. In all, there were 23 non-combatants.

'You lot, get out of your camouflage clothing now. You are not soldiers. You are nobodies now. You are not fit to wear military uniform. You are not allowed to wear anything again that could lead to you being mistaken for a fighter. I don't want to waste my time with you. When there is the opportunity, you will be sent back to São Salvador and assigned non-combat duties. If you want to leave Angola before then, you can try walking.'

That day, Callan received a report that Cuban forces were closing on the town of Tomboco and would soon bear down on Santo Antonio, where Peter McAleese's group was stationed. In his haste to attend an emergency meeting with Holden Roberto, Callan left Sammy

Copeland in command. The Portuguese mercenaries ('the Porks', as we called them) must have hoped the colonel would not be gone long. They would have followed Callan over a cliff but had scant faith in Copeland.

Copeland announced his plan to ambush a much larger enemy convoy that night. '*Não bom*,' said one of the Portuguese guys, which translated as 'not good'. Indeed.

To scare the non-combatants, Copeland told them that he expected them to take part in his suicidal attack, organising a demonstration of how to fire a 66-mm rocket launcher for those who had neither seen nor used one before, which was the majority. Fearing for their lives, they met in the bungalow complex where they were billeted to discuss their strategy. Barry Freeman and Chris Dempster were invited to listen to their complaints. Two of the men, Ken Aitken and Brian Butcher, spoke up, saying that they were worried Callan would have them all shot for refusing to fight. Freeman tried to allay their fears, telling them that Callan wouldn't do that, if only because the morale of the other men would suffer. The non-combatants looked far from convinced.

'The best thing you can do,' said Dempster, 'is to volunteer for tonight's attack. You'll win your way back into Callan's favour. He'll go easier on you all after that.'

The non-coms replied that some of them were willing but they needed time to think about it.

'OK. Barry and I will be returning here later this evening from Quibocolo before the mission in order to pick up Callan's Toyota. It's here for repairs. Those of you who are willing to bear arms, get yourselves back in uniform, pick up a rifle and be ready to leave for Quibocolo in a couple of hours.'

Dempster and Freeman left to attend Copeland's pre-mission briefing. Dempster reckoned it sounded more like a plan to kill him off.

'We will drive to Banana Junction in convoy before advancing towards Damba on foot in two separate columns, one led by Chris Dempster, the other by Spider Kelly. Under cover of darkness, we will silently approach the Cuban position then open fire with our 66-mm rockets. If the Cubans fire first, we will continue to attack. What do you think, Chris?'

'I couldn't think of a better way of getting rid of me, Sammy. Except if you burst into my room with a machine gun while I was asleep.'

As planned, Dempster and Freeman, accompanied by two others, Tony Boddy and Max Risbridger, returned to Maquela to collect Callan's Toyota. It was dark as their Land Rover passed through the abandoned checkpoints on the edge of the town. There were no lights on in any of the accommodation. The non-combatants' billets were also black, which suggested that those among them who had said they would consider fighting had thought better of it.

'Turn the torch on,' said Dempster. 'Flash it to let them know we're friendly.'

The Land Rover was within 300 feet of the bungalows when it came under fire from 66-mm rockets. The windscreen shattered. The blast, which stuck the front of the Land Rover, was followed by a hail of bullets, tearing the tyres to shreds.

'It's those bloody non-coms!' screamed Dempster. 'They must think we're Cubans.'

'Stop, you bastards, it's us, we're English!' shouted Freeman.

There was silence. They had escaped injury.

'Don't shoot!' Dempster shouted.

As if in reply, the Land Rover was raked by a fresh burst of automatic fire. Freeman dived out of the vehicle, running for cover, shouting at the others, 'It's the fucking Cubans!' The rest followed. Another burst of fire was directed at the area they had just left as they made it off the road; the firefight continued, the men shooting blindly as they raced out of the killing zone. Dempster took cover down the side of a building and the other three dived inside. When the firing ceased, Freeman joined Dempster outside.

'Look, Barry,' said Dempster, breathing heavily, 'this is shit. The Cubans have somehow got a small patrol inside there and wiped out those fucking useless non-combatants. There's no way the four of us are going to take this place back.'

'Chris, are you saying that we should leg it?' Freeman asked.

'Yeah, I am,' Dempster replied.

Around two the following morning, Terry Wilson, a soldier attached to Callan's group, was guarding a checkpoint when he was surprised to observe two trucks heading for the Zaire border from the direction of Maquela. Acting on Callan's instructions, he stepped into the road in front of the incoming vehicles and brought them to a halt. Aboard were the 23 non-combatants, including Aitken and Butcher. They told him that Maquela had been overrun by Cuban tanks in a major attack from the direction of the Damba road, claiming they had put up a fight but had been forced to withdraw. They told of Copeland's ambush plans and the assumption was that the attack had been a disaster or that Copeland's men had been ambushed themselves, leaving the way to Maquela clear.

Meanwhile, convinced that Maquela had fallen to the Cubans and that their only chance of survival lay in making their escape, Dempster and Freeman crawled for hours through undergrowth. As dawn broke, they arrived at a neighbouring village, reaching an abandoned roadside checkpoint. It was a good location to observe any traffic in and out of town but there was no rumble of tanks and armoured vehicles, only civilians strolling to and from the market in Maquela as if it was any normal day.

'This is ridiculous, Chris,' said Freeman. 'Ask someone what's been going on.'

Dempster confronted a man and woman walking towards them from the direction of Maquela. Using a mixture of pidgin English and mime, he asked, 'What soldiers have you seen in the town. Any Cubans?'

'No, Fenla, Fenla,' was the response.

Dempster flagged down another villager on a bicycle. Again communicating largely through gesture, he told him to cycle to Maquela and tell the FNLA commander there were two Britons who needed collecting from the checkpoint.

Twenty minutes later, a Portuguese driver arrived in an armoured car to pick them up. In Maquela, they found Boddy, Copeland, Andy McKenzie and a few others assessing Dempster's Land Rover. The vehicle was a bullet-riddled wreck with its windscreen shattered and its doors hanging off. Boddy explained that he and Risbridger had walked to Quibocolo to apprise Copeland of the attack.

It was an Angolan mechanic called Joseph who provided the most illuminating account of the events of the previous evening. He reported that, after their discussions with Dempster and Freeman, the non-coms had dressed in camouflage uniforms and armed themselves. Under Aitken and Butcher's supervision, they had raided the ammunition and food stores and loaded their bounty onto three trucks. A small group of the most heavily armed among them then disappeared, walking in the direction of the Quibocolo road. Joseph had fallen asleep only to be awoken by explosions. He then saw the three trucks leaving the bungalows, heading at speed towards São Salvador. To verify Joseph's account, the mercenaries visited the stores, which had indeed been looted. To them, it was now obvious that the non-combatants, not the Cubans, had attacked Dempster's Land Rover and were now heading for the Zaire border.

Copeland was apoplectic. 'They've legged it, the bastards. They knew you [Dempster] were coming back here last night. That's why they ambushed you. So long as they killed everyone in your vehicle, there would be nobody to raise the alarm. They've got half a day's start on us. We'll never catch them standing here.'

Dempster insisted on sending a radio message to Callan before they departed. It read: 'Ambushed in Maquela by non-coms, 2000 hrs last night. They are proceeding your way with three trucks. Urgent you stop and hold until our arrival. Dempster I/C Maquela.'

Tony Boddy was the nominated driver as they sped away in Copeland's Land Rover towards São Salvador. Copeland sat in the front passenger seat, with Dempster, Freeman, McKenzie and two other soldiers squeezed into the back. Copeland demanded that Boddy drive faster and faster along the rutted track. Those sitting behind him were almost thrown from the vehicle. After travelling just a few kilometres, they found one of the non-combatants' vehicles lying on its side in a ditch. There was evidence of an attempt to right the truck: logs and large branches were jammed under one side. From this and the nearby tracks, the pursuit party deduced that the fugitives had been delayed some considerable time. 'We've got them now!'

Copeland screamed. 'They can't be more than a couple of hours in front of us.'

Like foxhounds with a scent of blood, the pursuers pressed on. Copeland was maniacal, standing in the front of the vehicle and waving his machine gun in the air. 'Faster, faster!' he screamed at Boddy. They reached a fork in the road. It had presented the non-combatants with two options: either to continue on the main road to São Salvador or to take the secondary Cuimba road. They would have known that had they taken the first option, they would almost certainly have bumped into Callan. The vehicle tracks indicated that they had indeed chosen to drive towards Cuimba. This road offered the shortest route to Zaire and the hunters were despondent, knowing they now had little chance of making up the ground before their quarry reached the border crossing.

Resigned, they drove on to Cuimba, where they met Terry Wilson.

'I'm surprised to see you,' he greeted them. 'I didn't think you would have survived an attack by so many Cuban tanks.'

'What tanks?' said Copeland.

'The Cuban tanks.' Copeland looked at Wilson as if he were deranged. He continued, 'Your guys said they had knocked out two of the tanks and killed twenty of the enemy. It sounded like quite a contact. I passed it on to Callan via the radio. He's ordered the bridge at Cuimba to be demolished in order to prevent the enemy outflanking São Salvador by that route.'

'Where are those men now?' asked Copeland.

'I forced them to turn back towards São Salvador.'

Copeland was relieved. His group swung their vehicle around and headed towards São Salvador. On the road, they met Callan and a group of Portuguese mercenaries sitting casually in an armoured car. Callan hadn't yet received Dempster's radio message and was emotional with relief at the sight of men he had assumed dead. He had just sent a message to Kinshasa – based on information from the non-coms, who were dug in at positions in the hillside some kilometres further down the road – telling Holden Roberto that Maquela had fallen and his men had been killed in action. He listened impassively, stony-faced and cold-eyed, as he was told the facts.

Callan was beside himself with rage, spewing out obscenities in Greek and English. 'Those bastards! Trying to kill my men. I'll fuck 'em good.' The expression on his face suggested he was already imagining punishments for them. However, he wasn't so angry that he forgot the non-combatants were heavily armed. He warned Copeland not to lose his temper when he came face to face with them. Callan wanted to cajole rather than threaten them. They would be lured into his vehicles and then retribution would be swift.

As I lay in hospital listening to Barry Freeman's account of all this, I was amazed by how badly the non-combatants had played their hand. They could have blown Wilson away and sped over the Zaire border. How was he able to persuade 23 heavily armed men to turn back? There must have been some breakdown within the group, a lack of leadership or conviction. They bottled it when freedom was within their grasp. I found it hard to believe the extremes that Callan would go to in order to punish them but it was even more difficult to understand why men so desperate to get away from Callan and Angola that they would fire upon their own side to achieve that goal would ultimately go to their deaths without a determined fight. Maybe they had yet to grasp the insanity of Angola and the lunatics who ran the circus.

Most of the non-combatants were found hiding in foxholes near the side of the road. These were potential ambush positions, remember, but the men had no will to fight an armed enemy. All it took was for Dempster, Freeman and two others to saunter towards them and suggest they follow and they duly trudged behind the four men towards Callan. In spite of a numerical advantage of three to one over Callan's group, they made no attempt to resist capture or punishment. They carried their weapons by their sides.

'Six of you, any six of you, get in the back of the Land Rover. The rest of you get aboard the trucks and follow behind,' said Callan, his face hardened by simmering anger. He then confronted the six. 'Throw down your guns.' They followed Callan's instruction. With the men disarmed and out of sight of the others, Callan vented his fury on them. 'You will pay very dearly for trying to murder my men. Strip to your underwear.' The six shook with fear. They had heard that being stripped was a customary preliminary to a Callan execution. 'We're now going to retake Maquela from the Cubans.' It was a sick joke. The convoy drove back to base at a funereal pace.

At Maquela, half an hour passed and one of the trucks in which the non-combatants were travelling had not shown up. Suspecting they might have made another try for the border, Callan sent Dempster, Boddy and Freeman back to find them.

When all the transgressors were present, they were lined up in front of their billet. The Portuguese mercenaries, fiercely loyal to Callan after his early escapades, trained their heavy machine guns on them. Callan addressed the mutineers, his voice guttural with anger: 'You tried to murder my men, who have been up here for two weeks, with hardly any sleep, holding back the enemy. You tried to cover it up. You stole all the food and ammunition, and left everybody else with nothing. One of my men is worth ten of you cunts.'

The non-coms faces showed a mixture of fear, nervousness and disbelief. Callan drew his Browning pistol. 'I demand to know who fired the rocket that hit the patrol vehicle last night.'

Philip Davies, a 22-year-old ex-soldier from Birmingham, stepped forward and said, 'Me, sir.'

Callan raised his weapon. 'This is the only law here.'

He shot Davies in the forehead at close range, pumping a further two bullets into his head as he fell groaning against the wall. As the rest of the non-combatants looked at Davies, Callan ordered, 'The rest of you strip or you'll get the same.'

He glanced contemptuously at Davies. His brains were seeping from his skull and a puddle of blood was spreading around his head. 'Get that cunt out of here,' he ordered. The corpse was thrown over a wall.

Fearing there was going to be a massacre of the remaining 22 non-coms, one of Callan's men suggested a compromise. Those facing the death penalty could be used as cannon fodder for the next full-frontal attack on Cuban lines. This amused Callan and he called for volunteers. Only four saw this as a potential lifeline. Kevin Whirity and David Paden, both ex-Paras, Colin Evans and Mike McKeown stepped forward. When Callan added that the Land Rover would require a driver, Kevin Marchant, a former physical-training instructor, stepped forward. Barry Freeman pointed to another man and said that he had patrolled with him in Northern Ireland and that he was a good soldier. 'You can have him, he's yours,' said Callan. In fact, Freeman had never set eyes on the man before. He just wanted to spare someone's life.

The condemned men obeyed an order to strip to their underpants, all except 52-year-old Jock McCartney, the Russian interpreter, who was protesting that he'd only wanted a change of job and meant no harm. Copeland opened fire with his Uzi, the rounds biting into the dust at the Scotsman's feet. 'You will die here and now if you don't stop whining and hurry up undressing.'

He addressed the men again: 'You stupid cunts. All you had to do was behave yourselves and you'd all have gone home safe. Instead, you're all going to die.' He ordered Copeland to get the prisoners aboard a Dodge troop carrier. His final words on the matter were, 'Take them away, Sergeant Major. You know what to do with them.'

The Dodge left Maquela as part of a three-vehicle convoy. Travelling with Copeland were Dempster, Boddy, Freeman, McKenzie and one of the Portuguese mercenaries. The non-combatants were quiet, in a subdued state. Some cried gently, others prayed. Even at this late stage, they could have mounted some sort of defence. The floor of the troop carrier was littered with weapons: 66-mm rockets, grenades and automatic weapons of all kinds, Kalashnikovs and Uzis, all loaded. Any prisoner who wanted to arm himself only had to reach down. If they had made a concerted collective effort, they could have wiped out their escorts with minimal losses but it seemed that none of them was prepared to attempt such an operation.

Copeland, who appeared to find the whole spectacle highly amusing, ordered the convoy to a halt some five kilometres outside Maquela, where he knew a lush green valley. The prisoners could see that there was little cover to aid any escape bid. Copeland lined up a five-man firing squad and had the condemned men stand to attention.

'In a few minutes, you're all going to be dead,' he said, 'and I'm the one what's going to kill you. I'll blow an arm off here, a leg off there. Maybe gut-shoot some of you. I'm really going to have myself a ball. But I will give you a sporting chance to run first. So turn and face the valley.' The 15 remaining non-combatants obeyed his order and surveyed the green expanse. 'Get running, you bastards,' bellowed Copeland in his parade-ground voice.

Some did make a dash across the pasture. McCartney was one of those who stood his ground. He must have known his old legs would not carry him far enough fast enough. Others, like Harry Webb, just strolled across the grass, as if beginning a morning walk. Webb, a 36-year-old from Leeds, had left a wife and three children at home in Yorkshire, having been offered the chance to work as a training instructor in Angola. Billy Brooks, a 22-year-old truck driver from Hertfordshire, walked a few yards then turned to face his executioners and folded his arms. He had signed on as a driver and had been promised he would not have to fight. Thousands of miles from home, facing certain death, he stared in open defiance at his captors. Dempster said Brooks never once took his eyes from his face.

Copeland let those who had chosen to run get about 60 ft down the slope before he opened fire. The 9-mm bullets tore into their flesh. There was some dissent in the firing party. Dempster and Freeman adjusted the gas-regulator settings on their FN rifles, knowing this would cause their weapons to jam after firing only a few rounds. Copeland continued firing until his magazine ran dry, by which time most of the prisoners were lying stricken on the ground, crying out in agony. Boddy seemed to enjoy the event, screaming that it was a 'turkey shoot' and exclaiming excitedly, 'I've got one!'

Copeland replenished his weapon and brought down the remaining four runners. This left Brooks, standing, Webb and an unidentified younger man, walking, and McCartney. With a sweep of his Uzi, Copeland accounted for Brooks and Webb.

Now only McCartney remained, standing close to Copeland and repeating in his thick Scottish brogue, 'I only want a change of job.' Unmoved, Copeland fired a short burst into his stomach. McCartney toppled backwards, hugging his belly, his fingers clawing at his entrails in a vain bid to prevent them pouring from his midriff. Copeland seemed impervious to McCartney's suffering. He stared straight ahead as his victim's screams rang out across the valley. Finally,

Dempster took aim and shot McCartney in the head, killing him instantly. Copeland flinched, Dempster's shot having taken him by surprise. He spun round and stared at Dempster, perhaps fearing his colleague might shoot him next.

An execution party of Copeland, Dempster, McKenzie, Freeman and Boddy then moved down the valley, passing from one wounded victim to the next to administer the *coup de grâce*. Still Copeland wanted to cause more suffering, engaging in conversation with the injured, who by this stage were begging to die.

'Kill me,' one pleaded. Part of his face was missing and there was a ragged line of entry wounds across his chest.

'It doesn't really hurt, does it?' Copeland replied, as if in disbelief.

'Kill me!' the man screamed.

'You mean you want to die?'

'Yes!'

'What, now?'

'Yes!'

'Oh, OK, then.'

Finally, Copeland executed him.

With all the non-combatants dead, the execution party withdrew. The victims' bodies were left where they fell. Callan cancelled plans for a burial detail, saying he wanted the sight and smell of the dead to remind others of the price of desertion.

The longer I listened to this story and tried to analyse the events, the more difficult it became. As I had not seen it happen, at first I gave the benefit of the doubt to those who were said to have done so. The description of Sammy as a cruel and sadistic killer was at variance with the man who had looked after me as I lay injured at the Palace in São Salvador. I had thought he was a good soldier with lots of bottle. But Demspter was a friend of mine and I believed what he told me. The atmosphere had turned brutal and many people's personalities had been adversely affected. I knew that if you lived in an atmosphere of fear and violence, it could become a necessity for survival to run with the pack. Our pack was led by Callan and some were trying to emulate him.

CHAPTER 9

RETREAT WITHOUT HONOUR

AS SOON AS I WAS ABLE TO HOBBLE AROUND, I DISCHARGED MYSELF from hospital and checked into the Intercontinental Hotel. I returned to Mama Yemo daily for dressing changes and antibiotics. My mind repeatedly flashed back to when I was blown up. I knew I had not tripped the mine and set it off. The explosion could only have been caused by a crop of elephant grass springing back after it had been trampled down.

Hundreds of miles away, against ever-increasing odds, Callan continued to take the war to the enemy. It was like a personal crusade for him. He achieved some successes, albeit at a high cost. His tactics were near suicidal. It shocked FAPLA that such an outnumbered and outgunned military force would launch such daring raids. On one occasion, when Callan drove his men directly towards an enemy camp, a FAPLA tank fired its main gun down the road, hitting a Land Rover used to carry spare ammunition. Nineteen men were wounded in an enormous explosion that showered them with shrapnel. In a rare moment of common sense, Callan ordered everybody to withdraw so that they could be treated.

Sammy Copeland described another mission, in which Callan led his men towards Damba in search of the bulldozer that had eluded us the day I was wounded. He found it on the second afternoon of searching. He also saw enemy tanks, trucks and Land Rovers parked in the distance. He didn't realise at first that these vehicles were merely the tip of an enemy convoy stretching a mile further down the road and including 1,600 Cuban and Angolan soldiers. Callan launched a series of rapid attacks on the enemy lines, his ever battle-hungry Portuguese mercenaries making best use of their 'gimpies' (general-purpose machine guns). Inevitably, Callan attempted one attack too many and, as dusk fell, mortar rounds started raining down on the FNLA forces, one landing close to Copeland and Callan, blowing them 15 ft apart from each other. The tank guns started firing into the bush, one of the rounds decapitating a Portuguese commando.

The group was very close to the road, trying to get to a position where the enemy would have to cease firing mortars or risk hitting their own troops. Someone fired a 66-mm rocket at the Cubans. It hit a truck carrying munitions and suddenly there was a huge explosion that devastated the area, killing or wounding all FAPLA troops in the vicinity. The FNLA mercenaries caught in the blast were tossed about like rag dolls. Callan received injuries to his legs and could not stand. One ginger-haired young lad had his leg blown completely off. In the smoke and dust, men were screaming, in total confusion, their hearing affected by the deafening blast. Kevin Marchant and another of the recent recruits were ordered by Copeland, who had suffered a head wound, to carry Callan, while two others supported the boy who had lost his leg.

As darkness closed in, they retreated deep into the bush. The mercenary force was now reduced to fifteen men, including wounded. Nine were either dead or missing in action. The ginger-haired kid died overnight from loss of blood. Callan went into shock and Shotgun Charlie had to lie beside him all night trying to keep him warm and quiet, as he was moaning loudly in a delirious fever. The group's numbers fell to twelve early the following morning when two men Callan had sent on a scouting mission were shot on sight. The beleaguered party retreated further until they stumbled across a hut belonging to a leopard hunter. Callan ordered Copeland, with three others, to march back to Maquela and arrange a rescue party to collect the rest of them. When Copeland made it back, however, he found that fuel and ammo supplies were too low to allow him safely to head back out into the bush.

Meanwhile, news of the executions of the non-combatants had reached Kinshasa. A shocked Holden Roberto was baying for Callan's and Copeland's blood. He flew in Peter McAleese, with Mick Rennie, from their detachment at Santo Antonio. Roberto deposed Callan as FNLA field commander and appointed McAleese as his successor, demanding that he investigate the massacre.

At Santo Antonio, the five remaining men received a message from McAleese telling them that intelligence reports indicated trouble at Tomboco and to expect the same at Santo Antonio. At 8.30 the following morning, an alarmed Angolan ran into the marine depot, telling them that tanks had reached the first observation post on the approach to the town. His information was correct; within minutes, an armoured column had burst into Santo Antonio and FAPLA troops were rampaging through the hospital and other buildings shooting anything that moved. A Soviet-built BTR armoured car roared into the marine depot and disgorged heavily armed men, who ran for cover. The mercenaries opened fire with their sub-machine guns but it was obvious they were not going to win the firefight as more armour converged on the depot.

The group, among them several dozen panicking Angolans, as well as Robin Wright, an attractive reporter from the *Christian Science Monitor*, made a run for the jetty to get onboard a boat. Many of the Angolans were cut down in the intense gunfire and Mike Johnson, the former Legionnaire, was also killed as he reached the jetty. Brummie Barker was the first to reach the boat but he made no move to get aboard, instead trying to organise the evacuation. McPherson, Tilsey and Saunders, along with Robin Wright and 16 Angolans were onboard when the craft pulled away from its mooring. As the boat moved into the estuary, Barker remained on the jetty giving covering fire. At the last moment, he ripped off his combat clothes and dived into the water, swimming after the boat, which was now heading into the morning mist. A hail of bullets hit the water in front of him.

Barker took this as a warning and swam back to the enemy. Soviet advisers had given FAPLA orders to capture British and American mercenaries alive when they could, as living mercenaries were better propaganda than dead ones, so Barker was spared, at least for the moment.

In Kinshasa, McAleese questioned Dempster and Freeman about the massacre. Both insisted they had participated in the shootings only under great duress. McAleese then headed to Maquela with Roberto, Wainhouse and a new American mercenary, Tom Oates. Their mission was to arrest Copeland – and Callan, should he make it back from the bush. The only way to bring them into custody peacefully was to entrap them. As the party stepped off the plane, Shotgun Charlie welcomed them in a friendly fashion only to receive a smash in the face with a rifle butt. At base camp, unaware of Shotgun Charlie's arrest, Copeland agreed to point to Callan's approximate position on the map. The moment he put down his Uzi, it was snatched away and Oates put a gun to his wounded head.

Shotgun Charlie and Sammy Copeland were charged with murder. Stripped to the waist and with their hands clasped behind their backs, they were brought before an FNLA kangaroo court. Nick Hall began proceedings: 'I, Major Nicholas Hall, do hereby swear by the power invested in me by Holden Roberto, President of the FNLA government of the northern territories of Angola, to listen to the evidence both for and against these men and to judge them as fairly as possible.'

Thirty minutes later, Copeland was found guilty of murder and sentenced to immediate death by firing squad. Shotgun Charlie, who had not been present at the executions, was found guilty of 'unmilitary behaviour'. He was stripped of his rank and sentenced to serve six months on the front line without pay. This probably didn't worry him too much, as he wasn't getting paid anyway. (The four original British 'mercenaries' were in truth volunteers, although they had been promised land if the FNLA won.) Callan was convicted in his absence and the order was given for him to be shot on sight.

Given that Shotgun Charlie had been guilty of many atrocities, his punishment seemed ludicrous. McAleese appealed to Holden Roberto to reverse the sentences and execute Christodoulou as a warning to others. Nick Hall, on the other hand, threatened to leave the FNLA if this reversal took place, and Tom Oates said that he would withdraw his support and take the American mercenary intake currently in Kinshasa with him. Holden Roberto confirmed the original verdicts and sentences. As the arguments continued, Copeland made a desperate dash for freedom, cutting left and right as he ran in a bid to avoid the rounds fired at him. He was struck down just a few yards short of cover in the bush. As he lay in agony in the foetal position, Wainhouse marched over to him and fired three rounds into the back of his head.

In the days following the trial, those of us who were still on our feet found ourselves in the more serene surroundings of Holden Roberto's office, drinking beer and discussing what was next for the FNLA. In spite of intelligence reports that suggested the enemy was poised to capture Tomboco, which would open the way for them to take São Salvador as well, Roberto was adamant that we should continue. I agreed with him. I didn't want my Angolan adventure to end and I felt I had a contribution to make: there was the Tomboco Bridge to blow up. Dempster wanted out and declined McAleese's offer of $500 per week to return to the front line. Because I was still pretty badly wounded, some people thought I was a couple of beers short of a six-pack for not following Dempster home. Maybe they had a point. I was in considerable pain and I couldn't sit down, even to go to the toilet. I was no longer entitled to medical treatment at Mama Yemo. Outpatients were a luxury the hospital could ill afford. Without bandages and dressings, I resorted to using torn-up sheets held in place with insulation tape. In the dying days of our resistance, it was the likes of Canada Newby and Bryan Lewis, all civilians, who remained up for the fight. When McAleese told the ex-military men we could still stave off defeat if we held onto São Salvador, they did not seem convinced. I was no more optimistic about victory but my adventurous spirit was insatiable. I also wondered, crazily perhaps, what new experiences each day in Angola would bring.

That day, Bryan, Canada and I visited the armoury at Kirkuzi, the villa where we had stopped off on our arrival in Angola. To our surprise, we found new uniforms and weapons. I flew to Maquela with Bryan Lewis and our new CO Peter McAleese; the withdrawal from Maquela was organised and Wainhouse was left to supervise this. Then we boarded our small plane again and headed for São Salvador. The following day, the evacuation convoy arrived at São Salvador. Once again, Maquela was a ghost town – at least until FAPLA came. The men from the abandoned camp waited nervously in the Palace for several days for the Fokker Friendship to come and take them to Zaire. None of them wanted to stay in Angola a moment longer than necessary.

Then, for a change, some encouraging news came through. President Mobutu of Zaire had offered the FNLA two Chinese Type 59 tanks. The drawback was that we had to collect them from one of his military bases. McAleese asked for volunteers to go and bring them back and it was Bryan and I who ended up travelling to Mbanza-Ngungu to collect them from the depot there. Nobody else wanted to be absent when the plane to Kinshasa arrived. I thought the mission seemed like the ideal opportunity to learn to drive a tank but I was to regret volunteering as soon as I got in the troop carrier to travel to Zaire. Rumbling over every bump and pothole in the road caused me extreme pain and almost immediately I was sweating profusely.

Perhaps the world's least inviting toilets were to be found at Mbanza-Ngungu. Two cubicles stood in a corridor; one had no door and the other's was hanging from a single hinge. There were no seats, lights, windows or paper. In the gloom, I reached down to find a cardboard box containing office paper, only to discover that this paper had already been used for the same purpose. Feeling sick to my stomach, I heaped abuse on every man ever born in that country; had any Zairian soldier heard my outburst, I would probably have been shot. With hindsight, my reaction was indicative of my distorted state of mind. This incident caused me greater repulsion than all the death and destruction I had witnessed.

Bryan and I killed time by strolling around the enormous open-sided hangars that housed row after row of unused tanks, armoured cars, field guns and rocket launchers. Holden Roberto arrived at the camp for the formal handover of the military equipment from the

Zairian authorities. They added two Chinese guided-missile systems and two six-tube rocket launchers to the tanks they were giving us.

After my excruciating outward journey, I managed to hitch a ride back in Roberto's Range Rover and enjoyed the air conditioning, comfortable seating and cold drinks that came as standard when you travelled with the FNLA president. We had time on our hands to chat, as our convoy had a maximum speed of 30 mph, the top speed at which the guided-missile systems could be towed. Roberto did most of the talking, explaining how the Intercontinental Hotel in Kinshasa was filling up with US mercenaries, Western reporters and TV crews. The biggest story in town was the massacre at Maquela.

'The versions being reported are distorted and exaggerated,' said Roberto, 'they are doing a lot of harm to the cause of the FNLA.'

'Why don't you put out an official statement, present the facts?' I asked.

'This is a very painful subject for me, Dave,' Roberto continued, shaking his head. 'I just don't understand why Callan would do such a thing. Why did he kill so many innocent civilians?'

To my mind, Roberto's flaw as a military leader was his conscience. I knew that in life you had to stop at nothing to achieve your aims. Earlier in the conflict, Roberto's forces could have captured the capital city, Luanda, had he not given the order to halt. In doing so, he saved civilian lives but lost the initiative. When the Cubans arrived, they seized control of the city and began their inevitable roll towards victory. The only piece of Angola the FNLA now controlled was equivalent proportionally to the corner-kick box on a football field. The time when we could have altered the war had long past.

As the journey continued, Roberto and I talked about our families. I felt he was genuine in his concern for me and for my wife and children back home in Britain. Our progress came to a halt after nightfall and still 60 km short of São Salvador. I looked out of the car to see a large crowd gathered around a bridge. It had collapsed beneath the weight of a bulldozer. The vehicle had rumbled halfway across before the structure gave way. Both bridge and bulldozer were now in the river below. I watched from the bank as Shotgun Charlie and FNLA chief Sonny Lima led attempts to build a temporary crossing. Roberto said

he was going to turn around and drive back to Kinshasa. He asked me
if I wanted to go back with him. He was concerned about my welfare
and suggested that I receive medical treatment in Zaire. I considered
his offer but it was only 60 km to São Salvador and it was 350 km
back to Kinshasa. 'Thank you, but no. I've come this far and I don't
fancy the long haul back.'

'Very well.'

As we shook hands, Roberto thrust $1,500 into my palm.

'For your family.'

I was struck by his generosity. 'I'm getting paid. It really isn't
necessary.'

'Please, I insist, for your family.'

I joined Shotgun Charlie as he sat by a fire, trying to keep warm.
When I told him about Roberto's gesture, he said that when the
FNLA leader offered him money he had turned it down.

'Why did you do that?'

'It wouldn't be any use to me. I'm not getting out of Angola alive.'

'Well, you could have given it to me,' I replied cynically.

I completed the journey to São Salvador in Sonny Lima's Fiat 124.
The Palace was almost deserted on our arrival. Mick Wainhouse was
organising our final, inevitable withdrawal. With Callan still missing,
presumed dead, I headed for his bedroom. The terrifying spell he had
cast on the men was such that his quarters had been left untouched. I
navigated through the weapons lying on his floor and pointed myself
towards his double bed. As a good night's sleep beckoned, a familiar
voice cut through the darkness.

'You can join me if you like.'

The voice was Canada Newby's. I thanked God it wasn't Callan's.

'Hello, mate. I'm so tired I would sleep next to a corpse.'

'Good. So don't try and rape me.'

I awoke the next morning to the sound of Chinese tanks. The
Portuguese mercenaries were receiving their first driving lessons.
Learning to fire the rocket launchers was altogether more challenging;
all the symbols and instructions were written in Chinese. As I sat
on Callan's bed nursing my increasingly smelly wounds, Canada
persuaded me to pose for some photographs. I grabbed an Uzi with

one hand and bundles of escudo bills with the other. Later, Wainhouse, Lima and I drove to Quiende Bridge, which I was supposed to prepare for demolition. No one seemed to know what the game plan was, however, so in the end it was a pointless exercise. There were several human bodies downstream, their heads bobbing up and down like fishing floats. We blasted at the corpses with our automatic weapons, hoping we could sink them. Though we punched great holes in the bodies and whipped up fountains of water around them, they refused to disappear, stubborn symbols of man's inhumanity to man.

McAleese returned from Kinshasa with 23 British mercenaries. They had been part of a group of 200, recruited by Banks, who had been refused entry at Kinshasa airport. These were the lucky (or unlucky) ones who had sneaked through security and taken taxis to the FNLA bureau downtown. The immigration officials wanted to fly the remainder back to Belgium on the same plane they had arrived on. Meanwhile, in London, the Foreign Office was doing its best to dissuade mercenaries from entering Angola. Harold Wilson's government considered our activities an international embarrassment.

It was now clear that I was not going to be able to contribute much to the war effort and Peter McAleese told me to leave and get medical attention. Reluctantly, I agreed and boarded a supply plane to Kinshasa. As I was owed money, my first stop was the FNLA bureau. The office was deserted but for wounded mercenaries denied a bed at Mama Yemo. I took a cab to the Intercontinental Hotel, where the FNLA tab remained open and where Nick Hall, Tom Oates and Canada Newby were staying. Hall returned just before dawn, having spent the wee hours drinking at the Scotch Club. When I knocked on his door, a stranger poked a gun in my face. He was introduced as Vince Canning, formerly of the French Foreign Legion and a cohort of Banks. Oates opened his door gun in hand, too. It seemed everyone was paranoid, even though the enemy was hundreds of miles away.

David Bufkin, the guy who'd recruited Oates, the US equivalent of Banks, I guess, was staying there, too. He was a Californian pilot with a penchant for cowboy boots. He had advertised for bored Vietnam veterans seeking Communists to fight and offered $1,200 a month for the pleasure of doing so. Bufkin boasted he would bring a thousand former US servicemen to Angola. He arrived with six, all of whom had paid their own way to get there. Daniel Gearhart had placed a notice in *Soldier of Fortune* magazine reading, 'Wanted: employment as mercenary on full-time or job contract basis. Preferably in South or Central America, but anywhere in the world if you pay transportation'. Another recruit was George Bacon, a political science major and holder of the CIA's second-highest award, the Intelligence Star. He was considerably overqualified for the work; he should have been a CIA station chief in Kinshasa, not a grunt in Angola. Bufkin himself was press-ganged into joining his recruits as a private soldier.

That evening, I said my final farewell to Holden Roberto. He said he was sorry I was leaving and insisted on giving me his personal and official telephone numbers. 'I'll be back as soon as I can,' I told him, although both of us knew that was unlikely.

I almost wished I could have stayed on but I was worried about my wounds, as they were now bordering on gangrenous. I was looking forward to seeing Mary and the kids again – they were the only stable thing in my life – but I also knew I would head off somewhere else again as soon as the opportunity arose.

I had been in Angola for only a month but what I learned in that short period would stand me in good stead in the years to come. It was like an instruction manual on how not to do it, at all levels, from Roberto down. Regrets? I had many. That we didn't win and that so many lost their lives for nothing. That many families would grieve and children would miss a father. That the US didn't have the courage to put its money and weapons where its mouth was. But most of all that some who should have died didn't.

At ten that night I was driven to the airport and it looked like I was going home without any further complications. Then the FNLA bureau secretary handed me my tickets: Swiss Air to Zurich, with a connecting flight to London. I was barred from Switzerland and did not want to take another holiday at Zurich Stadtpolizie. When the plane reached Switzerland, I felt thankful when passengers for connecting flights were ushered straight into the transit lounge. My relief lasted only as long as it took for the London flight to be announced and I saw my luggage had to pass through a metal detector. I was pulled to one side and my bag opened. The airport officials looked surprised to find my combat gear, a red beret, a webbing belt, three sniper scopes, a sheath knife and a Kalashnikov bayonet. I had wanted to take home the tools of my new trade. I had visions of an imminent return to the maximum-security cells but the Swiss officials contented themselves with making a note of my passport number. The weapons were bagged and handed back in London.

Waiting for me at passport control at Heathrow were five smiling members of Special Branch. I was questioned at the airport for most of the morning then taken to New Scotland Yard, where members of Detective Chief Superintendent Harry Mooney's murder squad asked me about the Maquela executions. I told them that those involved had acted under considerable duress. The detectives drove me back to Heathrow and left me to find my own way home. I was allowed to keep my bayonet and other military equipment but not my army training manuals, which were marked 'restricted' and offered advice on jungle warfare and the sabotage of oil and electrical installations. My passport was confiscated at Heathrow. To get it back, I had to sign an undertaking that I would not use it to travel as a mercenary. When I got it back it was stamped with the words 'Confiscated' and 'Returned'. Not long after that, my passport suffered an accident. It got soaked and the stamps were illegible. I sent it off with a note explaining that my wife had inadvertently put it in the washing machine and was issued with a new one.

Six days after my departure, the FNLA were defeated. At the end, there were only about 45 British, American and Portuguese mercenaries and a dwindling number of Angolan soldiers attempting to hold back the Cuban and FAPLA tide. They continued against these impossible odds with great professionalism, although the writing was on the wall. McAleese had drawn up plans for counteroffensives to retake Maquela and other places. On the morning of 14 February, two small patrol groups set out in the direction of Cuimba to assess the enemy's progress. One was led by Shotgun Charlie, the other by one of the recently arrived US mercenaries, Gus Grillo. One of the vehicles broke down and the two patrols became one, with all the soldiers squeezed into a single Land Rover. A few kilometres short of Cuimba, the vehicle was raked by heavy automatic fire. Shotgun Charlie died instantly. The survivors dived into the elephant grass at the side of the road. As he lay nursing a wounded leg, Gus Grillo returned fire. Finally, when it was impossible to escape and all his colleagues were either dead or captured, he threw down his Uzi and surrendered to the Cubans.

The following day, Canada Newby set off on the patrol that cost him his life. He ran into a truck full of FAPLA troops and a firefight ensued. His Land Rover was riddled with bullets. In less than thirty seconds, five of the seven men inside were killed. Canada was mortally wounded. The bodies were driven to Cuimba and put on display for the benefit of Cuban and Eastern bloc war correspondents.

No further patrols were ever sent out. Peter McAleese took a flight in a Cessna light aircraft, saw 2,000 enemy soldiers and 75 vehicles below him, only a few miles from São Salvador, and decided it was time for Operation Breakout to be implemented. This was the contingency plan for the evacuation of São Salvador by the remaining Western mercenaries. The vehicles were loaded with supplies and fuel, while surplus explosives and ammunition were stacked inside the Palace. The explosives were detonated once everyone was clear and the Palace was reduced to a pile of burning rubble.

On 17 February, the mercenaries crossed into Zaire. Their last ordeal was a clash with border guards over the fate of the 15 Porks. They were separated from the British mercenaries and told that they had no authorisation to be in Zaire and would have to cross back into Angola. It would mean certain death for the Portuguese if they were captured by the FAPLA. A deal was struck for them to remain in a refugee camp inside Zaire while President Mobutu considered their plight and they were taken away under armed guard.

The British contingent reached Kinshasa later that day. At Kirkuzi, McAleese spoke to them about going back to Angola to carry out guerrilla operations but several hours later they were told that their services were no longer required and were paid off. The reasons given for the dismissal were the continuing bad publicity over the Maquela executions, concerns about future political relations between Zaire and Angola, and lack of funds. Most of the men flew back to England the next day; McAleese and several others stayed on but returned a few weeks later. Only Nick Hall remained behind in Zaire, as an aide to Holden Roberto, but he was eventually deported after spending three weeks in a Kinshasa prison.

On 1 April 1976, I heard the MPLA-controlled Angolan News Agency's announcement that ten British and three American mercenaries were to be placed on trial in Luanda. Callan was among them. Injured in the bush, he had been involved in a firefight with FAPLA troops, resisting in spite of his wounds and fighting until his ammunition ran dry. He had insisted that the able-bodied soldiers around him make their escape. Andy McKenzie, wounded by the FAPLA, would stand trial with Callan. I had mixed feelings, as McKenzie was accused of laying mines: they were not his mines; I had laid them. Daniel Gearhart, Gus Grillo and Satch Fortuin were also to face Angolan justice. Satch had been captured in the bush after attempting to limp to the Zaire border. The villagers treated his injuries and then put him under house arrest before handing him over to the MPLA.

What followed was an international show trial, a sham of justice. Five days before proceedings opened the Angolan government issued a statement saying: 'There is no doubt that the men in the dock are guilty. It is just a question of how much we will punish them.' The indictment covered 139 charges and took almost an hour to read out. The 'guilty men' were charged with being mercenaries, invading Angola, murdering civilians, fighting for the FNLA, planting mines, using explosives to destroy bridges and buildings, robbing and looting. Callan was charged with multiple murders and incidents of torture. The charges were supported by written evidence from Joe Akoo, who had been presumed dead but had in fact survived the ambush that killed Jamie McCandless. Joe had cut a deal to avoid being deported to Ghana. He never attended court and Callan's defence lawyers were not provided with an opportunity to cross-examine him.

On the opening day, Kevin Marchant gave a moving account of how he had refused to fight and the events that led up to the massacre. He told the court how he had escaped death only by volunteering to become Callan's driver. The world was watching as Callan strutted defiantly into court the following day. The prosecution described him as 'a man of despotic power and satanic terror'. He stood to attention in the dock as if he was before a court martial. Asked by the judge if Tony Callan was his real name, he replied, 'My name is Costas Georgiou, known as Tony Callan.'

He was reluctant to answer further questions but told the court, 'All I want to say is this, and I want it taken down. All my men who were captured, the so-called mercenaries, for instance McKenzie, he was not my second in command, OK? And all the rest of my soldiers who you captured were all under my direct command. So any responsibility and any charges against them . . . they were following my orders. They were just soldiers. That's all I want to say and I don't want to answer no more questions, OK? No disrespect.'

Callan's acceptance of full responsibility signed his death warrant. Towards the end of his trial, he told the court, 'I am not a criminal. I am not proud of my actions and I want to pay for my crimes. The truth is that I am afraid to go to prison and I don't want to go to prison. No one wants to die . . . but I am prepared to die.'

A less than defiant Gus Grillo heeded advice to show full cooperation with the judges and to publicly denounce the United States in order to save his own skin. He told the court, 'US society – of which I am a product – is a monster . . . it's a society of power seekers, status seekers and waste makers. The weak get weaker and the strong get stronger. Angola has a more developed society than the United States. I entered the Angolan people's back yard, which I had no business to do, yet these people saved my life, gave me medical assistance, clothed me, fed me, many other things, all in a superb manner. For all these things I am grateful. But words are not enough. I will fight, work and do anything else for the people of Angola and I accept the sentence of this court.'

The state prosecutor praised Grillo's 'high political consciousness', and promised his statement would be taken into consideration. Grillo's life was spared; he was handed down a 30-year prison sentence, as was Kevin Marchant. Satch Fortuin received a 24-year sentence, while Callan, McKenzie, Brummie Barker and Daniel Gearhart were sentenced to death by firing squad. Gearhart had been in Angola only for a few days. His crime was advertising his services as a mercenary. Callan had told the court that McKenzie was never his second in command and, as I knew better than anyone, he had not laid the mines. Had McKenzie refused to participate at the Maquela massacre, he would have been shot.

After receiving appeals for clemency from Queen Elizabeth, Prime Minister James Callaghan and President Gerald Ford, President Agostinho Neto announced on 9 July that the death sentences would stand. He said, 'We are applying justice in Angola not only in the name of our martyred people but also to the benefit of the brother peoples of Namibia, Zimbabwe and all the people of the world against whom imperialism is already preparing new mercenary aggressions.'

Callan's sister Panayiota 'Blondie' Georgiades had travelled to Angola to be with her brother during his trial. When she visited him for the final time, he told her, 'Don't let them see you crying. Remember you're a Greek.' His last words to her were, 'I'm not afraid, you know that, sis.'

On 10 July, the four condemned men stood on a firing range, about two metres apart. In an act of final defiance, Callan refused a blindfold. McKenzie, who had had a leg amputated and needed to hold his crutch, was spared having his hands tied. Twenty Angolan military policemen armed with sub-machine guns took aim. Callan was hit twice in the chest and once in the stomach. He remained conscious for several minutes before dying. Costas Georgiou was given a Greek Orthodox burial service at a cemetery in north London.

✳ ✳ ✳

The publicity surrounding the executions, much of it focused on John Banks' role in recruiting the men, acted as an incentive rather than a deterrent to those romantically inclined towards war. Camberley became a Mecca for those seeking such adventures. Ever the enthusiastic recruiting sergeant, Banks sought volunteers to liberate those whom President Neto had imprisoned. As I was on a retainer from the FNLA (modest sums but welcome nevertheless), I attended meetings to discuss our options.

At one of these, I was introduced to Victor Fernandes, a former FAPLA officer who had acted as court processor. I was wary of his claim to have switched sides. I knew him but he did not know me and, although he might have assumed as much, I did not tell him that I had served in Angola. One day, we were at lunch in a Kensington hotel and I noticed that Fernandes kept looking at me as though he was trying to figure me out. Suddenly, he extended his arm across the table, pointing his finger at me, and said, 'You've been in Angola.'

I hesitated before answering. 'What makes you think that?'

'I've seen photographs of you there,' he said.

'That isn't possible,' I responded flatly. 'I don't think anyone besides Callan had a camera and I don't recall ever seeing him take pictures.'

'But I have seen a picture of you,' Fernandes insisted. 'I saw you in a photo lying on a bed covered in money, with money in one hand and an Uzi in the other. Your hair was cut very short, not long like now.'

How could Fernandes have seen this photograph? As far as I knew, the film had never been developed and Canada was dead. 'Where did you see this photo?' I asked.

Fernandes responded without hesitation or emotion. 'I killed your friend Canada. He had a plastic box inside his backpack. The camera was inside there and I developed the film myself. So I know it is you in the picture.'

Anger stirred in me. Canada had been a nice guy and a friend of mine. To be confronted by his smiling assassin, who claimed to be on our side, was unsettling. 'Do you still have this photograph?' I asked calmly.

'It is on display at the war crimes museum in Luanda,' he replied.

I guessed any publicity was better than none.

That afternoon, Fernandes and I visited the Royal Geographical Society to study maps of Angola and he explained, 'Your friend was too badly wounded to save. I shot him again to put him out of misery. That was all. Soon after that, I was appointed to the court as the chief processor of evidence against the captured mercenaries. The prisoners had a hard time. They were beaten and kicked, often threatened with execution. There was a fourteenth mercenary whose name I don't know. He never made it to the trial. He was shot behind the knee and in the back of the head.'

Callan had resisted interrogation. 'I was trained by the KGB in Moscow,' Fernandes recalled. 'I knew how to break people. Most of the prisoners were easy, resigned to their fate. But Callan, he was different. I was under strict instructions to ensure he was repentant in the courtroom. I knew it was going to be difficult but I had to break his spirit. My bosses did not like it when on that first day he strutted into the court. They wanted to see him break. That was my job. I did not have much time. So I placed in his cell the remains of the Maquela victims and his friend Sammy Copeland. There was a note attached to Copeland's skull. It read: 'This is your friend Sammy Copeland. He joined those he killed and you are going to join him very soon.' This was what broke Callan down. He went berserk, screaming and shouting incoherently, unable to escape the nightmare sight that was the end result of his orders.'

Fernandes evidently knew how to screw with a man's mind; he also got Callan's sister Blondie pregnant. She was escorted daily from her hotel to the court by Fernandes. This led to their becoming lovers and in due course she would bear his child.

CHAPTER 10

ALL SMOKE AND MIRRORS

COLIN TAYLOR, MY MAIN FNLA CONTACT AND A 'SECURITY ADVISER' (one of those titles that tells people everything and nothing), introduced me to his brother Stanley, always cheerful and full of deals and schemes. He knew people all over the world, although they were not always the most desirable characters. They usually had colourful, if not downright dubious, backgrounds. Much of his time was spent in the Caribbean islands; his base was usually St Vincent, where he was very well known. Stanley's seedy little office in Croydon was at odds with his appearance. He was a dapper little man, always immaculately dressed. In February 1977, we were sitting in Stanley's office swapping gossip about the security circuit and drinking coffee when he told me of an enquiry he'd received about 40-mm M406 grenades for the regime of President Anastasio Somoza Debayle of Nicaragua. At the time, Nicaragua was in the middle of a civil war between Somoza's National Guard and the revolutionary socialist Sandinista guerrilla army.

This enquiry about sourcing, purchasing and delivery had been passed to Stanley by Frank Sturgis. Sturgis could have done the job himself but there were complications. He was known to have connections with the CIA – he had been one of the Watergate burglars, no less – and consequently, he could not touch any deal to arm President Somoza, as the CIA did not support him at that point. Stanley wanted my help because, after Angola, I was familiar with the M79 and M203 launchers that fired the M406 grenades.

Stanley placed a telephone call to a Vietnam vet called Don in the United States. We had met Don after the Angola fiasco. He was one of the many who had made their way to Camberley in search of John Banks, in the hope of finding a war to fight in. He was well over six feet tall, bulky but not well muscled and with a slight paunch brought on by excessive drinking. He was pleasant enough, at least in small doses. The American word 'redneck' would adequately describe him. He had a lot of the characteristics of Americans that Europeans find irritating, in particular bragging and bullshitting. He spent a lot of time talking about himself, Vietnam and everything he had done. One of his idiosyncrasies was to carry around with him a huge butcher's carving knife. When asked why, he delighted in saying, 'You stick this motherfucker in 'em, walk around 'em once and they fall in two pieces.'

Don told Stanley that he could source the grenades but Stanley would need to fly to Colorado to collect them. According to Don, these items had been 'liberated' from the Rocky Mountain Arsenal, a demilitarisation site in Colorado, used for the destruction of munitions. I think the first price that was mentioned was $200,000. Obviously, there would be no export licence application under these circumstances. Don, who was an ex-pilot and knew the country, would arrange transportation of the weapons to Nicaragua.

We flew from Gatwick to the United States. Neither Stanley nor I had much spare cash, so we took the cheapest flight available, which was with Laker Airways to New York. From there, we caught a bus to Baltimore and got on a plane to Miami. Sturgis lived in Miami's Little Havana district. With his classical Italian looks (his real name was Frank Angelo Fiorini) and mobster's dress sense, Frank made an immediate impression. He looked like a Mafia heavy straight out of central casting. He told us that the guy paying for the arms on President Somoza's behalf was called Freddy, a Jewish importer and exporter who had all the trappings of success – the Rolls-Royce, the beachfront offices and membership of the exclusive Jockey Club, where he took us to dinner.

A covert deal to purchase grenades on behalf of a Central American president against the interests of the CIA was never going to go smoothly. All the usual wrangles were compounded by the fact that none of the parties trusted each other. Negotiations over terms of payment, inspection and delivery went on and on. Freddy needed to show proof of funds, while Don had to assure Freddy, Stanley and I that he had the merchandise and the means of exporting it from the United States. Finally, it was agreed that Freddy, Stanley and I would travel to Colorado to inspect Don's grenades. Freddy was to bring $40,000 to cover transportation costs and a bank letter to prove that he had $200,000 to fund the deal. The $40,000 was payable once the goods had been inspected, found satisfactory and placed aboard a suitable cargo aircraft; the balance was to be paid on delivery.

Prior to inspection day, I flew alone to Denver, Colorado, to meet with Don and introduce him to one of President Somoza's sons, who wanted to meet the seller before approving the deal. On arrival at the airport, I was met by Don and a companion, a freaky-looking guy called Roy, who had a scar running down his cheek and wore a leather top hat. The Rocky Mountains of Colorado are quite impressive; less so was the beaten-up Chevrolet they were driving. We stayed outside of Denver at the Ponderosa Motor Inn, not far from Cripple Creek, awaiting the arrival of Somoza's son. When I pushed him on the type of plane he intended to use for the journey to Nicaragua, Don told me it was a Douglas DC-3. I questioned whether a DC-3 had the range capability required but he claimed that it was fitted out as a forest-fire fighter, with water tanks that could hold sufficient fuel to fly halfway around the world.

Nothing smelled right about this deal but it wasn't my call, so I went with the flow until Somoza junior and his minder arrived two days later. During the wait, Don and his hillbilly sidekick seemed to do little but drink Jack Daniels and six-packs of beer. To my surprise, Somoza and Don instantly struck up a rapport. Don, it was revealed, had flown Cessna aircraft to Nicaragua for the Somoza family's business empire. The Cessnas were used as crop dusters over the cotton fields. The meeting between Somoza and Don was the crucial factor in convincing the parties to go ahead with the deal. One other condition was placed on the sellers: the inspector, that being me, would travel with the aircraft to its final destination. As my role expanded, so did my potential compensation and the trip might also prove quite instructive. It seemed the sort of opportunity not to be missed, in view of the main players involved and the credibility I might be able to establish.

Now nearly everything was in place and the route to Nicaragua from Colorado was confirmed. We would fly across the Gulf of Mexico to Puerto Cabezas on the Nicaraguan coast. But just as I was beginning to feel optimistic, the deal almost fell through the next afternoon at Denver airport. Stanley, Freddy and two minders arrived and although Freddy showed Don a large envelope of money and the proof-of-funds letter, Don refused to allow Freddy and the two minders to accompany him to the location (a ranch with its own airstrip) where the grenades were in storage and the DC-3 was waiting, as he felt this would compromise the security of the operation. Don wanted me to travel alone with him to the ranch. Freddy argued his case and Don relented but insisted that Freddy would have to lose the muscle.

It was late in the afternoon when Freddy and I set off with Don and Roy, just the four of us, to this mystery location. In the gloom of the car's interior, I kept my eyes on the pair in front. From their body language, both seemed relaxed and they kept up the pace of their beer drinking. But after some time, I began to notice, looking at the rear-view mirror, that Don kept glimpsing sideways towards Roy. This made me uneasy. I wished I were armed but all I could do was keep my fingers crossed and hope that my gut instincts were wrong. We were now into cowboy country. There was very little traffic on the road and it was getting dark.

'How much further do we have to travel?' Freddy asked, his strained voice revealing his agitation.

Don pointed towards a small cluster of lights some way off in the distance and, from what I could tell, off-road. 'That's the airstrip over there,' he said. 'The ranch is right by it.'

We continued for a couple of miles in the general direction of the lights before turning off the blacktop onto a dirt road. By now it was very dark and the car's headlights tunnelled into the surrounding blackness. Eventually, we pulled up just a few yards short of a barbed-wire fence. Roy got out and I half expected him to pull a gun but he only unhooked the fencing like a gate and pulled it to one side. Just for a moment, I thought maybe I'd read the situation wrong and paranoia had got to me. We continued through the open fence and a short distance later the dirt road gave way to a two-rut track. Now I knew something was wrong. I could no longer convince myself that my fears were simply the products of an overly fertile imagination or the results of past experiences. The twin tracks had obviously been made by a vehicle but it looked as if it had been some time since anyone had driven down this route. There was no way this was the track to a ranch and private airstrip. The grass suddenly became a couple of feet high between the ruts. All at once, the car came to an abrupt halt and the barrels of a sawn-off shotgun were resting on the top of the front seat, pointing directly at me.

'I guess we don't need to tell you what this is, do we, Dave?' Don's words were delivered in his customary drawl. Roy had a pistol – my brain registered that it was a Walther PPK – pointed at my head.

I felt the blood drain from my face, while Freddy looked like he was about to have a heart attack. At least my brain continued to work. Fight or flight was the usual choice in these circumstances. Fight? Well, neither Freddy nor I was armed, so that option was out. Flight? Well, that was out of the question as well, given that the rear doors were fitted with child locks and could not be opened from the inside. I sat in the enclosed gloom and smelled the fear – mine and Freddy's.

'Is it OK if I smoke?' I asked, breaking what had been a prolonged silence. Don and Roy granted my request. I pointed towards my breast pocket to indicate that my hand was going for nothing more than cigarettes.

'Open your briefcase, Freddy, and hand over the money,' said Don. This was by no means an easy request to fulfil, as Freddy was shaking and blubbering. 'You can have my Rolls-Royce, just don't kill me,' he replied. I did not have anything to offer in a bid to convince them not to end my life in Cowsville, Colorado, or wherever we were. When Freddy opened the combination lock on his briefcase, it was discovered that the envelope he'd flashed at the airport contained only $20,000 cash. The remainder of the agreed fee was in American Express traveller's cheques. This pissed Don off.

'What happens now?' I asked.

'This is the end of the road,' he replied.

I struggled to think of a further question; anything would do, so long as they kept talking and didn't shoot us.

'Define "end of the road"?'

Don smiled as he replied, 'At this moment, I am guilty of armed robbery and kidnapping, which in this state carries a sentence of 50 years to life imprisonment. Now I'll tell you the fucking truth: I haven't got 50 years left.'

I thought it was a great answer but I was damned if I was going to tell him so. I wished I could think of something witty to throw back at him. Freddy's blubbering grew louder. He really thought he was done for. Freddy had his briefcase in his lap; he was signing the traveller's cheques with a shaking hand. The only illumination came from the car's interior light. This was a lonely place for Freddy – and for me. On the other hand, sure, our lives could end at any second; but if Don and Roy really wanted to kill us, they would have done so by now, wouldn't they? And Don wasn't going to shoot either of us with the shotgun, as it would make too much of a mess to clean up afterwards. It was Roy who was more likely to squeeze the trigger. He was the quiet one of the two and he seemed unpredictable. I would rather Roy shot me than Don did it. With the Walther, it would be quick and clean.

'Shut the fuck up, Freddy,' I said, finally growing tired of his cries. I wanted to enjoy what might be my last cigarette. Through the smoke, I peered down at his hand clasping the pen as he tried to countersign the traveller's cheques. It vibrated violently in his grasp. He could just about hold it but writing his name was proving difficult. My frustration got the better of me. The old red mist came floating down. 'You're fucking stupid, the pair of you,' I snapped. 'What is shooting us going to achieve? Why are you even considering it? Just take the money. Think about it. What happens when we don't return? Everyone knows who you are and eventually someone, even if it's my wife back in England, is going to put out a missing persons request. There'll be an investigation. Do yourselves a favour and take Freddy and me somewhere civilised. He can sign the cheques properly and you guys can fuck off wherever you want.'

They heard me out, so I continued, hoping I had set off some alarm bells in their heads. 'Come on! What do you think we're going to do afterwards? Call the police ourselves? We can hardly report the fact that we've just been ripped off on an illegal deal to supply arms to Nicaragua, can we? I can really see that. "Yeah, officer, I've just been held up at gunpoint over some stolen grenades I was sending to Central America." He's really going to help me out, isn't he?'

'OK,' said Don suddenly, and I stopped ranting. 'But if you try any funny business . . .' His eyes indicated the shotgun, which had remained pointed at me throughout my speech. Don looked a little nervous and kept glancing at Roy. They were on the back foot now. They had probably expected to have this over and done with by now. We drove to a Tomahawk Truckstop in the nearby town of Brighton and pulled in to the well-lit parking lot alongside all the semi-trailers. The confidence Don had had in the darkness of the cow patch seemed to be ebbing away and I was determined to hang on to the initiative. 'Are we going to sit here all night?' I asked, adding, 'Are you going to shit or get off the pot?'

Again, a glance passed between Don and Roy, each hoping the other would come up with something clever to say or find some way of regaining the upper hand. Don could hardly stroll into the café with his shotgun and he didn't know what to do.

'Look,' I said, softening my tone, 'you don't need the shotgun. Roy's got his pistol.' They agreed and we walked into the diner like a group of regular guys who worked unusual hours. There were a few truckers around but the place was pretty quiet. We sat in a booth and a waitress soon took our order for coffee. Roy had the pistol under his jacket, sticking it in my ribs none too gently to remind me it was there. Don marched a sweating Freddy to the toilet to clean up and sign the traveller's cheques. I guessed this went smoothly, as they returned a few minutes later and Freddy had managed a reasonable signature. Our business was done. We had been screwed but at least we were still alive.

They offered us a lift back to Denver but there was no way I was getting back in the car with them. I decided to get in a few last words. 'You stick that fucking gun in my ribs again and I'll make you use it,' I said to Roy. 'You've won this time,' I continued, 'but don't you ever come to England or anywhere else where we might meet, because you won't be going home again if you do.'

Don and Roy looked satisfied with their night's work and told us they were leaving. Roy added, 'You guys stay here for ten minutes after we're gone before you leave.'

I couldn't resist a response to his idiotic demand. 'What are you going to do, you cunt?' I snapped. 'Wait outside to check? Fuck off now while you've got the chance.'

At that, they left, taking Freddy's briefcase, the money and the cheques. We sat there drinking coffee, relieved to be alive. A couple of hours later, we found ourselves back at Denver airport, having accepted a lift from a guy at the diner who said it was on his way. Our three companions knew something was wrong as soon as they saw us. Stanley told me that I'd looked ghostly white and Freddy like the living dead. We filled them in on what had happened and the muscle responded in true Mafia fashion, calling their buddies and putting out a death warrant for Don and Roy. I handed over the film on my camera, as I'd taken some photos of Don. Stanley and I said our goodbyes and flew back to England with 30 pence in our pockets between us.

Don was traced to Colombia but unfortunately he was in prison in Bogotá. He must have been the only inmate who didn't want to be released, knowing what faced him on the outside. About a year later, I received a letter with a printed PO box return address on the envelope. It was an apology of sorts from Don. He said he wanted to explain why he had had to bring down our deal. He claimed he had been working for one of the rebel groups in Nicaragua. I lodged the letter with my solicitors in case it was a prelude to something more damaging. The address was traced to a US federal prison. Don had declined to mention in his note that he was in jail. I passed the information on to parties who should know. With luck, Don and Roy would get a trip to a cow patch themselves.

CHAPTER 11

A HOLIDAY WITH MALICE

TOGO IS ONE OF AFRICA'S SMALLEST COUNTRIES. IT LIES ON THE
continent's western coast, a narrow strip of land sandwiched between
Ghana and Benin. Once a German colony, after the Second World
War it was divided and administered by the French and British,
who benefited from its rich phosphate deposits. While British
Togoland was absorbed into Ghana in 1956, French Togoland
gained its independence in 1960 and was renamed the Republic
of Togo. Its first president, Sylvanus Olympio, promptly banned
political parties and repressed all opposition to his rule. Many of
his enemies were imprisoned or fled the country. Three years later,
in a military coup led by army sergeant Étienne Eyadéma (who
later changed his given name to Gnassingbé), President Sylvanus
Olympio was assassinated outside the US Embassy while trying to
seek refuge inside. It was widely believed that the fatal shots were
fired by Eyadéma himself. Nicolas Grunitzky, Olympio's brother-
in-law and political opponent, returned from exile immediately and
shortly thereafter became president of Togo. He rewarded Eyadéma
with promotion to military chief-of-staff. In 1967, Eyadéma led a
bloodless overthrow of Grunitzky and installed himself as president.

Like Olympio before him, Eyadéma banned all opposition and instituted a one-party state.

Togo was of no strategic or economic importance to the West, so its internal disputes and human-rights abuses were, for the most part, ignored. However, Eyadéma's exiled political opponents took every opportunity to remind the world about Togo and its politically bereft people, while some schemed to overthrow the regime. In 1976, a prominent Togolese exile met a former Canadian army officer turned arms dealer, Tom Finan, in Ghana. Lieutenant Colonel Finan had a distinguished military record. He had led troops in Italy and the Middle East during the Second World War and commanded the Royal Canadian Dragoons at the time of his retirement in 1967. As an arms dealer, he specialised in spares for obsolete weapons and equipment still in service in Africa's poorest countries. Finan, or 'Colonel Tom', was well connected in Ghana, where he had served as a military instructor. He registered his arms company as Teshi Team International, the name derived from a Ghanaian military camp.

After meeting the Togolese exile, Finan hired four former SAS soldiers to conduct a feasibility study on the assassination of Gnassingbé Eyadéma. The four men travelled to Ghana for a briefing and then on to Lomé, the Togolese capital. They made a detailed appraisal of the president's movements and security arrangements and appraised the ability of the army to react to a hostile attack by a relatively small number of highly trained soldiers. Their report concluded that Eyadéma's assassination was achievable by a small but well-armed number of highly trained soldiers. Their caveat was that while killing Eyadéma could be straightforward, seizing power would not be. This aim required the defeat of the Togolese army. Therefore, the support of military leaders would have to be won before any assassination attempt was carried out. It could only be hoped that the general population would rise up in support of the coup, or at least go along with it.

Finan approached the same quartet of ex-SAS men again in the spring of the following year and invited them to participate in the operation that had been the subject of their report. The exile had satisfied himself that they would be able to count on the support of officers within the Togolese army. These disaffected officers had informed him that Eyadéma was paranoid about a *coup d'état* by his own army and therefore refused to give his soldiers more than a few rounds of ammunition. The four men declined the offer, however, on the grounds that they were committed elsewhere on the security circuit. Instead, they recommended two Special Air Service veterans. Both men had served very briefly as officers in John Banks' Security Advisory Services. After travelling to Togo to make a feasibility study of their own, they accepted Finan's offer and terms and hired 13 mercenaries, almost all of whom were former members of the same Hereford-based regiment.

The two former SAS men applied the usual security precautions, sending their team into Africa in twos and threes and assigning each party a circuitous route to avoid attracting attention from Special Branch officers or security 'flags' on airport computers. However, one pair were already well lubricated when they boarded their flight from Heathrow to Ghana via Zurich. Their drinking continued in transit until a dispute ensued and blows were exchanged. The Swiss authorities were duly notified and when the flight disembarked the men were earmarked for special attention. They found it hard to support their claim to be tourists after customs officials found a cosh and a pair of wire cutters in their luggage.

This breach of security resulted in the pair being put on a return flight to Heathrow, where Special Branch detectives were waiting to ask more questions. A ticket for a car park at the airport was discovered on one of the men and a search of the vehicle revealed a list containing the names of all the men on the team due to assemble in Ghana. The intelligence services are not stupid; enquiries would reveal that most, if not all, of the men on the list were ex-special forces, and alarm bells would soon be ringing. Two men missing from the watering holes of Hereford might mean nothing, but thirteen going covertly to the same location in Africa meant a whole load of grief for someone. The team was now compromised, on the 'watch list' at ports and airports, and the mission was put on hold.

In the autumn of 1977, the project passed to Harold Davidson, known as 'David' or 'Darkie', and John Pace, again both ex-SAS soldiers. Darkie and I were friends and he asked me to recruit a B team of ex-military personnel, with all operational details to remain secret. If the new A team – again to be recruited from among the many former special-forces men in the Hereford area – was compromised, the B team would be put into play. On 4 October, I booked a small private-function room in the Cambridge Hotel, Camberley, under the name Fire Protection Ltd. Applicants were ostensibly there to be interviewed for opportunities in the fire-protection industry. All of them were former members of the Parachute Regiment, the Marines or the French Foreign Legion. Tom Finan attended and gave a general briefing to those selected on what might be attempted overseas. I had chosen the candidates carefully and each of them was able to leave England at short notice if required. They were all ready to sign up for the job.

While my preparations continued quietly, Darkie received word – via his former commanding officer – that the Foreign Office had wind of a number of ex-SAS troopers who were about to leave on some mission to an unknown destination. He was asked to supply them with the details. I followed developments closely, as the more heat the Foreign Office put on Darkie, the more likely it was that my B team would be called off the substitutes' bench. Darkie declined the FO's invitation to let them in on his plan – no surprise there. When he refused, it was made very clear to him how embarrassing it was to Her Majesty's Government that while it sought to encourage African democracy, soldiers it had trained were plotting a bloody *coup d'état*. Unless Darkie revealed his destination and target, the Foreign Office would alert the governments of a number of likely African countries, via diplomatic channels, that an assassination attempt was in the final stages of planning, giving the names of the men involved. Such a move would make Darkie's plans to vary the infiltration patterns of his team into Togo useless. His men would be apprehended wherever they landed. Deciding he could not commit men under such conditions, Darkie provided the FO with the target. A few days later, and much to his surprise, the FO backed off. He was told, 'We wash our hands of the matter.' This response, perhaps deliberately ambiguous, he interpreted as a tacit indication that the operation would proceed without any interference from Her Majesty's Government.

Meanwhile, the exile behind the proposed coup had been exploiting the chilly relationship between Togo and Ghana. Historically, the two countries had often been in dispute. While Ghana could not be seen to assist in any hostile incursion into Togo, it could come to its neighbour's aid in time of crisis. The plan, hatched with senior officers in the Ghanaian and Togolese armies, was that after the assassination of Eyadéma and an attack on the army base at Camp Tokoin by the British mercenaries, the Togolese army would request urgent military assistance from Ghana. This 'friendly' military response would come in the form of an armoured unit and hundreds of heavily armed troops. With the arrival of the Ghanaian forces, the mercenaries would be allowed to escape.

Personally, I thought an arranged escape for the attacking force all sounded a bit too good to be true. The Togolese army was 800-men strong and not all of them were aware of their officers' plan. Camp Tokoin, lightly manned and poorly equipped, would fall to the mercenaries very quickly. Holding it for any length of time would be a different proposition. An 800-man army, even with only a few rounds of ammo each, would eventually win against a small group in a fixed location. The Togolese officers who were on side were going to have to perform miracles.

By various routes, Davidson's and Pace's team travelled to Africa in the second week of October, with the takeover attempt pencilled in for the 15th. In Ghana, they merged with a team of international mercenaries chosen by Finan. His outfit comprised two Americans, two Italians, a South Korean and an Irishman. The plan was to hit Eyadéma en route from the presidential palace to his private residence at Tokoin military camp. The fact that he chose to live at an army facility was an indicator of Eyadéma's paranoia. He trusted his personal bodyguards but each night he selected a senior army officer at random to stay with him, so fearful was he of attack from within his army. Perhaps he was taking the advice of Sun-Tzu's *Art of War*: 'Keep your friends close and your enemies closer.'

Unbeknown to Davidson and Pace, the intelligence services in

London and Washington were on the brink of intervening to halt the coup – so much for the 'washing of the hands'. Either the CIA or MI6 had by now probably fingered Tom Finan as the architect of the plot. His company, the Florida-registered Teshi Team International, had recently purchased a cargo plane, a Lockheed C-121 Constellation, for $200,000. The aircraft and its American flight crew were now in Africa but not where their flight plan had indicated they would be. Finan had concealed the military hardware, purchased in the United States, among other, innocuous cargo. This aircraft was next seen at Lomé airport, where it had been given permission to land for emergency repairs. The weapons were offloaded over several days by men posing as repair crew engineers. Then Finan ran into a problem: his flight crew, unaware that they had been carrying weapons for a coup, saw the hardware being concealed in a maintenance vehicle. They told Finan what they thought of him and that he could fly the plane himself. The crew abandoned the aircraft, crossed the border and left Africa as quickly as possible. But at least the weapons were now in country.

In Whitehall, the decision was made to alert President Eyadéma to the imminent threat to his life. He was tipped off on 13 October, just 48 hours before the planned assassination attempt and with the mercenaries preparing to cross the Ghanaian border. The warning, delivered via the US Embassy in Lomé, included the names of all known participants. President Eyadéma closed the border and reinforced it with troops. Fortunately for Darkie and his men, a contact in the Togolese army warned them the job was blown.

The story of a failed *coup d'état* in Togo by British mercenaries was leaked to the media and a multitude of conspiracy-theory stories were published. It was open season on Darkie's team. Typically, the media made up whatever they didn't know and it was suggested that the paymaster for the operation was none other than the president of Libya, Colonel Gaddafi. Supposedly, Darkie's men had been ambushed and captured by waiting Togolese troops – a figment of the reporters' imaginations. The Ministry of Defence was forced to deny reports that it was serving (as opposed to former) members of the SAS who had been poised to kill the Togolese president. Meanwhile,

President Eyadéma threatened to kill all the mercenaries implicated in the plot and chided them publicly for daring to try to topple 'the Immortal One', as he referred to himself. Darkie and Pace's failure to surface in Hereford in the immediate aftermath of the incident increased the level of speculation that they had, in fact, been killed. Finan, too, was keeping his head down. The Royal Canadian Police wanted to interview him about gunrunning. When Darkie and Pace eventually returned to the UK, Pace told the press that he had merely been working on a sugar plantation in Ghana. Darkie offered no explanation.

I was left disgruntled. My time and effort had come to nothing. Fortunately, I escaped any mention in the national press, although one story made its way into my local paper speculating that my fire-protection business meeting might have been a cover for recruiting mercenaries. It never ceases to amaze me how after such revelations staff at hotels always seem to recollect burly men with short haircuts, well built and obviously soldiers. If the speculation had been about a naval operation, I'm sure they'd have seen men with parrots on their shoulders and the odd wooden leg or hook.

Some weeks later, I got back in contact with Darkie. The man behind the plot was not happy that everything had gone tits up and it looked as if it would be virtually impossible to get the operation back on the road. The Hereford team was compromised and most of them didn't care, as they'd been paid anyway. It seemed that Togo was going to fade away into another fuck-up best forgotten and I was beginning to have serious doubts about the way these operations were planned. I kept pushing Darkie to put me in contact with the Togolese guy. I was confident that an alternative team of mercenaries could enter Togo and do the job without the Foreign Office getting advance warning. Finally, Darkie gave me his contact details and I travelled to the Continent in a bid to persuade him to stage another attempt on Eyadéma's life. I was promised a meeting on 22 December but I got no further than the airport, where I made a call only to be informed that the guy was out of the country and would not be back until the New Year. I spent five more days waiting for him, from 11 January 1978, but again I left without seeing him. Then I was promised a face-to-face meeting with him on 19 January.

I could afford only one night in a hotel room with a television and a minibar from which I was too broke to drink. I spent most of the day confined to the room waiting for my potential client. Finally, he arrived but he seemed less than pleased to meet me, launching into a tirade about the harmful publicity caused by the failed operation in October. He was particularly angry with Finan, exclaiming, 'I paid him $600,000!' I made the usual sympathetic noises while trying to distance myself from the mess. Given that the man was smarting over the financial cost of the failure, it seemed unwise to suggest he get his wallet out again. At the same time, I wondered whether I would get a second opportunity to present my pitch, so I went for it.

'Please give me the chance to present an alternative plan to achieve the same objective.'

'No,' he replied, 'such an operation is now impossible given the increased security inside Togo. Eyadéma is on the lookout for suspicious Westerners.'

'But my name wasn't on any of the team lists. I have at least a fair chance of being able to mount a reconnaissance operation and present an alternative plan on the back of it.'

He paused. 'I will consider the suggestion overnight.'

I was less than optimistic about my chances of getting the green light but the following morning, shortly before my check-out time, he returned. The deal he offered was atrocious.

'I will give you $1,500 and not a cent more to come up with a feasible way to kill Eyadéma. You will be paid more on production of the plan if I approve it.'

I had not liked this guy from the moment I met him – he had acted as if the earlier cock-ups were my fault – and I liked him even less now. But my back was against the wall financially, so I took his money.

We agreed that I would leave for Ghana within a week. I was to book a room at the Meridian Hotel in Tema, a port just east of the capital, Accra, and stay there until I was contacted by someone from Ghanaian military intelligence, who would give me assistance and update me on the security situation in Togo.

I arrived in Accra on 26 January. The hotel, near the docks, was almost deserted. Leaving it on foot was not recommended during the day and out of the question at night. My room was tatty and the dim light bulb added to the unwelcoming atmosphere. Meal times were less than exciting, too. I was usually the only person in the restaurant and the menu was a waste of time: every dish consisted of chicken and rice. There was no beer or wine; I could have any drink I wanted so long as it was Fanta. Still, I was operating on a tight budget, so the main thing was that the place was cheap.

I did not hear a peep from any of my client's sources on my second day in the country, so I decided to go it alone, heading for the Togolese Embassy in Accra, where I applied for a tourist visa. As President Eyadéma's security restrictions remained in place, visas were valid only for 48 hours. I took a battered yellow cab to the border crossing at Afloa. The job was nearly over before it started. The Ghana crossing was heavily militarised, with steel-helmeted soldiers on patrol and large signs informing civilians that all photography in the area, which was otherwise a bustling market, was forbidden. An old man spotted me taking pictures from the back of the taxi and began waving his arms about like a lunatic. His behaviour alerted the soldiers and I was marched to a command post with this silly old bastard shouting at me all the way. He caused so much fuss that the soldiers became less concerned about the security aspect of my transgression than about the old man's ranting that I'd captured his spirit in my camera. With the help of the cab driver, I explained that I was a tourist and had taken a picture of the marketplace and not of him in particular. The matter was resolved by removing the roll of film from my camera and presenting it to the old man. He seemed happy that he could now die with his soul intact. I would gladly have assisted him on his way.

I walked across no-man's-land to the Togo control post. I was about to discover if my name appeared on any list of suspect foreigners. As it turned out, my fears were unwarranted. An immaculately uniformed gendarme stamped my passport, wished me a good day and waved me through. I told a cab driver to take me to any hotel and he dropped me at the Hotel de la Paix. It had four stars and looked very good; it was also full. The concierge told me that all the hotels in Lomé were fully booked due to an international convention of African politicians but he was very obliging and phoned around to find me a room. Numerous calls later and looking very apologetic, he told me that he'd found me a room but it was in a very poor hotel, rarely used by tourists. I just wanted to get out of the limelight of the hotel lobby, so, address in hand, I took a cab to Hotel la Patience, a pink, two-storey house converted into a seven-bedroom hotel with a shared bathroom. As the concierge had warned, it was situated on a dusty, unpaved street. There was no restaurant, no air conditioning and no television in my room.

I had two days to get a result in what was to me a strange and unknown city. I had never visited Lomé previously and there were no decent maps available to assist a tourist wanting to explore the city – or a potential assassin looking for a prime location to kill the president. However, it was easy enough to find one's way around Lomé, which was no bigger than a minor English provincial town. The road system consisted of inner and outer circular roads, with most of the important buildings situated on a series of wide avenues within. Walking west from my hotel on Rue du Sous-Lieutenant Gnemegnah, I turned onto Avenue de la Libération. President Eyadéma travelled this road twice daily en route between the military camp and the palace. I recalled from my discussions with Darkie a rough description of his intended ambush position: a land-clearance project of unoccupied slum dwellings. The site was in front of me now. The southern edge of the rectangle flanked the road on which my hotel was situated; the northern edge was adjacent to Boulevard Circulaire and was directly opposite the gendarmerie; the western edge bordered Avenue de la Libération and was directly opposite the Commissariat Central de la Sûreté, the police headquarters. The ambush spot was well chosen. At the junction of Circulaire and Libération was a crossroads with a roundabout. The presidential convoy would have to slow down at the roundabout. Darkie's ambush party had intended to hit the presidential car at the crossroads, while two support groups would have pinned down any vehicles coming to Eyadéma's assistance from the police and security-service buildings. Afterwards, they would have raced on foot to their escape vehicles and it would have taken no more than two minutes to reach the front gate of the Tokoin military camp. The rest would have been up to the Ghanaian army.

This ambush option was now ruled out, however. The buildings where Darkie's team would have lain in wait had been razed to the ground. The site was as flat as a billiard table. At dusk, I made my way back to the hotel, fearing the trip might be wasted. But, for once, I got lucky. There were several old armchairs in the reception area and sitting in one of them was a local man. While I was awaiting the proprietor's return with my key, he enquired in perfect English if I was American.

'English,' I replied.

He didn't have the look of a cop, so I sat down and offered him a cigarette. He told me his name was Koffi. He seemed surprised by my choice of hotel and asked how I was coping without air conditioning and television. I explained that all the other places were full. Koffi told me that he had learned English on merchant ships; like me, he had been a sailor for many years. I asked him if, for a fee, he would be willing to show me around Lomé the following day. He readily agreed and we arranged an early start.

I went up to my room and was contemplating whether to go out for a meal and a drink at one of the local French-style restaurants when there was a knock on the door and Koffi appeared with a radio cassette player and a bunch of tapes. 'I don't want you to be bored in an empty room. The radio is a loan.' I invited him to join me for dinner. Careful questioning brought me up to date on recent events in Togo and the increased security situation in the country. I had been looking for the hook with this guy since we met but he didn't appear to be a hustler. He wasn't gay, that was for sure, he hadn't offered me drugs or women and he seemed too naive to be an intelligence agent. When I told Koffi that my visa expired the following day and I would like to stay longer and look around at leisure, he told me that he could get me an extension. The deal was that I was to give him my passport with the equivalent of $25 inside it and he would take it to the Commissariat Central de la Sûreté to get the extension. However, the one thing I never parted with voluntarily was my passport; it was a vital part of my escape kit and never left my person. Koffi suggested that for my peace of mind I should accompany him to the office where I would wait outside while he spoke to the necessary officials. He said they would not agree to the bribe in my presence.

The next day, I watched him enter the building and kept my fingers crossed. It was nearly an hour before he returned, handed me my passport and said that everything had gone smoothly. It certainly had, as in full colour and taking up a whole page of my passport was a visa for ten days, ramped, stamped and signed by the *commissaire principal*.

For the next few days, Koffi was like my shadow. I met his family, who lived in very poor conditions and yet were unfailingly hospitable. We walked the streets and visited his ancestors' graves. At around 6 a.m. and 3.30 p.m. each weekday, sirens and whistles could be heard as the president's convoy travelled along its route. Each afternoon, with my cameras hidden in a bag (as well as an ordinary still camera, I had a Cine 8 movie camera and a Minox B spy camera), I stood with the local children who clapped and waved as his motorcade passed by. The children acted as an effective cover. They always wanted their pictures taken and I obliged, snapping them in front of a background scene of relevance to my mission. Things were a little more difficult in the early mornings, when there was no one around and I had to choose my vantage point with care in case Eyadéma's security noticed me. Once I was satisfied that the composition of the president's escort never changed and that his route was always the same, I began my search for a location and method to kill him. Obviously, I could not involve Koffi in this task, so made my excuses and apologised for spending less time in his and his family's company.

Access to the military camp at Tokoin was through a main gate near the junction of Route Circulaire and Avenue de la Libération. I strolled daily towards this location, buying fruit from a local shop to make it look like I had a reason to be in the area. I took time to observe the ordinary goings-on in the area as well as the movements of the guards on the camp gate and in the watchtower. Of course, it was imperative that they took little interest in me and I was always very cautious. The camp was surrounded by a concrete-block wall topped with barbed wire. There was no high point on the perimeter that could be accessed for an inside view. The president's convoy was at its slowest at the entrance to the camp but, on the downside, there was no cover from which to spring an ambush and the road was always cleared of traffic before his vehicles exited the front gate. After several days' research, I was forced to rule out a conventional attack. Darkie had chosen the optimum position the first time around and this location no longer offered the same advantages.

I took a growing interest in Lomé's drainage system. The surface drainage was basic, with no network of subterranean pipes to disperse rainwater. Instead, it drained into gullies, concrete ditches that formed a grid network across the capital. Excess water ran from these into the Mono River, which in turn fed the water into a large inland lagoon and then out to sea. The river flowed between Boulevard Circulaire and Route Circulaire, crossing beneath Avenue de la Libération. At this location, it was a mere 40 ft wide, shallow and still in the dry season. There were never any children swimming or playing with boats in the river. The homes on each side were built with less than satisfactory sanitation systems and it was a very unclean stretch of water.

Togo's government had not wasted much money on building bridges. Instead, they laid five equally spaced pipes, about sixty inches in diameter, in the river, parallel with the direction of its flow, and poured concrete between and over them to create a roadway. The tops of the pipes were only 12 inches from the surface of the road. Add a guard rail for pedestrians and a bridge was the end result. Exactly 240 yards north of the bridge on Avenue de la Libération the road crossed a main drainage gully; here, a single pipe surfaced with concrete ran under the road.

Looking north from the bridge, the 240-yard gap between the water crossings was flanked by open grassed areas. The left side was used as a football field, with two sets of dilapidated goalposts and a public toilet in the south-east corner, its contents discharging into the river. The area to the right was an open space of several acres, with three drainage gullies, equally spaced, running north to south into the river. South of the bridge, on the bank opposite the football field, was a wooden building with a corrugated sheet-metal roof painted a dirty red. This was a cinema, with the usual street vendors' stalls in front and what appeared to be makeshift squatters' huts to the rear.

This presented two possible scenarios, both of which were dependent on the use of explosives. The first option was to place charges in the north and south pipes that crossed Avenue de la Libération and detonate them from either of the grassy areas using command wires while the presidential car and escort were between the two charges. The destruction of the road behind and the bridge in front would trap the vehicles in a 240-yard linear killing ground. The vehicles would have no escape to the left or right, as wide rain gullies ran parallel to the road. The football field was my first choice as a location from which to mount the attack but there was the problem of concealing the ambush party. Two football teams of white men with machine guns at six in the morning might have looked a bit suspicious.

The second option, which I preferred, circumvented this drawback. The idea was a bit radical but several late nights in the vicinity of the cinema convinced me of its potential for success. When it came to selling a plan to my client, it would be my first choice. I spent another couple of days on calculations and measurements before I was satisfied that I had all the necessary information. I said goodbye to Koffi, who had no idea how helpful he had been. On 8 February, I flew back to London and drove to Hereford to meet Darkie. I felt obliged to show him the fruits of my labours in Lomé and offer him a chance to make the pitch with me. His reluctance to involve himself again came as a disappointment. He said all the Hereford team had been paid off and had spent their earnings buying racehorses. Togo was dead and buried as far as they were concerned. It looked like I was on my own.

Five days later, I returned to the Continent to meet my client. For once, he did not keep me waiting.

'Why have you taken so long?' was his opening gambit.

'I've been in Togo all this time,' I explained.

'I don't believe you,' he said. This really infuriated me. 'Show me your passport,' he demanded. I thrust it at him already half-open on the page displaying my visa issued in Ghana. I could tell he was looking for an entry stamp. He turned over the page to the visa issued in Lomé. 'My God, they must be so stupid!' he exclaimed. 'The Togo authorities should have arrested you, not issued you with a visa. Your name was on a list of the plotters in the coup attempt.' I hadn't been

Off duty at the Roma–Joyce gold mine, Rhodesia, 1979

At the remote Buchwa iron-ore mine, Rhodesia

With my family in 1984. From left to right: my daughter Jay, my wife Mary, me, my daughter Kelly, my mother Alice and my son Billy.

My yacht, *Elim*, moored at Shoreham in Sussex

The case of guns I collected in Spain and took to Monzer al-Kassar

In the Colombian
rainforest, 1988

Fantasy Island, Puerto Boyacá – our base for Operation Phoenix

Peter McAleese with the cocaine-lab helicopter we found hidden in the jungle near Combat Camp 50

A rehearsal briefing for Operation Phoenix

The San Miguel River from the lookout point at our last jungle training camp. The far bank is Ecuador.

A paramilitary patrol leaving camp

Dean Shelley and me having a beer at the cocaine-lab guards' jungle bar

Kit and stores
arrive by pirogue

A makeshift
demolitions
classroom

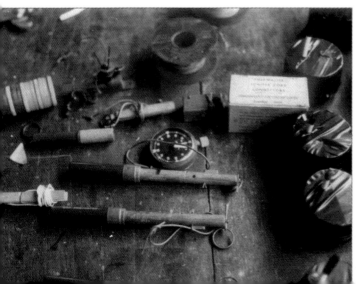

Home-made bunker-
clearance charges

Training for the mission to
assassinate Pablo Escobar,
La Guagua camp,
Colombia, 1989

Our police-liveried Huey helicopter

Taking a break
from training at
La Guagua

Our Hughes 500, crashed on a
mountainside en route to
Haçienda Napoles

Our interpreter Omar, bloodied
in the aftermath of the crash

At Opa-locka Airport, posing in the Dragonfly bomber during the
deal that would lead to my arrest 12 years later

aware that my name was on any list. Now I liked the guy even less; he should have warned me.

My mistake was to provide my client with a detailed explanation of my plan for the assassination of Eyadéma. With hindsight, I told him far too much. He was really pleased with the idea. I could sense that I was about to be shafted but I'd gone past the point of no return and the situation couldn't be turned round.

'How much do you want to carry out this operation?' he asked.

'$350,000.'

He told me that my plan was so straightforward his own contacts could carry it out and he would not need to hire expensive Western mercenaries. Then he offered me £15,000 to do the job. Even I was not so stupid or strapped for cash that I would have accepted such a paltry fee for a job that might have cost me my life. We parted on bad terms. He must have concluded that I was a complete idiot when I had accepted the $1,500 fee a few weeks previously. I left with less money than I had arrived with.

A sympathetic Darkie set up a meeting with another exile in the hope that it would have a more positive outcome. As we sat in his plush mansion, he informed Darkie and me that he did not share his countryman's taste for insurrection. More was the pity. I returned to scratching a living betting on horses. The bad days outnumbered the good and I cursed myself for not having played my cards better.

CHAPTER 12

THE OTHER SIDE
OF THE COIN

DURING THE SPRING FOLLOWING MY RETURN FROM TOGO, ON 21 March 1978, I received an unexpected telephone call. Neither the gentleman's name nor his voice was familiar. He claimed to be the honorary consul for the Togolese government in the United Kingdom and told me that a Togolese diplomat based in Europe had asked to be put in touch with me, as he wished to speak with me in person. I questioned the consul as to the matter concerned but he could tell me no more about it.

Adrenalin and paranoia is not a cocktail designed to result in a good night's sleep. As I lay awake, various scenarios that might arise from this phone call ran through my head and most of them had a very bad ending. The next day, I called international directory enquiries to check that the number I had been given for the diplomat was in fact that of a Togolese Embassy before contacting him. When we spoke, I agreed with considerable reluctance to meet him.

'The matter is of some urgency, Mr Tomkins,' he told me. Then he added, 'Of course, the embassy will pay all your expenses in advance.'

DIRTY COMBAT

The offer of expenses was the clincher. I had no wish to be packed in a crate and shipped to Togo as diplomatic baggage, so the main restaurant at a Continental airport was chosen as the venue for our meeting and I stipulated that no security agencies or police were to be alerted. I travelled via London, where I picked up my expenses (more than reasonable compensation for the trip) from the honorary consulate, a one-room office above a dress shop in New Bond Street.

I arrived a couple of hours earlier than agreed and played the watching game. One dubious advantage of my years belonging to the criminal fraternity was that I had an enhanced awareness of people and their actions . . . or lack of them. I identified a number of plain-clothed security officers all over the airport doing nothing but playing the same observation game as me. I didn't think that anything too dramatic would happen to me in the terminal but I was somewhat anxious that the Togolese might attempt to have me arrested on some charge relating to conspiracy.

The diplomat was sitting alone at a restaurant table. I recognised him from his description. I wondered whether it was even worth going over to talk to him. As far as I was concerned, the Togolese had breached the terms set for this meeting by bringing surveillance teams into the equation. I concluded that it was worth giving him a piece of my mind before heading home. When I introduced myself in a less than friendly manner, he strenuously denied planting the security officers and pleaded with me to sit down and talk to him. I would have none of it and left him sitting at the table. We spoke for no more than two minutes.

When I returned home, he had given Mary a message apologising for any misunderstanding and asking me to call him back. I waited for a day before getting in touch with him. In the interim, the newspapers revealed the real reason for the heightened security presence: a continent-wide hunt for Red Brigade terrorists. The Marxist group had kidnapped an Italian politician, Aldo Moro, in Rome. I made no apologies but agreed to a second expenses-paid meeting. On 31 March, I arrived at the location for my second meeting with the diplomat to find a bottle of champagne waiting for me.

He began, 'The Togolese government is aware that your recent travels have taken you to Lomé.' I suspected that this information had been passed on by the French intelligence services. The diplomat continued, 'This is of concern to President Eyadéma. He is disappointed that you were able to enter and exit his country seemingly at will. President Eyadéma wishes to be your friend, Mr Tomkins, not your enemy. The president is also afraid of what might happen to him as a result of your work. He fears that an attempt on his life is imminent. Will you work for my master instead?'

So I was a potential beneficiary of the president's paranoia. This placed me in a difficult position. I conceded that I had visited Togo but I neither confirmed nor denied who my client had been. As a villain, I had principles that could not be traded for money or freedom. If my client had taken me on to do the job, no amount of money could have persuaded me to sell out my plans to Eyadéma. Similarly, if I had been aware of any operation that would have been compromised by my passing information to the other side, no figure could have persuaded me to assist the Togolese government. However, as neither of these conditions applied, I proceeded, albeit cautiously.

'If I may point out, just coming to this meeting puts me at some risk. What is the nature of this job offer?'

'The president wishes to know what you might know about any plans to send him on a visit to his ancestors.'

I realised that, for once, I was in charge – an all too rare occurrence. I could call the shots in this conversation.

'I am just a small cog in a larger wheel. Information regarding operational details is shared on a need-to-know basis. I couldn't tell you even if I wanted to when the president should cancel his milk.'

'We will offer you a passport and safe haven in Togo if you help us.'

'Not possible. I have a family to support and I don't want to be blacklisted for any future security work.'

President Eyadéma was seeking to purchase my betrayal, something about which I felt uneasy. Or did I? I was the architect of my own plan. I owned the unofficial copyright, not my client, Darkie or anyone else. It was mine and mine to sell for the right price. But what was the right price? It was difficult to put a value on the information I had. I decided to aim high.

'If, and I stress "if", I accept the president's offer, my terms and conditions will be as follows. My fee will be $250,000, 50 per cent of which will be payable in advance in pounds sterling, cash. Under no circumstances will I travel to Togo. Should those terms be acceptable, I will supply all details of my proposed methodology, including photographs and film. Where possible, I will detail other areas of vulnerability that should be addressed by presidential security staff.'

The diplomat's only response was, '$250,000 is a nice round figure.' I wasn't sure whether we had a deal or not. Before I left, I casually said, 'I would advise the president that he shouldn't screw his girlfriend in the house near the Gabonese Embassy.'

'Why?' he asked, startled.

'The president sneaks out of Camp Tokoin with minimal security, usually on a Thursday night. He has a liaison with a woman who lives in a house close to the Gabonese Embassy. It could cost him his life.'

The guy looked mortified, not, I don't think, because I had brought up his master's secret sex sessions but rather because he wondered how he was going to raise this delicate security matter with Eyadéma.

I didn't hear from him for almost two weeks and assumed I had blown it by demanding too much money. To my relief, he called on 12 April and requested to see me the following day. The Togolese Embassy at which he was based was a large Victorian-style building. A very attractive secretary escorted me to a tasteful room with red walls and dark wood surrounds. She told me that the diplomat would see me shortly. He greeted me like an old friend and asked the secretary to bring us some champagne. Either he liked a drink or there was something to celebrate.

'You have just missed the bank manager,' he said. 'There is a slight problem with the money.'

Story of my life, I thought. 'That is a shame,' I replied, hoping not to sound too concerned.

He explained that the exchange rate from CFA francs (the Togolese currency) to French francs and then to sterling had created a small problem. I expected him to make me a lower offer but he said, 'There is slightly more than the 50 per cent you requested but it's not all in sterling.'

'That is not a problem,' I replied.

He unzipped a large leather document case and tipped a shitload of money onto the table. The dollars were made up in $5,000 bundles in yellow bank wrappers, the sterling in £20,000 plastic packs. My heart was banging like a trip hammer. I thanked him calmly, as if I received sums like this every day. With a very dry throat, I was glad of the champagne. 'When do you want me to start?' I asked.

A cine projector and a blackboard were sent for. Anticipating that I might get the go-ahead, I had had the foresight to bring my material with me. I began the presentation, providing as much detail on the plan I'd pitched to my client as I could recall.

'A team would need six prefabricated canisters with flat bases and convex tops, each packed with fifteen kilos of plastic explosives. The canisters should be sixteen inches long, nine inches wide and six inches from base to top. Two canisters would be placed into each of pipes one, three and five. The canisters should be situated approximately two feet either side of the middle of each pipe, directly underneath the road. They should have base detonation points to facilitate initiation by detonating cord. Each canister should be secured against the top radius of the pipe by a slim, lightweight aluminium prop painted black. The explosive charges would be connected by detonating cord. The det-cord from each would be weighted to run under the water round to the centre pipe three. The individual cords would be connected to a single main line. This would be run further along the river-bed for connection to a detonator fired by command wire from a suitable distance.

'I do not believe there would be much difficulty in placing the charges in the river pipes late at night, even if it required more than one trip. Once the explosives were in place, there would be little chance that they would be discovered, as no one would be likely to go into the waist-deep stinking water. The charges would be invisible from the banks. The lone policeman guarding this bridge as the cavalcade passes never checks under the bridge or the river below. The timing of the detonation would be critical. All the charges would need to explode simultaneously while the presidential Mercedes was on the bridge. The bridge is only 40 ft in length and the presidential car needs to be within this area for the explosion to achieve the desired result.

'Twice a day, the route is cleared of traffic. Uniformed police with electronic batons man all junctions and intersections along the way. First to pass is an outrider on a police BMW motorcycle. Twenty seconds later, a Mercedes 450 saloon passes the same point. This vehicle carries the bodyguards, armed with Uzi sub-machine guns. The target car, which is the same model of Mercedes, follows 50 yards behind. A third car, a Citroën saloon carrying more bodyguards, follows a further 50 yards behind. All the vehicles have flashing lights and sirens. I used a stopwatch to time the president's car as it crossed the bridge. As a rule, it takes 3.4 seconds to travel 100 yards. This equates to a speed of 60 mph or 88 feet per second. The timing is vital: one second too late and the president's car would be over the bridge and gone. If there is any margin for error, it is in the other direction. If the explosives were to be detonated slightly before the president's car crossed the bridge, at least then his Mercedes would be travelling at 60 mph into a hole.

'I suggest that it is likely that a team of assassins would choose to hit the morning rather than the afternoon escort because there would be fewer people around and the likelihood of collateral casualties would be reduced. If executed with precision, the explosion would destroy the president's car and its occupant. While the Mercedes is armoured, built to withstand small-arms attack and has a strengthened underbelly, it could not withstand a 90-kg blast from immediately below. An ambush team of six to eight men equipped with good communications could do the job. The team would not be going into a confrontational situation; rather, it would be there to provide protection to the demolition party while they worked under the bridge. They would be most likely to choose trail bike motorcycles for their escape vehicles, which would allow them to travel faster off-road. Given the proximity of the Ghanaian border to the capital city, Lomé is the perfect location for such an assassination attempt. It is the only capital city in the world that is situated on the border with another country. The distance from the ambush point to the Ghanaian border is only four kilometres. The team could extract to another country before the police and security services in Togo reacted to the bomb.'

Even I thought I had given them value for money. The diplomat was particularly impressed with my knowledge of the streets of Lomé and that the speed of the president's car could be gauged against the equally spaced lampposts using a stopwatch. I showed him film and photographs of the drainage systems where the explosive charges could be hidden and also explained how it was possible to enter the covered drainage gully at the north wall of the army camp and travel unseen to a position beneath the front gate over which Eyadéma passed daily.

A diplomatic car dropped me at the airport in time to catch the last scheduled flight to London. Running the gauntlet of Special Branch and customs at Heathrow unchallenged provided the proverbial icing on my cake. I took a black cab home, glancing out the rear window in disbelief that I had made it this far. Exhausted, I walked in the front door. Mary woke up and asked how the trip had gone. I tipped the money out of the bag and went to bed, leaving her to stare at it and contemplate a new way of life.

I heard nothing from the Togolese for a couple of months. I enjoyed the change from struggling to make a buck to making a buck work for me. Meanwhile, Banks was persevering with Security Advisory Services and getting nowhere. He had to meet a prospective client in Milan and asked me if I'd come along. After the meeting, I rang home and Mary said that the Togolese diplomat had called and wanted me to contact him urgently.

I called him back. He was as friendly as usual; he had begun to call me 'Mr David'. He asked me to come to Paris, adding rather ominously, 'The President wishes to see you.' I bet he does, I thought, hanging from a meat hook over hot coals, no doubt. Eyadéma was attending a pan-African summit in the French capital. I enjoyed the irony: all these African heads of state pledging friendship and cooperation between nations; yeah, right, I thought, only when they weren't starting wars with one another. Banks and I drove to Paris, stopping at Chamonix overnight, and met my diplomat friend in a hotel lobby. He was accompanied by two men, a middle-aged French security-service officer and Major Assi, a Mike Tyson lookalike who acted as President Eyadéma's chief security officer. While the Frenchman sought to reassure me that he had been advised that my presence was by invitation and that everything was above board, Major Assi stared at me coldly. He was shorter than me but very intimidating. It was a racing certainty that I was one of his least favourite people, as news that a fresh plot had been circulated to kill his boss was hardly going to make him employee of the month. The diplomat passed on President Eyadéma's invitation to a reception that evening. He and I would travel there together and be chauffeured there and back by a French diplomatic protection officer.

President Eyadéma's residence was situated on an avenue where many of the African heads of state in town for the summit were staying and the entrance to the street was guarded by tall gates, security cameras, dogs and police officers armed with MAT-49 sub-machine guns. The interior of the building was as opulently appointed as I had expected, with huge, highly polished wooden doors, lavish reception areas and sofas and chairs lining the walls. There must have been 50 people in the hallway but it didn't look crowded. Each door leading from the room was guarded by a very large bodyguard. Dotted among the suited men were the most beautiful young women; I admired President Eyadéma's taste. The diplomat sat me down and instructed me to relax while he attended to some business. He disappeared through a giant set of double doors. Thirty minutes later, he returned amid a procession of dignitaries ahead of the president himself. The bodyguards stiffened as Eyadéma approached. Everybody else was told to stand. He was introduced to everyone. Some he would shake hands and exchange pleasantries with but mostly he just moved on.

I wondered which approach he would choose with me. I was introduced as Monsieur David Tomkins. President Eyadéma stopped and stared at me. I held his gaze. He was powerfully built, with a thick neck; his most striking feature was a set of tribal scars curving from the sides of his nose across his cheekbones. We exchanged nods. After the reception, the diplomat told me that he would contact me shortly regarding the balance of my payment. The trip to Paris was an anticlimax; all Eyadéma seemed to have wanted was the chance to see the man who'd planned to kill him in person. I could do nothing now but wait.

During the two months that passed without further word, I accompanied Banks to Kenya on a job providing protection for a photographer from a French magazine. He was supposed to go into Uganda but Banks fed him so many stories about atrocities committed by Idi Amin's troops that when we reached Kitale he refused to cross the border.

Then, during the second week in August, the diplomat made contact. 'I am sorry for the delay, Mr David. The president is now ready to pay you the balance owed. He wants to pay you personally, in Togo.'

I had not forgotten the terms of our agreement; neither had he. 'Our verbal arrangement excluded that possibility,' I replied sternly.

'Mr David, I am very sorry. Very sorry. But the president insists he wishes to invite you to Togo to thank you for your cooperation.'

Such a visit constituted a significant threat to my personal security but, as I had $125,000 to collect, the decision was easy. In my earlier career as a safe-beaker, I would have taken a lot of risk for that amount of money. Besides, I had looked the president in the eye; there was no way I'd give him the satisfaction of thinking he'd spooked me. So I was going to Togo.

I took some precautions, including notifying the Africa desk at the Foreign Office. The FO staff were aware of my involvement in the attempted coup, so I stressed that I had received an official invitation to Togo, at President Eyadéma's personal request. In the absence of any British diplomatic representation in Lomé, they promised to monitor developments from the embassy in Ghana. I figured I needed a psychological edge as well. While I knew that John Banks was no tough-guy soldier, his international reputation as a mercenary recruiter was synonymous with Colonel Callan and the bloodshed in Angola. I offered him a deal to come with me. In fairness to him, he agreed to go and didn't bottle out. I suspected that Eyadéma and his entourage would be suckers for his bullshit. The diplomat told me that I could bring my own interpreter, as proceedings were to be conducted in French. I invited Anthony Debono, whose company,

Bata International Airways, had a London office but also operated in the Republic of Guinea, where French was the official language.

Banks, Debono and I flew to the Continent on 24 August to collect our visas. At our hotel, we were surrounded by European politicians wining and dining at the taxpayer's expense. I asked that the diplomat post written confirmation of President Eyadéma's invitation to Mary. The letter was stamped with the embassy seal and posted to Camberley from the airport.

When we stepped onto the tarmac at Lomé, officials ushered us into two Mercedes saloon cars as troops aboard Land Rovers observed proceedings. This was quite a reception committee – and something of a contrast to my first visit to Togo. The diplomat took our passports to be stamped. I rode with him, while Banks and Debono travelled in the second Mercedes. I had insisted prior to our arrival that we be billeted in a hotel rather than in government accommodation. A visit now in the darkness to Camp Tokoin would have spelled danger. At the junction of the airport approach road and the Route Circulaire, we turned right. The turning we took from the next roundabout was crucial; if we went straight over, our destination must be the army camp. My pulse rate accelerated and my throat tightened. I stared at the car in front of us hoping to see a flashing indicator. It seemed an eternity before the driver granted my wish.

We came to rest at the Hotel de la Paix, the four-star place that had been fully booked many months earlier. I was not given a room there this time, either. Instead, we were put up in an adjacent white-walled compound of luxuriously appointed bungalows reserved for international VIPs. Armed soldiers patrolled the perimeter walls, as much to keep us in as to keep anyone else out, I couldn't help feeling.

When the next morning we pulled in to the palace courtyard, I was reassured by the sight of a gunmetal-grey Jaguar Mark VII, the wing standard flying the Union Jack. I knew it must have belonged to the British High Commissioner to Ghana. When we were introduced, he told me that President Eyadéma had summoned him to reassure me that I was 'an honoured guest in his country' and that the British government was aware I was here as a 'friend'.

A photo session was held, presumably for the local press, or the 'wanted' posters should I abscond. Upstairs, we entered an anteroom leading to the president's office. His bodyguards seemed to have been selected for their exceptional height; I am 6 ft 2 in. tall and they towered over me. We entered the office through a steel-plated door and sank into deep white carpets. The president was dressed in a beige uniform with brass buttons and campaign ribbons under the left breast pocket. His staff, and some gentlemen whom I assumed were tribal leaders, were seated on a row of chairs. Eyadéma rose to his feet behind his ornate desk and shook my hand. Once the introductions were over, the British High Commissioner stood and said, 'That's it, then. I must drive back to Accra now. Good luck.'

I was mightily relieved that his departure did not precipitate a change in atmosphere and felt that now was an appropriate juncture to voice my appreciation of the president's hospitality. 'May I thank the president for his generous invitation to Togo. I must say I am very happy to be in his country and I extend my apologies for the nature of the circumstances that first gave rise to my attendance.' From his expression, I judged that I had been forgiven.

President Eyadéma then addressed Banks. 'How many soldiers do you have?'

Banks, totally unfazed, immediately responded with, 'How many do you want?' Without waiting for a response, he continued, 'I can give you 1,000 men at a week's notice.'

Eyadéma looked impressed. 'There are only 800 men in my army, Mr Banks.'

I never could fault Banks when it came to bullshit. But I wanted to move the conversation towards the reason for my visit. I enquired whether the security recommendations I had suggested had now been implemented. When my question had been interpreted, Eyadéma looked blank faced then began a conversation with his staff. My interpreter could not help, as it was conducted not in French but in a Togolese dialect. The upshot was that I was invited to give the president his own personal presentation on the plan for his assassination. It was nerve-racking giving such a speech to the intended target of the operation. Eyadéma wanted specifics; clearly, he had not been fully briefed. My explanations were followed by a heated discussion. It was obvious that the president was furious. He ordered several people to leave the room. Since I had told the diplomat where a bomb might be placed, the president had been driven over the exact spot scores of times. Nobody had checked under the bridge or bothered to inform him that it was a prime spot for an assassination attempt. When I was asked if the weapons flown in for the initial attempt were in Togo or Ghana, I told the truth. All I knew was that they had come in on a transport aircraft that might well still be on the tarmac at Lomé airport. This gave rise to more heated words and more officials were ordered from the room.

Later, I accompanied members of the president's security detail and senior army officers to the intended killing ground at the bridge on Avenue de la Libération. Police officers sealed off the area and curious onlookers were ushered away. As time passed, the numbers of military personnel increased, yet the atmosphere was so sociable that we might have been at a barbecue. The officer in charge was the double of Antonio Fargas, who played Huggy Bear in *Starsky and Hutch*. 'Huggy' bounced around rather than walked and wore a red beret that sat on his head like a mushroom. When I asked what was taking so long, I was told we were waiting for a digging machine. Finally, to cheers from the soldiers, a bright-yellow JCB digger rolled up.

'What are you going to do?' I asked.

Huggy looked at me as if I was stupid. 'Dig up the bridge, of course.'

It seemed a shame to spoil the party atmosphere and risk denting Huggy's ego but I couldn't resist. 'You don't need to do that. If one man with a mirror lies on the ground and leans over the side of the bridge, he'll be able to see right through each pipe to the other side.'

This was relayed to the soldiers, who started laughing. The interpreter told me that someone had commented, 'It takes a clever man to think of a simple solution to a problem.' This remark might have been flattering but it did not endear me to Huggy, as he found himself the butt of his soldiers' jokes. He yanked angrily at a mirror on the cab door of a truck, incurring more laughter. Finally, after the drainage systems were officially declared free of explosives, we retired.

The following day, we were taken to a conference hall to meet the heads of Togo's religious groups. Nuns and priests in their habits and dog collars were seated at a long table. At one end of the hall was a platform with a lectern and microphone. President Eyadéma addressed the audience: 'I am misjudged by many external elements and certain governments who do not understand that I am trying to protect my people from those who would exploit them for their own benefit. There are those who condemn my rule of Togo.' He introduced John and me as mercenaries, saying, 'Mr Tomkins had been told a pack of lies about a brutal dictator with a regime, akin to that of Idi Amin, that subjugated the Togolese people. But when he came to our country with the intention of assassinating me, he found a free and open society with a happy population. This was when he realised the truth and his conscience no longer allowed him to carry out such an act. Mr Banks has also found Togo to be progressive and open, unlike other African nations in which he has fought wars.'

I found this line particularly amusing. Banks never fought in the wars; he just supplied the soldiers.

To my horror, I was beckoned forward to say a few words. With half of God's army awaiting my wisdom, I approached the microphone. 'I would like to apologise for the cause that first brought me to Togo. I echo the president's sentiments and am happy to have come back into the fold again from the brink of committing a tragic error of judgement.' I glanced up to see nodding heads.

Banks' speech did not disappoint. Had he been running for president, they would have elected him. 'I have witnessed the atrocities of conflict. Now I have seen the smiling faces of the Togolese people. Africa should look to Togo as a role model, a country to be emulated and admired.'

President Eyadéma was pleased with our performances. That afternoon, we went swimming, I looked on in amazement as our armed escort ushered all the other swimmers out of the pool. In the evening, we had a surprise visitor, Major Assi, who drove us down some seedy alleys to a restaurant close to the Ghanaian border. I think he must have chosen the route for its maximum fear factor. It was a pleasant meal, although nobody gave much away. I got the feeling that Major Assi still wanted me lightly grilled with fresh vegetables.

The following day, I was taken to meet diplomats representing the United States, Libya, China and the Soviet Union. The staff from the various embassies were not so much addressed by President Eyadéma as given a lecture. The interpreter had a job keeping up as Eyadéma berated them for their lack of concern for his well-being. He told them that their intelligence services should have known what had been planned against him. He said they had abused his hospitality, having had the hand of diplomatic cooperation and friendship thrust towards them. President Eyadéma told them that I was his 'only friend', who had warned him of another attempt on his life. When he said that, I wished I had charged him a million dollars. Alas, I knew there was a flip-side to this compliment. I envisaged my ability to move freely around the world being compromised. As far as the assembled diplomats were concerned, I was *persona non grata*.

When the floor was opened to questions, the Russian ambassador had a dig at his United States counterpart. 'Mr Tomkins, was it not the case that this was an American-sponsored operation against President Eyadéma? The company of the principal instigator, Tom Finan, is based in Florida and the aircraft that delivered American weapons to Togo was also purchased and registered in the USA.'

The US representative responded, 'Mr Tomkins made it perfectly clear that the coup attempt was not sponsored by any US agency and that the principal recruiter was, in fact, a Canadian citizen. The aircraft was a normal commercial purchase. Its location and registration in the United States are coincidences that should not be misconstrued as part of any conspiracy involving the United States government.'

I kept my counsel. Neither superpower had been involved. Only the Ghanaian government had been implicated and President Eyadéma had decreed that no representatives of its government were to be present.

Meanwhile, Banks and Debono had a stress-free morning. Reunited, we were informed that Togolese commandos had attacked a mercenary cargo plane at the airport. This was intended to serve as a warning that the Togolese were not to be underestimated as a military force. Finan's Constellation had sat on the ramp unclaimed for months. The Immortal One had skilfully turned a fuck-up into a propaganda victory.

The issue of my $125,000 remained outstanding. I did my utmost to appear relaxed about this until our time of departure approached. I had one final meeting with Eyadéma in his office. The room was full of very old men, elders from his home village. Eyadéma thanked me for my cooperation and said, 'You should return soon and stay at my home in the village in which I was born.' His interpreter claimed this great honour was only extended to a privileged few. Then the president produced my prize from beneath his desk. My payment was contained in a huge brown-paper parcel. I concluded immediately that the money must be in CFA francs, not sterling or dollars. Reluctant to appear ungrateful, I asked Debono to apologise for my impertinence, but could His Excellency say what the parcel contained?

Debono was slightly confused by the reply. He believed the parcel contained either 4 million or 40 million CFA francs. I had no idea what the exchange rate was and I feared that returning to Heathrow with such a physically large quantity of money would raise questions I didn't want to answer. As tactfully as I could, I ventured, 'If it is possible, I would appreciate a more convenient currency, such as US dollars, that could be carried with more discretion.'

Immediately, Eyadéma made a telephone call and a few minutes later I was presented with a bulging Manila envelope addressed to 'The Minister of Finance, Togolese Republic'. I thanked the president while, still curious, opening the envelope and quickly transferring its contents into my briefcase. The final payment was made in 500-French-franc notes in bundles of 50,000 francs. My mental calculations suggested that the payment exceeded the sum owed to me.

My lasting memory of Togo was the sight, as our flight took off from Lomé, of the Constellaton on the adjacent ramp. Hundreds of bullet holes had ripped through its fuselage, while its tail section had been left hanging by mere shreds of aluminium. The cockpit nose had been blown off and drooped mournfully towards the tarmac.

CHAPTER 13

A BETRAYAL

ON 2 SEPTEMBER 1979, ALMOST EXACTLY A YEAR AFTER MY RETURN from Togo, I received a telephone call from the Togolese Embassy in London. As far as I had been aware, Togo maintained only an honorary consulate in London. The call was from the ambassador, a Mr Yakoubou, who asked me to come to a meeting the next day. 'It is very urgent,' he said. 'The president is very worried.'

I met Yakoubou at the embassy, which was in Knightsbridge, very close to Hyde Park. He introduced me to a Togolese minister, who dismissed the ambassador from the room so that he and I could talk alone. He muttered some excuse about how it would have violated Yakoubou's diplomatic status to have been privy to the conversation.

The minister proceeded to tell me that Eyadéma was extremely anxious, so much so he had summoned the minister in the middle of the night. The president was in an agitated mood concerning Gilchrist Olympio, the son of Sylvanus Olympio, the man whom Eyadéma had overthrown. Olympio lived in Paris, where he was frequently on his soapbox stirring up anti-Eyadéma feeling. He had been sentenced to death *in absentia* in a Togolese treason trial a few weeks earlier. The minister stressed the urgency of the matter, telling

179

me that while his official reason for visiting the UK was to offer his country's condolences to Queen Elizabeth over the murder of Lord Mountbatten, the real reason he had come was to speak with me.

'Olympio's agenda is to create unrest and dissatisfaction among the Togolese at home and abroad. We cannot allow this to continue,' he said. The minister's background was probably in the legal profession. He chose his words with caution. 'You are a friend of the president and you may be able to help redress this situation once and for all.' He might not have said outright what he meant but his intention was perfectly clear. The words 'once and for all' seemed to echo around the room.

I used the analogy that the only way to prevent a poisonous snake biting was to cut off its head, which seemed to meet the requirements of the minister's word game. 'Your president's concerns for the future are of great importance to me,' I continued. 'However, there are of course considerations as to what it is possible to undertake in Europe, as opposed to other parts of the world. The matter will need to be considered carefully.'

'I understand entirely.'

My job was to find Olympio and place him under surveillance.

'How much would such an operation cost?' asked the minister.

'The initial expenses would have to be sufficient to cover several people to travel to Paris for a few days, locate the subject and assess his movements. I think we should review the situation and then discuss a price.'

Olympio's address was given to me and the ambassador was instructed to give me £3,000 for expenses.

While assassination in a small West African republic wouldn't raise an eyebrow in the West, and I would be unlikely to face extradition unless there was concrete evidence against me, if Olympio were to be killed in Paris, it would be called murder and there would be a storm of publicity and protest. I had no moral qualms, however. Assassination or murder – it was just a question of semantics, really. In any case, it was business. Many of the special-forces veterans I knew made me think of the old joke 'Join the army, see the world, meet lots of people and kill them', and there were others like them looking for work all over the world, so I was unlikely to have problems finding men prepared to undertake the operation – providing the money was right.

It was early days yet, however. I would have to find out what the potential problems were before I could resolve them. Darkie Davidson agreed to conduct the initial location survey with me. The address I had been given for Olympio was at the Rue de Courcelles. The first problem to arise was that the number I'd been given did not exist on that street. The street did not feel right. It seemed out of keeping with a man of Olympio's money and style. Rue de Courcelles was fairly narrow with many small apartments in very old buildings, and towards the junction with Boulevard Haussmann most of the premises were clearly commercial offices. It might best be described as anonymous, which didn't seem to fit Olympio's profile.

We wasted most of the day satisfying ourselves that the address did not exist. With hindsight, we should have done the obvious much earlier: eventually, we checked in the phone book to see if there was a listing for our target. His address was 72 Boulevard de Courcelles. A broad avenue with grand apartments and off-street parking, it was more the kind of place one might expect a former president's son to live. Number 72 was a nineteenth-century apartment block, overlooking Parc Monceau. One entered the building through a tall archway and a set of ornate wrought-iron double gates. From a surveillance point of view, its location was perfect: there were parking spaces on either side of the wide road and Parc Monceau bordered the pavement of Boulevard de Courcelles, with a set of railings running its length, behind which bushes and trees created a perfect covert vantage point to observe the entrance to the apartment.

I was satisfied with this brief survey and felt we could now move on to the next stage. I arranged to meet the minister the next day and we headed home. There were some negative vibes on Davidson's part. He rightly considered undertaking the operation in Paris very dangerous because of the rigorous police investigation that would surely follow. My prior association with the Togolese government was no secret. I decided that I would undertake the surveillance but that, in order to protect myself and others involved, I would find a hit man who had no previous connection with Togo or me.

DIRTY COMBAT

There were two meetings with the security minister the following day. The first took place in the embassy, where I advised the minister that my price would be $750,000, plus expenses for the surveillance team. In the late afternoon, we met again in his suite at the Ritz Hotel, Piccadilly. He provided me with a set of photographs of Gilchrist Olympio and his brother Benito, along with $125,000 for expenses. He told me that his master was very happy to know that I was working to protect him. When I had told him earlier that my price was $750,000, the figure had seemed ridiculously high and I would have negotiated if pushed. But, to my great surprise and chagrin, the minister told me that the president felt he has not been charged very much money. He said that when the matter was over I would be 'greatly recompensed'. I was even offered a position on Eyadéma's security staff in Lomé. I thanked him but there was no way I was going to live in Togo.

The surveillance team numbered eight: me, two men recently returned from Rhodesia, where they'd served in the special forces, three British ex-paratroopers, a former French Legionnaire and a French connection who was not introduced to the rest of the team. Our accommodation was a large penthouse in a self-catering 'aparthotel', rented on my behalf by the anonymous Frenchman, so our ID was never required. There was no concierge, so we came and went unobserved. We rented vehicles and mounted our operation. The initial watch period provided encouraging results. The behaviour and movements of Gilchrist Olympio suggested that he was not surveillance conscious. Paris, however, is not the easiest place in the world for mobile surveillance, even with multiple cars, and we lost our subject's Peugeot 504 on a couple of occasions in the nightmare traffic round the Arc de Triomphe.

One evening, I paid a visit to Olympio's apartment block. The ornate gates led into an arched passageway with a set of unlocked double doors to the left. These led into a hallway with a winding set of stairs fitted with red carpet. The lights at each level were operated by push-button timers that allowed time to get to the next floor before they switched off. All the private apartments had strong doors with good security locks.

In the short space of time during which we watched Olympio,

no regular pattern was established. He was not trying to hide and I was satisfied that he could be taken out quietly as he entered his apartment block one night. My French connection introduced me to someone prepared to pull the trigger. He came highly recommended and had a background of working in the strictest confidence. He was Algerian by birth, a former member of OAS (Organisation de l'Armée Secrète), an anti-Gaullist far-right group. He was in his mid-40s and spoke passable English. Terms and conditions were agreed. Every detail known about the target was given to him, with photographs, to enable him to conduct his own surveillance operation. I paid 12,000 francs for several weapons. The one that really mattered was a SIG P230 with customised silencer and subsonic 380 ammunition. We arranged another meeting, when I would accompany him to confirm target identification before pulling my surveillance team off so that he could begin his own operation with a clear area. The plan was for my team to have left France before the hit took place. To further protect them from legal repercussions, they never met the Algerian and nor were they told the reason why they were watching the target. Even a conspiracy charge would be hard to prove.

I returned to the UK on 13 September to arrange payment terms with the Togolese, leaving my team in place, with instructions to watch Olympio in the mornings until he left the apartment and to do a late check to see if his car was parked for the night. I told them to do nothing more than this and to avoid anything more heavy-handed, which might compromise the situation. On the morning and evening of the 12th, Olympio had not been sighted. I checked in with the team late on the evening of the 13th and he had still not been seen entering or leaving the apartment. The Peugeot 504 was still in its parking space. On the night of the 14th, the story was the same.

The next day, I received an urgent call from the Togolese government. 'Do not go to the embassy and under no circumstances go back to Paris. The police are looking for you.'

'What? Why? Explain what you mean.'

'One of the people working for you has informed the Olympio brothers of your plan.'

'Not possible,' I replied with indignation.

'It is true, I'm afraid. It's all over the news. The papers are calling the embassy for their comments. You know a Mr Davidson?'

'Yes.'

'Mr Davidson made a sworn affidavit on 11 September at the offices in London of Benito Olympio's lawyers stating that the Togolese government contracted you and him to kill Gilchrist Olympio. The press are printing a photograph of Olympio holding up the affidavit for the cameras.' I was shocked. But the news was about to get worse. 'And a bomb has been found under the Peugeot parked outside his apartment.'

I instructed my surveillance team to close the shop, split up and make their separate ways home from Paris. There was no possibility that the authorities knew who they were, as I had not told anyone and Davidson had not been involved in the surveillance operation.

The team returned with the Parisian newspapers. Gilchrist Olympio was front-page news. L'Aurore carried a spread beneath a headline that translated as 'Tribal War of the Boulevard de Courcelles'. The story included wild speculation, spinning a tale of coup attempts, double agents and triple agents. It read like an extract from a cheap spy novel. At least they had managed to spell my name correctly.

According to Olympio's version, his nephew, who was going to drive him to the airport very early on the morning of 15 September, had noticed a plastic container on the ground beneath the driver's seat of the Peugeot. On closer examination, this turned out to be a container with magnets attached to it. This had apparently become detached from the car due to rust preventing the magnets from performing adequately. Attached to the container was a trip switch that would detonate the two kilos of explosives that it contained. Gilchrist Olympio was obviously a very cool customer, as he called the media and held a photo opportunity and press conference straight away.

The accusations and denials between the Togolese government and Olympio went on and on, the Togolese authorities wishing it would go away and Olympio making certain it didn't. He demanded police protection, which was refused. What spoiled the party for him was the involvement of the press: there was considerable scepticism as to how the media had been able to cover the story almost simultaneously with the discovery of the bomb.

What motivated Darkie to betray me, I may never find out; but the Olympios surely betrayed him as well, as I'm certain he was not anticipating the release of the affidavit to the press. As for the bomb, who made it may also remain a mystery. It certainly wasn't something I would have attempted, not in a Paris street, anyway. In any case, France was now off my travel itinerary, at least until the dust settled.

I had a five-month stay of execution before the tentacles of the Parisian investigation reached Basingstoke, where I'd moved with my family. On the morning of 22 February 1980, officers from the Serious Crime Squad requested an interview. They made it perfectly clear that the investigation was outside their jurisdiction but they had been requested to assist as a matter of courtesy and cooperation. There seemed little point in avoiding the issue and the interview might give me some clue as to what future problems might be heading my way. In the afternoon, two Scotland Yard officers, one of whom spoke French, and a French detective knocked on my door. They explained that, in accordance with French legal practice, a magistrate had been appointed and a number of parties were being interviewed. Presumably, they had checked flight records and hotel-registration cards, as they were aware of my travel schedule in September of the previous year. They stressed that they knew of my relationship with the Togolese government. Choosing my words carefully, I admitted mounting a surveillance operation on Olympio.

'Do you know anything about the bomb planted underneath the car?'

I told them that if it had been my intention to kill Olympio, I would not have chosen such an indiscriminate method likely to cause considerable collateral casualties.

'Could you have made such a bomb?'

'Possibly, depending on how it was fabricated.'

The French officer produced a set of photographs of the explosive device and its individual components. The container was an opaque Tupperware box with one small hole cut in its side and another about the size of a coin in the end face. Another picture showed a coil of sash cord with a loop at one end. More pictures were presented; these were of individual components: batteries, electrical switches, magnets, a detonator and ten cartridges of Gomme F15 dynamite. I was asked to describe how a bomb using these components might be operated but I was reluctant to answer, not knowing where this line of questioning was leading. I was assured that there was no sinister intention behind the question and told that I could speak freely.

I laid the pictures out on the table and studied them individually and collectively. The sash cord puzzled me at first and there was apparently no mechanism, such as a mercury tilt switch, to operate the detonator. Then I worked it out. The small hole in the side of the box was for a safety switch for arming or disarming the electrical circuit, while the hole in the end was for a second switch. This was pull operated. One end of the sash cord was attached to the pull switch, while the other was attached to the prop shaft of the car. Once the device was in place and secured using the magnets, the safety switch could be set to the armed position. The bomb would only detonate once the car was in motion, when the sash cord would wrap itself around the turning prop shaft, tighten and pull the switch that closed the electric circuit to the detonator. Then it would be goodbye, with a very large bang.

My interpretation of the photographs seemed to amuse the French cop; he then showed me the picture of the fully assembled bomb . . . I'd got it right in one! My record, and whatever they considered they knew about me, led them to believe that while my mission in Paris might have involved a little more than surveillance, it did not include anything to do with the bomb. The French officer summed it up by saying, in effect, 'Methinks Olympio doth protest too much.' The police left me with the understanding that for their part I was ruled out of any further investigation and could return to France without legal repercussions.

CHAPTER 14

THE LEARNING CURVE

DURING MY INVOLVEMENT WITH TOGO, I ALSO TOOK AN INTEREST in events in another African nation. I had long been a supporter of Rhodesia's Ian Smith, because he had had the balls to snub the international community with his Unilateral Declaration of Independence in 1965, and I was a card-carrying member of the Anglo-Rhodesian Society. By the late '70s, I felt that my moral support was not enough. Civil war was raging and Rhodesia was surrounded by antagonistic states. Zambia and Botswana were safe havens for Communist organisations outlawed in Rhodesia, while Angola and Mozambique were already Communist.

The largest Communist group was Robert Mugabe's ZANU (Zimbabwe African National Union) and its military wing, ZANLA (Zimbabwe African National Liberation Army), which drew its supporters from Mashonaland, home of the Shona tribe, the country's biggest population group. Another major Communist faction was Joshua Nkomo's ZAPU (the Zimbabwe African People's Union) and its armed wing, ZIPRA (the Zimbabwe People's Revolutionary Army), which recruited from the Ndebele people. The guerrilla fighters lived in camps in Zambia, infiltrating Rhodesia from the north or, looping south through Botswana, from the west. International sanctions were having a crippling effect on Rhodesia, worsened by American pressure brought to bear on the country's closest friendly neighbour, South Africa, to shut the door on its arms and oil supply.

It was another alphabet-soup war and I wanted in. I had been corresponding with a friend, Derek, who had left his Sussex home for Rhodesia and joined the Ministry of Internal Affairs (Intaf) as an armourer. He guaranteed me a temporary roof over my head if I showed up on his doorstep, so in January 1979, I did. Derek lived in Salisbury, the capital city, and worked in the Intaf central-armoury workshops at Chikurubi, on the outskirts of the city. His rank was WO2 and he was second in command of the armoury. Much of his workload consisted of repairing weapons damaged in ambushes or in firefights between guerrillas and Rhodesia's armed forces. Ordinarily, these weapons would have been declared beyond repair. But sanctions meant that arms were thin on the ground and necessity was the mother of invention. I saw modified weapons in Rhodesia I had not seen before or since. When an FN or G3 rifle barrel was damaged, it was sawn short and its breechblocks re-machined so that gas regulators could operate the ammunition feed mechanism. Browning machine guns from aircraft were converted to manual operation for automatic and repetition firing, to be used mounted on vehicles. These were just a couple of the many innovative engineering feats I saw accomplished in the workshops.

The principal role of Internal Affairs was the running of and preservation of order in the 50 or more administrative areas of the country. The war had added a further dimension to Intaf's role, however, that of protection, and it was this element of their work that I was interested in getting involved in. Rural communities, many in very remote regions of the country, were the most vulnerable to attack by guerrilla groups. Exposed regions contained 'protected villages' or PVs, where local people could work the land by day and sleep at night in purpose-built fortified complexes, protected by armed personnel from Internal Affairs or from Guard Force, an arm of the security services established for this purpose. The protected villages had a number of advantages. They freed the fighting units of the military from the increasing burden of taking a protective role and they restricted guerrilla access to the local population, depriving ZANLA and ZIPRA of a source of food, shelter and information, forcing them to operate less efficiently. Communist propaganda labelled them 'concentration camps'.

Taking advantage of Derek's connections, I spent a couple of weeks at the Intaf battle camp, a training programme for new recruits to the service. The instructors were excellent, with years of combat experience, and imparted expertise in the tactics of the terrorists and how best to combat them. Although the role of Intaf was to protect, much of the training was more suited to a fighting unit, which instilled confidence in the trainees. Live-fire weapons training and anti-ambush drills gave a sense of the realities of what you might encounter but rather hoped you wouldn't.

Unfortunately, joining Intaf as part of the National Service Unit was a commitment that I was not in a position to make. I had bought land in Basingstoke and was in the process of building a house on it. When I left for Rhodesia, it was just a small field with ranging rods stuck in the ground to show the layout of the house. I needed to be free to travel back to the UK should a problem arise with my family or the building. The problem was resolved when Armaguard offered me a position. It was a private company operated along lines similar to Guard Force but its major advantage for me was that it did not come under the umbrella of Intaf, which meant that I had more freedom to come and go. Armaguard's role was key-point security, protecting so-called 'vital asset ground'. This term referred to sites essential to the country's economy and we were posted to isolated and vulnerable tobacco farms, mines, power installations – any strategic or economic target at risk from terrorist attack.

My first posting was to the Roma–Joyce gold mine, approximately 50 km south of Salisbury. I turned off the main road to Fort Victoria at Beatrice, onto a winding dirt track through the bush. I had been sent to replace the previous security officer, who one afternoon had talked the mine manager's 14-year-old son into letting him borrow his trail bike. He handed his rifle to the kid, who rode pillion as they set off up the dirt track towards the general store. They were ambushed on the ride back as they came around a bend. A bullet passed through both the guy's legs as well as the petrol tank. The boy fared better, only being shot through his knee. The bike crashed in the bush. Like most white Rhodesian children, the kid was comfortable with a weapon and he fired at the guerrillas through the long grass. Not knowing that his ammunition was nearly expended, the attackers withdrew. Both the guard and the boy survived but the incident illustrated how easily an error of judgement could cost a life.

This was no luxury posting. My accommodation consisted of one small room in the powerhouse that operated the mineshaft machinery. It was furnished with a metal cot, a table, a chair and a gun cabinet. About five kilometres from the main shaft was a compound in which the manager and his family lived. Near that was the processing plant, where gold was extracted from crushed ore. It was not the richest grade of ore – it averaged a mere ten grams of gold per ton – but Rhodesia needed all the revenue it could get.

Working with me were eight black guards. We had to secure and patrol a fenced area of about twenty acres surrounding the main mineshaft. Bunkers had been built using rocks brought up from the mineshaft, with pit props to form the roofs. These were strategically placed around the inside perimeter of the compound. Most of my work was done between early evening and morning. The late afternoon, which the Rhodesians referred to as 'terr time', was considered the most dangerous period, as most attacks occurred at dusk, when the cloak of darkness would fall to hinder the trackers terrorists knew would come with the 'reaction sticks', the small units of men, usually four, who arrived by the quickest means possible when an attack was reported. It was difficult to sleep during the day because of the noise of the mine, with shaft machinery hauling up the ore, which was transported by narrow-gauge rails to the crushing plant.

My guards were not the brightest bunch in the world and the long, boring nights were mainly spent checking they hadn't gone to sleep and trying to build a rapport with them. When I wasn't on the prowl round, I would read in my room, my one small window covered by a sheet of corrugated iron. One night, having joined my sergeant in his bunker, I asked him, more out of politeness than curiosity, if he had seen anything in the pitch blackness that surrounded us. He replied, 'Only *mhondoro*. Two mhondoro come, they meet each other shake hands and go.' Mhondoro, as it turned out, were ancestral chiefs from the spirit world. This was told to me in absolute sincerity and who was I to question it?

In a previous attack on the mine, several workers had been killed. The main objective of the attack had been to disrupt mining. Many black Rhodesians believed that the white man was hollowing out the world and that when the indigenous Africans won the war, everything that had been mined should be put back underground. During the attack, the guerrillas had pushed everything they could physically move back down the mineshaft. For security reasons, night shifts had been stopped.

My roster was two weeks on and two days off. Very little happened to break the monotony. I'd spend time at the main plant watching the extraction process and I got to ride shotgun into Salisbury with the finished product. The manager's armour-plated Land Rover bore little resemblance to the original vehicle. It was like something out of *Mad Max*. The cab was doorless; in fact, the cab was cableless – sitting on the chassis was an open-top steel cocoon, its sides a zigzag of metal plates, with sheets of bulletproof glass for the windows. The wings and bonnet had been removed and replaced with armour plating to protect the engine. It was all topped off with a canvas roof like that of a covered wagon in a cowboy film.

To walk around Salisbury was to step back in time to the 1950s, with immaculate Morris Minors and Ford Anglias parked on the streets. Courtesy and politeness were the norm, not the exception, while the dress code in restaurants and for social gatherings was on the formal side of smart. With modern consumer goods in short supply, the goods for sale in the Salisbury shops were often museum pieces. Household appliances such as refrigerators and washing machines were usually second-hand and 10 or 15 years behind those available in Britain. It seemed a great shame to me that these people should be fighting for their lives and for the continuation of a way of life that was becoming alien to the rest of world. United Nations-supported economic sanctions were bringing the country to its knees and increasingly few international governments were sympathetic. The ban on financial transactions with Rhodesia bit hard and travel abroad was difficult. The business community relied on a handful of sanction-busting companies. Meanwhile, the civil war had claimed over 4,000 lives. This was not many in relation to the wars in Vietnam or even Angola but Rhodesia was a small country by comparison. The war was a dangerous game of hide and seek in which both sides paid a heavy price.

Rhodesia's rural population were very switched on with regard to security. Homes had strongpoints or 'keeps', where, as a last resort, the occupants could take refuge until assistance came. These strongpoints contained weapons and ammunition, had three-foot-thick walls and weapon-firing points like the slit windows you find in medieval castles. Much use was made of close-link chain fencing around homes and installations. Its main purpose was to defend against rocket-propelled grenades. When fired at a building surrounded by chain-link fencing, the rocket might fail in two ways: the nose cone's electrical fuse might be short-circuited as it forced its way through the mesh; or the fins that stabilised the warhead might shear off, preventing accurate flight.

A system called Agric-Alert (agricultural alert) provided emergency communications between isolated properties and armed-response assistance from the nearest police unit or JOC (joint operations command). Pressing the Agric-Alert button would bring a police anti-terrorist unit (PATU) or a military 'fire force' unit by road or air. These units would bring combat trackers known as 'sparrows' and, daylight permitting, these would follow the terrorists on foot. They might be supported by a variant of the Alouette III helicopter called a K-car, fitted with a 20-mm cannon that was operated by a gunner swinging outside of the chopper on a canvas seat. He would only be able to fire in single- or double-round bursts due to the force of the recoil. It was amazing to watch.

After some weeks at the mine, I was, thankfully, redeployed to convoy protection. Whenever and wherever possible, civilians travelled with a military escort. Lone civilian vehicles were not encouraged to drive on roads outside of populated areas, particularly if the route went through regions designated as operational. The guerrillas were always looking for soft targets. They set ambushes for those who took the gamble and many had lost. Certain days and times were set for vehicles to travel in groups between cities and towns. Armaguard vehicles would join heavily armed police escorts to protect the convoys. The line of vehicles could stretch for miles, as they were spaced out to minimise the number that could be caught in one swoop if an ambush was sprung. All escort vehicles were in radio contact with one other, with set procedures for breakdowns or enemy contact.

Of the many dangers in Rhodesia, landmines were perhaps the most insidious of all. Many roads were unpaved, offering ideal conditions for the laying of anti-tank mines, usually Soviet TM46s. When driving, one had to be constantly observant, alert to changes in the terrain that might offer ambush cover, aware of ground disturbance that might indicate mines. Even tarmac roads were to be driven with caution, as the guerrillas had developed a trick for laying mines under these. The top was cut off a five-gallon metal drum, and the edges heated in a fire. Then it was screwed into an asphalt road surface like a pastry cutter. The asphalt disc was then lifted out intact and the subsoil removed to accommodate an anti-tank mine. The asphalt disc was then replaced and engine oil spread around the cut, so that it looked like nothing more than a minor oil spill.

On trips to isolated places, the military sometimes escorted us for the last few miles, preceded by another of Rhodesia's innovative vehicles, the 'Pookie'. It was named after the bushbaby with its big, all-seeing eyes. The concept was brilliant in its simplicity and effectiveness. It was essentially a long wheel-base chassis stripped to nothing but the axles, to which wheels with wide racing tyres kept at a low air-pressure were fitted. Mounted on the rear of the chassis was a Volkswagen engine and in the middle was a steel box, the driver's position. This was open-topped with roll bars and a V-shaped blast-deflector bottom. Mounted crosswise under the chassis was a long plastic drainpipe containing the electronic circuitry of a metal detector. A long steering column protruded from under the armoured-glass slit windscreen. Spotlights were fitted high on either side, like a pair of eyes, and the Pookie resembled a cross between a giant go-kart and a gravel hopper. The low-pressure tyres distributed its weight so effectively that it could drive over a landmine without setting it off; in fact, it could drive over your foot without breaking a bone. An electronic boom would signal to the driver that it had passed over a buried metal object such as a mine, the mine would be lifted and the convoy continue.

In March, I was put in charge of Armaguard's training camp at Kintyre, a temporary position while the senior instructor was absent having a prosthesis fitted, having lost his leg below the knee in a mine blast during active service with the army. The camp was barely 25 km from Salisbury and the posting gave me the opportunity to get into the city on occasions. It's a small world when you chase wars and those who choose to fight in them – and survive – seem to pop up in others. I was walking along deep in thought one day when an old Volvo car suddenly came to a halt before reversing towards me, blowing its horn to get my attention. Wandering over to see what the problem was, I was greeted by the smiling face of Peter McAleese, whom I hadn't seen since Angola. McAleese had been in Rhodesia for more than two years, doing what he does best: soldiering. I spent several hours with him and a bunch of special-forces men at a curry party, celebrating some completed mission or one about to be embarked on. Peter had spent two years in the Rhodesian SAS. His professional soldiering skills had brought him safely through the sharp-end battles with guerrillas and raids on enemy camps across the border. Now he was with the country's Special Branch, engaged in covert operations. He seemed to be in his element and I was happy for him.

As guerrillas poured into Rhodesia in increasing numbers, there was little that even soldiers of McAleese's experience and expertise could achieve. Rhodesian forces were taking the war to the enemy's doorstep, carrying out daring cross-border raids on Zambia and Mozambique, some of which were covert missions and some direct attacks. Aircraft well beyond their sell-by dates – Dakota planes and Alouette helicopters – would drop fewer than 200 men deep inside Mozambique, straight into enemy training camps containing thousands of guerrilla fighters. With the support of ageing Vampires, Hawker Hunters and Canberra bombers, the Rhodesian armed forces went straight for the enemy's throat. It was still not enough to win, however. It only postponed the inevitable.

As attacks increased, the white population reacted in different ways. Some saw the writing on the wall and left the country for Europe or South Africa (colloquially referred to as 'taking the gap', a term derived from a rugby manoeuvre) with what little they could salvage. Others adopted a siege mentality and were digging in, metaphorically and literally. Travelling the country with the convoys, I met die-hard Rhodesians prepared to fight to the bitter end to protect their way of life. They were not prepared to hand over what they held dear and what had taken them a lifetime to build up to the Communist guerrillas.

Before I took up my final posting, I had to go to the eastern border of the country, to a timber mill near the Chimanimani Mountains where several of our guards had been captured, mutilated and killed. The logging camp had shut up shop – there was no need for guards any more. The closer we got to the Mozambique border, the more deserted the country became. Nearly everywhere was closed. It was a ghostly place, hastily deserted, it seemed, by a population seeking safety in other cities or other countries.

My last assignment was to protect an iron-ore mine at Buchwa in the Belingwe Tribal Trust Land, 300 km south of Salisbury. We drove to Shabani, where the road ended and a dirt track began. Shabani was home to the largest asbestos mine in Rhodesia. The population was made up almost solely of employees of the mine but it was the nearest thing to a town where I was going.

Buchwa Mine, which belonged to the Rhodesian Iron and Steel Company (RISCO), turned out to be a densely foliaged mountain – a mountain of iron ore that was being removed from the top downward. Our team comprised eight white senior security officers and sixty African armed guards with a black sergeant major. Our unit liaised closely with the police anti-terrorist units and military patrols active in the region. The mine had been closed on occasions due to attacks on the workers, who were vulnerable in the slow-moving vehicles that transported them daily up the steep, twisting road to the top. On the mountain, we had problems with *mujibas*, young lads, many not more than children, who were the eyes and ears of the guerrillas. They would sit in the foliage on the ridges and watch the daily security detail for the works convoy preparing to leave, gathering information on which vehicles should be targeted. To deter them, we would lie up in ambush positions on the mountain in the early hours and scare the shit out of them if they turned up.

Landmines and sabotage of equipment were our biggest concerns. We had established a strong visual presence, which seemed to prevent further attacks on the mine, and we had many auxiliaries operating in the area. The auxiliaries were former guerrillas who had been captured or switched sides. The auxiliaries who remained loyal to internal African political parties were retrained by the likes of Peter McAleese in Special Branch, which was responsible for the control and deployment of these 'tame terrs', as they were called. Many auxiliaries were placed in the peasant kraals, traditional villages, to prevent ZANLA guerrillas from mounting raids from tactically important tribal lands. In the mornings, we did mine and counter-ambush sweeps on roads used daily by vehicles travelling to the rail sidings at Iron Ore Junction, and we also did escort duty on trips to Shabani for stores.

All talk now centred on the forthcoming elections. In 1978, Smith had negotiated an agreement known as 'internal settlement', with moderate black nationalist leaders, notably Bishop Abel Muzorewa, leader of the United African National Council (UANC). For the first time, black Rhodesians would be entitled to vote, although ZANU and ZAPU were not represented. Part of our job was to explain the electoral process to our black guards. Time and again, they told me they would vote for Ian Smith. I explained that they now had the choice of putting a black African in charge of the country but they seemed horrified at the thought, saying there would be conflict between the Shona and Ndebele tribes without Ian Smith. As March drew to a close, increased daily sweeps around the local area were ordered. The election bandwagon of Bishop Muzorewa was coming to Buchwa, to tell the workers and locals how life would improve if they voted for him.

The day he arrived and gave his talk from the back of a flatbed truck turned out to be a bad day for me. When the election circus departed and I stripped off my camouflage gear, I was smothered in ticks, in every nook and cranny. The little parasitic bastards were having a field day on me. Three incredibly sweaty days later and in the grip of tick-bite fever, I was transferred to Salisbury's Andrew Fleming Hospital. Meanwhile, they got somebody else to do my job at Buchwa. Once I was back on my feet, it seemed appropriate to return home. I left Rhodesia in April 1979 and stuffed the last of my wages into a glass globe at Salisbury airport, a collection point for soldiers injured in the civil war.

The elections were held and, unsurprisingly perhaps, the UANC was victorious. Rhodesia became Zimbabwe Rhodesia, Josiah Gumede became president and Bishop Muzorewa prime minister. However, because the hard-line black nationalist parties had not participated in the elections, the civil war that Ian Smith had hoped to end continued.

I met Ian Smith and Bishop Muzorewa in September 1979 when Mary and I attended an Anglo-Rhodesian Society reception at the Carlton Tower Hotel, London. Smith and Muzorewa were attending the Lancaster House peace conference. I reminded the bishop of his visit to Buchwa and joked that I held him responsible for my sickness. Fresh elections were held in February 1980 after a campaign in which Mugabe's ZANU party was accused of intimidation. Mugabe won the leadership of the newly independent Zimbabwe and the rest, as they say, is history.

* * *

Around the time of the Lancaster House conference, on 24 September 1979, my former boss at Armaguard, David Saddington, invited me to dinner at a private club in London. There was another person at the dinner; in fact, he was actually the host. Kevin was a long-time friend of David's, although the exact relationship was never discussed. Kevin was an ex-cop. He had been an officer with the criminal-intelligence branch of the Metropolitan Police – not the sort of company I'd usually dine with. When polite chat came around to the subject of my background, I didn't duck any questions. If anything, I took a perverse pleasure in knowing that my host was an ex-police officer who knew that I was an ex-villain.

DIRTY COMBAT

As social evenings go, it was very pleasant; our host was likeable and didn't seem perturbed by my dubious background. Kevin said that he was now a director of a security company, not the sort that supplies uniformed security guards, more a high-class investigative agency. It was basically similar to his old job but in the commercial sector. As I understood it, Kevin's company had been created to do most of its work for a US investigative agency. This corporation was one of the largest such agencies in the world, with offices throughout the USA and in over 30 countries around the globe. The numerous institutes and federations that governed the conduct of private-detective and security agencies took violations of their standards and codes of ethics very seriously. Such agencies were required to stay within the framework of the law: burglary, illicit phone tapping and other illegal use of electronic surveillance equipment were frowned upon. Companies with a reputation to protect used 'deniable assets', smaller companies unaffiliated with them (on paper at least) and specialising in 'black-bag work': that is, gathering information through less than legal means.

I accepted Kevin's offer of a job to retrieve a file from an office situated in a private apartment at the Grosvenor House Hotel. These apartments were rented out on a medium-to-long-term basis to wealthy patrons who demanded privacy, a fancy address and all the amenities of a good hotel without the inconvenience of checking in and out. With a little help from a friend and an excellent locksmith, I gained entry to the office of a Liechtenstein-registered company and began my search for a contract for a Gulf State shipping company to transit grain to the Islamic Republic of Iran. I located and copied the file. One sheet of paper caught my eye: it was a copy of a banker's draft, payable in rials and drawn on an Arab bank. There were so many noughts and commas in the amount payable it stretched along two lines of the draft. This was a multi-million dollar deal, no question about that. I delivered the copies to Kevin and, in spite of my curiosity, considered the matter closed. It should have been just another discreet black-bag job done and dusted but I was soon to learn that the square mile of Mayfair is a very small and incestuous world when it comes to villains, arms dealers and spooks.

CHAPTER 15

TRUST ME, I'M A DOCTOR

BY THE END OF 1979, I HAD VISITED GERMANY, HONG KONG AND South Korea, to name only a few, in an effort to get my business off the ground. However, all my travels were to little avail. I was trying to break into the arms business, which was proving more difficult than I had imagined. Dealers and suppliers guarded their sources closely and resented newcomers. I was short of arms to sell and contacts to buy them.

Not everyone in the arms business worked out of an office. There was a crowd of us budding brokers who operated from hotel coffee shops and lounges. My usual place of work was the Kensington Hilton, where I was fortunate enough to enjoy a very good relationship with the management. I was able to use the phones and send and receive telexes. The hotel's PA system would even announce our incoming calls. An added advantage was that when you received a call through the switchboard, the caller assumed you were a guest. The hotel proved a great place to meet people and there were some real characters around. Ted was one such gentleman. We referred to him as 'the Tardis' because he spent so much time in phone booths. Ted had an ingenious scam, which he used whenever he had to make a long-distance call. First, he selected a phone booth from a list he kept of those that were well used, so that the coin-slot mechanism was always slightly clapped out. He kept the nails of the thumb and index finger of his right hand extra long. When he dialled a number anywhere in the world and the other end picked up, the call box waited for coins to be deposited before connecting. Ted could grip the edge of a ten-pence coin with the long nails acting as pincers, insert the coin and pull it back, all in a split second. By pumping the same ten-pence pence coin in and out of the slot, he was able to make long calls overseas for free.

One evening in November, I met Leslie Aspin in the Intercontinental Hotel, Park Lane. I'd first encountered him years before, through John Banks' recruitment activities, and he was now working as an arms broker. At the conclusion of our business, he invited me to join him and a friend just around the corner for a drink. I agreed and soon found myself on Park Street, round the back of the Grosvenor House Hotel. The last time I had been here, it wasn't on a social visit. To my surprise, Leslie led the way to the apartment block. Surely it wasn't going to be a case of déjà vu? But indeed it was the same office that I had broken into the previous September. It was let to a Dr Benham Nodjoumi. He wasn't in but I was introduced to his British business manager in his absence. Nodjoumi was enjoying a very interesting, varied and now profitable life. Formerly an officer in the Shah of Iran's secret police force, he had escaped the country in the immediate aftermath of Ayatollah Khomeini's rise to power. He presented himself as a doctor of law (not medicine) who was travelling on business. I asked his colleague about the Iranian's business interests and was informed that he was a commodity broker in foodstuffs and produced a glossy marketing magazine for overseas companies. We had an interesting discussion but it didn't lead anywhere, not that evening, at least.

A week or so later, I received an invitation to drinks at Grosvenor House from Nodjoumi's associate. Leslie had almost certainly briefed him on my background and it seemed that his boss wanted to meet me. First, however, I had to get past the gatekeeper. In the comfort of the hotel bar, I found myself on the receiving end of what amounted to an interview. I felt entitled to pose a question or two about the man who was seeking to engage my services. I was not surprised (although entertained nevertheless) to learn that Benham Nodjoumi was so crooked he probably couldn't lie in bed straight. I heard the story behind the banker's draft with all the commas and noughts, neglecting to mention that I had seen it myself. For that job, which netted Nodjoumi a small fortune, he had been in partnership with a Pakistani family shipping business that had its own reputation for irregularity. Nodjoumi had signed a contract to supply a huge quantity of grain to the Republic of Iran. He undercut his rivals on price because he had a profit-making ace up his sleeve. He expertly manipulated the idiosyncrasies of the international shipping market and the fact that banks are only ever interested in paper and numbers, not grain or, as it would transpire, beef.

Most international trade payments are based upon letters of credit, payable by the bank against sets of documentation that purport to be evidence that the goods described have been shipped or are aboard ship. A bank is duty bound to pay the beneficiary of the letter of credit on sight of the documents listed in the letter, without seeing the actual goods, which can take months to reach their destination once shipped. A fraudster would be able to present faked documents that met the required criteria, having registered his company in an offshore haven with nominee directors who would be unlikely to have met him and would never hear from him again once the transaction had been concluded. The money would be moved through numerous offshore accounts, siphoned off or converted along the way to hide its origin.

Nodjoumi's grain scam, however, had worked on a different principle. The fixed penalty for every additional day a ship is delayed in port that is not the fault of the ship's captain is called demurrage. In this case, the buyer – the Iranian government – was liable to pay demurrage for any delay in the unloading of the ship. The contract between buyer and seller of the cargo made clear the agreed time period for the massive quantity of grain to be offloaded once it reached Iran. Nodjoumi's partner in crime was a corrupt shipping company. It chartered one of the world's largest bulk grain carriers. The ship duly arrived at the Iranian port but there was one small problem: the harbour was too narrow and the water too shallow for the carrier to dock. It had to be anchored offshore in deeper waters. The grain, which should have been industrially sucked from the belly of the ship into silos on the dockside, had to be emptied manually. It was bagged at sea and loaded onto barges, which were towed ashore. Given that Nodjoumi stood to collect a cut of the $25,000 per day demurrage, this was hardly a setback. The ship was still anchored off Iran nearly 12 months after it had been due to depart. Nodjoumi might not have made much of a profit on the grain but demurrage payments amounted to many millions of dollars.

Several days after my interview, I had lunch with Dr Benham Nodjoumi in the restaurant at Grosvenor House. He was of medium height, slim with olive skin, black hair, delicate features and a weak chin. Benham spoke perfect English, with only a hint of accent. He was an immaculate dresser. His clothes looked very expensive and his overall appearance reeked of money. He had obviously been briefed that I had a working knowledge of explosives; the purpose of the lunch was to explore the possibility of placing a bomb onboard a cargo ship. When I asked what the objective was, he was very open. A company controlled by Nodjoumi had been awarded a contract to supply 3,000 tons of beef to the Iranian Meat Marketing Company. Benham had a documentary letter of credit for $6,000,000 but had no intention of shipping to Iran enough beef to make a sandwich. The documentation to cash the letter of credit would be created and a vessel would be chartered or purchased, ostensibly to carry the meat to Iran. The captain would issue a bill of lading, the most vital piece of documentary evidence required by the bank as proof of shipment. The ship, now containing a cargo of invisible beef, would set sail on its journey. When the ship arrived in ocean water deep enough to prevent insurance investigators from doing their job, a bomb would explode in some part of the vessel, causing it to sink.

Nodjoumi's ruthless nature became clear when I asked him about the fate of the crew. 'Fuck the crew,' was his response. As the whole thing was purely theoretical, I expressed my interest in discussing the matter further when plans were further along. The truth was that, having been a merchant sailor, there was no way I would sacrifice a crew of seamen for a greedy bastard like Benham. However, I left him with the impression that I was prepared to do so. I heard nothing more about the invisible-meat deal for a long time. Months passed during which my time was taken up with other business and with refitting the yacht that I had purchased, *Elim*, at the Lady Bee Marina in Shoreham, Sussex.

Then, in January 1981, Leslie Aspin, who had been working with Nodjoumi, contacted me. I met him at the Holiday Inn, Edgware Road, where he had been staying. This in itself was strange, as before he'd always checked in to Grosvenor House when he wasn't at home in Norwich. When I arrived, he was just leaving to catch a train home. He asked me to go with him, saying he had a proposition that he felt sure would interest me and that I would get paid in advance that day. Curiosity got the better of me and we set off for the train station by black cab. As the cab pulled away from the hotel, Leslie could not resist a bit of one-upmanship. Asking the cabbie to stop, he got out and went over to a new black Mercedes-Benz saloon, opened the door and retrieved some papers from inside. Back in the cab, I asked him whose car the Merc was.

'Mine,' he replied.

'You lucky bastard! You've had a result somewhere.'

'Only a little bit,' said Leslie. 'It's not as nice as my Rolls-Royce,' he added, just to rub it in a bit further.

On the train to Norwich, Leslie brought me up to date on the skulduggery at Grosvenor House and what this latest job offer was about. Not long ago, Benham Nodjoumi had been ready to call me to discuss sinking the ship with its cargo of invisible beef. However, a war had deprived me of the chance to make a decision regarding the plan. Because of that same war, Nodjoumi was on the verge of making millions. The Iran–Iraq War was in full swing and the Iraqi air force was mounting bombing raids on Iran's vital infrastructure. Lloyd's of London had given notice to all shipping companies that vessels travelling to Iranian seaports would not be covered by marine insurance issued by them until further notice. For many, this would mean cancelled contracts. For Nodjoumi's company, the timing was absolutely perfect, as an Iranian bank had issued him with a letter of credit that contained a clause that could be exploited by a clever and determined fraudster.

That clause was 'Trans-shipment allowed'. The cargo was no longer insured to travel directly to Iran by ship and the trans-shipment clause entitled Nodjoumi to choose an alternative route and method of transporting the goods. To receive payment on the letter of credit, he needed only provide documentation stating that the goods had been trans-shipped. As always, the letter of credit required a bill of lading signed and stamped by the ship's captain. What Nodjoumi needed most was a captain or authorised agent of a shipping company who would stamp and sign the bill of lading as 'goods free on board', which would mean that responsibility for the cargo had passed to the shipping line, then sign an addendum stating that the goods had been trans-shipped back off the vessel to some other means of transportation. A small shipping company was duly found. Signing a bill of lading without the goods having been loaded is probably a criminal offence, particularly if it is done knowingly to help perpetrate a fraud. It might, however, have been done in good faith, to save the seller loading and then immediately unloading the cargo, which would be an expensive exercise purely to keep within the letter of the law. At the end of the day, however Nodjoumi managed it, a bill of lading was stamped 'free on board – goods trans-shipped'.

One major hurdle had been jumped, but there were several more to cross before the finishing post. Nodjoumi now had to create the illusion that he had organised alternative transportation for the trans-shipped goods – all 3,000 tons of fresh air. A meat-haulage company registered in Ireland was purchased, as a paper exercise only, of course. This company was supposed to have 150 refrigerated vehicles to move the meat; in fact, it had none. But banks are only interested in paper and as long as the letter of credit was accompanied by the required documents – just pieces of paper, after all – Nodjoumi would get his cash.

The final piece of paper he needed was the halal certificate, stating that the meat came from animals that had been killed in accordance with Muslim law. The letter of credit stated that this was to be presented to the bank, with a copy deposited in the files of Regent's Park Mosque. The Iranian buyers were sending a mullah, a man learned in Islamic theology and sacred law, to make certain that the abattoir that was ostensibly the source of the beef met the required conditions. On inspection day, the mullah set off in a car with three representatives of Benham's company, supposedly to a meat wholesaler in Boston, Lancashire. During stops for refreshment on the long motorway journey, the mullah's drinks were spiked with LSD. Before the inspection team reached halfway, they were heading back to London, with a mullah who now believed he was a butterfly and was trying to fly around in the car.

The mullah was taken to the Water Gardens, a luxury apartment block off the Edgware Road, where he remained, still drugged, with two minders. The halal certificate was found among the mullah's possessions and was stamped and signed, the signature copied from his passport. Meanwhile, in order to throw any investigation that might arise from the non-delivery of the meat off the scent, an Iranian associate of Nodjoumi's took the mullah's passport to a nearby branch of the Crédit Lyonnais, where he opened an account in the other man's name, depositing $25,000 in cash. Now any investigation would discover a corrupt mullah. Before long, a mysterious fire broke out at the mosque in Regent's Park, destroying the records office and disguising the fact that there was no duplicate halal certificate lodged there.

The operation was almost complete. The full complement of required documents was presented at the bank, where some concern was expressed about the fact that the goods had been trans-shipped by road. The bank was reluctant to pay out but, as Nodjoumi pointed out, every condition laid out in the letter of credit had been met. He threatened to take legal action and encashment of the letter was made in his favour. Benham Nodjoumi's company was now the beneficiary of over six million dollars – the cost of the most expensive beef sandwiches never to be eaten in Iran.

The job that Leslie was now offering me, for a sum of money difficult to refuse, was to man Nodjoumi's office at Grosvenor House, which, for obvious reasons, no one wished to go near until the dust settled. I could do as I pleased in the offices and run my affairs from them. All I had to do was fend off any enquiries from Iran. The first week or so was really pleasant – free phone calls, five-star room service, chocolate on the pillow if I stayed the night – but there was bound to be a catch. It came in the shape of a representative of the Iranian Meat Marketing Company. The man arrived at the office one morning with a female interpreter, requesting to see Mr Nodjoumi. I advised him that Nodjoumi was not expected that day. The following day and the day after, the ritual was repeated. Eventually, he decided to sit in the outer reception area for hour after hour waiting for Mr Nodjoumi to return, which, of course, he didn't. In the end, he became very annoyed and demanded to speak with Nodjoumi urgently. I contacted him and told him that this official was getting very irate and was not going away. After a meeting with Nodjoumi, it was time for me to earn my money. I had been briefed on what to say and awaited with trepidation the meat man's next visit.

When he arrived with his interpreter, I invited him into the inner sanctum.

'Mr Nodjoumi will be absent on business for the foreseeable future.'

The guy was furious. 'He must see him. This is a very serious situation,' the interpreter said.

'I am a temporary custodian of this office. But if you explain your problem, I may be able to help you resolve it.'

'He wants to know where 3,000 tons of compensated quarters of beef are, which his company, on behalf of the government of Iran, paid over six million dollars for. These have not arrived in Iran. Where is his beef?' she said.

There was no way to break it gently. However it was worded, it amounted to the same thing: he'd been fucked out of six million dollars. There was no meat. There never had been any meat.

The business of relaying the bad news through the interpreter seemed to me to have something of the comic opera about it. When we got to the bit about 'there never was any meat', the guy shot off his chair, ranting and raving.

'He does not believe it. How can you say this? He will have to call the police.'

All this was bad enough but we hadn't got to the really nasty bit yet. He was quite a big man and, in the state of rage he was in, he might have been a handful to contend with. God only knew what the interpreter thought. She looked more anxious and confused by the second.

'Perhaps he should consider his position,' I said to her. 'Has he signed any documents or contracts for this meat?'

'Yes, of course he has.'

'And he has read these closely?'

'No. He speaks and reads only Farsi. The papers were in English.'

Nodjoumi was a cunning bastard; the next bit was a real peach. 'Some of the documents you signed made you a director and shareholder of the company that stole your six million dollars.'

That took the wind out of his sails. I felt quite sorry for him as he slumped in his chair, looking very pale. Perhaps he was considering his options. Did he fancy living in a colder climate? Would the Revolutionary Guard allow him a last cigarette before they shot him? I never saw him again. I do hope he's all right.

More than two years passed before any investigation into the fraud took place. When it did happen, it was only as a result of the discovery of another fraud, this one involving arms and the kidnapping of six Iranian army officers, for which Benham Nodjoumi was sentenced at the Old Bailey to twenty years' imprisonment. The investigation came to nothing and the meat fraud was a complete success. The Iranian government didn't pursue the matter. The bank knew they'd been screwed, but then it wasn't their money anyway.

CHAPTER 16

MAD DOGS AND ENGLISHMEN

AS 1980 DREW TO A CLOSE, I WAS BEGINNING TO FEEL A LITTLE more optimistic about the arms business. In December, I had a meeting with two men: John Miley, a senior officer in the US Defense Intelligence Agency (DIA), and Captain Loftur Johannesson, an Iceland-born pilot. Both of these gentlemen worked as consultants for a company called Aviation Finance & Services, a front for covert DIA operations, which had its offices at Roebuck House, Victoria. The object of our meeting was to discuss the acquisition of SA-7 Strella M2 surface-to-air missiles, better known as SAM-7s. They had purchased SAM-7s before. Philip Sessarego, a former British soldier also known as Tom Carew, had been the loadmaster on board the plane that had carried the previous consignment to its final destination. That shipment had been purchased from Kintex, Bulgaria's state-owned arms-trading company. According to the flight plan and all other documents, the cargo was destined for Tripoli, Libya. In fact, the plane had flown to a US airbase in Germany and then on to Parachinar, Pakistan, where the missiles were given to mujahideen fighters resisting the Soviet occupation of Afghanistan.

DIRTY COMBAT

The United States was not motivated by altruism in offering these gifts of arms to the Afghans. The last thing the US wanted was a quick victory for either side. The Soviet Union was slowly sinking into a financial quagmire as it poured more and more resources into the fight and the Americans wanted to help the resistance to hold out as long as possible. Another object the Americans had in mind was gaining intelligence on Russian armaments. The Soviet military was using Afghanistan as a proving ground for a whole range of new weapons but the US Congress would not authorise a covert operation into Pakistan or Afghanistan to satisfy the US military's desire to acquire samples of these armaments. The solution was clandestine operations using foreign personnel as 'deniable assets' in case a mission should go tits up. Any such operation would require the blessing of the mujahideen, the two most accessible groups of whom were at that time the Jamiat-e Islami and the Hezbi Islami. The quid pro quo would be a supply of arms and ammunition, in particular SAM-7 anti-aircraft missiles.

Sessarego and several other mercenaries from the Hereford area had already been to Peshawar, in the North-West Frontier Province, to meet with mujahideen leaders and set up a training camp. The camp was not a success. The British instructor came down with hepatitis, jaundice and malaria. The muj had their own ideas and formal military training was definitely not on their agenda. The SAM-7 has a pistol-grip launcher that contains a battery for the weapon's infrared heat seeker and gyroscope. The soldiers had great fun trying to lock on to birds or other objects in dry-run training but ran the batteries flat. The object in supplying this weapon in the first place was to enable the guerrillas to shoot down the Soviet helicopter gunship Mi-24 Hind-D, which was high on the Pentagon's shopping list. The Americans were keen to get hold of any parts that could be recovered from a crash.

The Pakistani government, meanwhile, was becoming increasingly nervous about the whole operation. They had initially turned a blind eye to the Americans and their people, even assisted to a limited degree, but they knew the Soviets could not have been unaware of the operation and it wasn't long before the Pakistanis decided that it could lead to embarrassing exposure for them if anyone was captured across the border or snatched in Pakistan. After several cross-border trips, one of the team was held under house arrest in Islamabad and deported. This was the liaison officer from Roebuck House, who happened to be a knight of the realm and was therefore treated with some respect. The instructor who had been training the Jamiat-e Islami was now attached to a saline drip in a hotel room in Peshawar.

It appeared the operation was a risk too far for Washington and they pulled the plug on their involvement. There is an unwritten code of ethics in the intelligence world designed to give a limited modicum of protection to agents in the field. Superpowers play the 'exchange game' to recover their compromised assets. The Roebuck House outfit, using mercenaries to scavenge the Hindu Kush of Afghanistan and the Tribal Areas of Pakistan for Soviet weaponry, would not come under these rules, unwritten or not. In February 1981, Philip Sessarego and I flew to Washington DC for a meeting with DIA officers at the Pentagon in an attempt to get support for continued operations in Afghanistan. We didn't get it; we were on our own. However, we were told that items of equipment recovered from any independent operations would be negotiated for – 'unofficially', of course. It didn't really make a lot of difference to us; we understood that if things went pear-shaped, the US agencies would probably not have intervened to help us anyway.

With Sessarego and an ex-SAS trooper known by the nickname 'Paddy', I flew to Islamabad, travelling on to Peshawar, where we checked into Dean's Hotel. The place had the basic amenities required for civilised living but it wouldn't have got too many stars, that was for sure. Peshawar was a nice place if you liked exhaust fumes, dust and constant noise from the horns of trucks, buses and three-wheeled motorised rickshaws. It had atmosphere, though; it was reminiscent of the American Old West. In many ways, that was hardly surprising; it was a wild western frontier, after all, with the cowboys replaced by gun-toting warriors from over the border. The hotel was home to an assortment of Europeans, none of whom looked much like tourists. It was pointless asking even casually what anyone was doing there; everyone lied anyway. If anyone had asked what my business was, I was carrying letters of introduction from a London-based Pakistani with business interests in Karachi, where I was supposed to be negotiating a textile deal. But what's a thousand miles between liars?

War brings all sorts of people to the periphery of battle zones and although Peshawar was just another dust-blown spot at the arse end of nowhere, it was full of journalists, spies, photographers, charity workers, arms dealers and mercenaries. One of the more unusual characters was 'Airplane Annie', a platinum-blonde schoolteacher from New Orleans. She spent her time doing the rounds of the Afghan resistance groups looking for her English husband. It was from his business that her nickname derived. He was an aeronautical engineer who had offered his services to the mujahideen. He was convinced that he could help end Soviet domination of Afghanistan's skies by building the mujahideen a fleet of remote-controlled model aeroplanes designed to carry an explosive charge that would explode on impact or be detonated from afar. One group supplied him with funds and he was able to produce very fast and manoeuvrable model planes, some with six-foot wingspans. The models worked well in trials but the concept was never put to the test in the field. Peshawar had its share of spies and agents for the Soviets. Annie's husband had left Green's Hotel one morning in October 1980 and had not been seen since.

The next couple of weeks in Peshawar were taken up with a round of meetings with various mujahideen commanders, including Gulbuddin Hekmatyar, the leader of the Hezbi Islami. It was a frustrating period, as much of the time was spent waiting around for these guys, who had no apparent concept of time. Their propaganda bulletins were outrageous. If their claims had been true, the war would have been over very quickly. They would tell of brave mujahideen of Hezbi Islami who had attacked some Soviet military base, listing Russian casualties and military equipment destroyed. This might read: '22 tanks, 18 armoured cars, 7 helicopter gunships, 3 attack aircraft, 3,000 Soviet troops and 1,200 Afghan government soldiers killed.' The downside of this battle would be that two mujahideen had been martyred. I enquired of the mujahideen how these kill rates were achieved and was told that they based them on the approximate number of rounds of ammunition they had fired. This logic escaped me but it seemed that the rationale was that when a muj fired his rifle, Allah guided the bullet. With that kind of help, they couldn't fail to win the war – which, eventually, they did. I remember meeting Hezbi Islami's best 'tank destroyer', who was also their finest rifle shot. Further probing about the methods he used to destroy the tanks made me regret having asked. He told me he would shoot down the barrel of the tank's main gun, hitting the fuse of the shell, exploding it and thus destroying the tank. This was clearly more ridiculous propaganda. There was no way the fuse of a tank shell, a sophisticated piece of equipment, could have been detonated in this manner. The resistance groups' photographic propaganda was just as far-fetched. Both the Hezbi and the Jamiat-e had shown me photographs of downed helicopters with their fighters posing by the wreckage. But while there were different groups in the various pictures, the helicopter was the same one.

We were getting nowhere fast. The Hezbi would not allow us to cross the border with them now that the DIA had removed the promised supply of arms from the equation. They knew that the USA were interested in certain pieces of military equipment and were not about to let us scavenge for free. On 6 March, Sessarego met a Pakistani intelligence agent at the Holiday Inn, Islamabad, to try to get some local support for our venture. Late that evening in Peshawar, Paddy and I received a call from him saying he had been arrested and was being deported. He had been ordered to tell his associates to come to Islamabad or they would be arrested in Peshawar. According to Philip, they had Paddy's name but not mine. I decided to stay on and take my chances. Paddy headed for Islamabad and deportation.

Armed with the Yanks' wish list of goodies, I headed for the Tribal Areas, a region of the country only nominally controlled by the government. About 40 km south of Peshawar, the road passed between two oil drums and a bored-looking policeman lowered the chain strung between them. A faded notice gave warning that this point marked the perimeter of the area governed by Pakistani law. Anyone passing beyond here did so at their own risk. This region, on the border with Afghanistan, was, and probably remains, the largest inhabited area on earth that is beyond the authority of any government. It is home to the warlike Pashtun, who recognise no law but the Koran and Pashtunwali, a code of ethics and behaviour promoting hospitality and love but also revenge. A Pashtun must defend his land and his honour; a wrong must be avenged even if one thousand years have passed since its commission.

I was headed for Darra, perhaps the only town in the world devoted to the manufacture and sale of arms. It had only one street worthy of the name, about three-quarters of a mile long with small dusty alleys running off it, bustling with traders, trucks and camel trains loaded with goods. Sheep wandered loose against a backdrop of sandstone hills and the rattle and crack of gunfire added another note to the cacophony of noise and colour. Stores were single-storey, windowless, with open fronts and gaudily painted with the proprietor's name. Crude drawings of guns and bullets denoted their wares. These stores, none larger than a family garage, were crammed with every conceivable type of small arm. They were mostly copies of the originals, made from inferior-quality metals, but they weren't recognisable as such until you picked them up and felt the difference in weight. All the weapons were fully functional, although how accurately and for how long remained to be seen. The shelves packed with explosives and detonators would have given a health-and-safety officer a heart attack.

In small side-street workshops with basic tools, men forged and fabricated the weapons, while young boys learned the trade they would pass on in turn to their sons. Once-fired ammunition cartridges were re-primed and loaded with spoons of cordite by children not yet in their teens. Those who didn't have a workbench improvised by digging a short, narrow trench in the earth and sitting with their legs in the hole so that the ground itself became their workbench. Short chunks of railway line were used as anvils to hammer and shape the guns' working parts, while wood carvers fashioned the butts and stocks. Original guns could be bought as well, although, of course, the price was higher. The AK-47 Kalashnikov, the weapon of choice for most, was in evidence everywhere. Heavier weapons were also available; parked out the back of the stores were artillery pieces and mortars. There was a ZU-23 anti-aircraft gun at the rear of one store, which must have been fun for someone to smuggle over the border.

Day after day, I trawled the dealers searching for the items on the shopping list until I was sick of drinking the over-sweet tea and trying to explain what was required. The main priorities were the AGS-30 30-mm grenade launcher and the AK-74 rifle, along with any generic variants and a supply of its 5.45-mm, 39-calibre ammunition. Most of the dealers had never seen an AK-74 or they would have copied it in inside a week. Finally, I met two tribesmen who knew what I wanted. Haji Gul and his brother Haji Baz Gul actually recognised the difference between the AK-47 and the AK-74 and told me that they would try to obtain one from their mujahideen suppliers. Unlike its sister the AK-74, named for the year in which it was designed, had never been issued as a standard weapon to Soviet troops; it was only in service with Soviet special forces in Afghanistan. A sharp-eyed Western intelligence agent at a military parade in Moscow had spotted the subtle difference between the AK-74 and its better-known counterpart. Only one had so far been acquired by the Roebuck House operation, at a cost of millions of dollars. The Americans wanted more.

There were numerous other items on the shopping list, including gas-mask filters and atropine sets used to defend against chemical weapons. Other items in demand were a section of cockpit windshield, instrument panels and optical sensors from the Mi-24 Hind-D helicopter gunship, which the Russians would go to extraordinary lengths to protect. The muj had no chance of shooting one down and all evidence of any crashes was quickly removed from prying eyes or destroyed by bombing.

One item on my shopping list that was potentially more accessible was flechettes – steel darts dispensed in their thousands from air-dropped anti-personnel bombs, as indiscriminate a weapon as you could think of. Scouring the battlefields of Afghanistan was both impractical and highly dangerous, so I headed for the nearest Afghan surgical hospital. An appointment was made with the administrator of the hospital, who was given to understand that I was a photojournalist interested in the types of injury the hospital had to contend with as a result of Soviet aggression waged against the Afghan people. When I arrived at the hospital, a surgeon gave me the guided tour and a graphic description of each patient's injuries.

The stories were terrible. Many patients were victims of mines, the children in particular, some of whom had picked up a butterfly mine, easily mistaken for a toy. There were frostbite victims, now amputees, who had been so desperate to get away from the war or to join in the fighting that they had attempted mountain crossings in sub-zero temperatures. Everyone wanted their picture taken, for the world to see what the Russians were inflicting on them. To my surprise and despite my protestations, a photo shoot was organised, with all the walking wounded instructed to line up on their crutches in the back yard. One poor sod had a tube draining out of his side, running into an old sweet jar held by another patient.

I described the flechettes and, while the surgeon had removed many, the only ones in the hospital at that time were inside a patient. When I explained to the bedridden victim that my quest was to show the world the Afghans' suffering, he demanded to be cut open on the spot without anaesthetic so that I could go away with the evidence. I refused this fanatical offer and told him I would return after he had been under the knife.

On my return to Darra, things suddenly got better. Haji produced an AK-74, along with its bigger brother, the RPK light machine gun, which used the same ammunition. At first sight, the AK-74 appears almost identical to the AK-47, and in most respects it is. The only feature that is obviously different is the end of the barrel, which has what appears to be a flash hider attached. This addition is in fact a muzzle brake, which I had never seen on a rifle before but which was common in artillery and tank guns, acting to compensate for the recoil by reverse deflection of muzzle gases from the barrel. The magazine was made of plastic rather than metal pressings and longer than that of the AK-47, capable of containing 40 rounds instead of 30, an advantage that any soldier would appreciate in a firefight. The ammunition was markedly different in size; instead of the chunky 7.62-mm round, the AK-74 used the 5.45 mm, which was long, slim and designed to cause the maximum amount of tissue damage that a projectile of its size could inflict. If that little bastard hit you in the arm, it would probably amputate it.

Now it was time to drink lots of tea and haggle over price, which was eventually fixed at a horrendous $6,000 for the two units, with the proviso that Haji would also get me an AGS-30 grenade launcher for $15,000. All that remained now was to get in touch with Sessarego or another of the Roebuck House mob and set about making a profit. When I finally got back to Peshawar, I found that Sessarego had come back as someone else. Having adopted a new name, he was now sharing my room, as he couldn't check in under another passport since everyone in Peshawar knew his previous identity.

Just when it seemed as if things were going to work out, life dumped on me again when the bullshit brigade turned up. A group of wannabe British mercenaries arrived in Islamabad, the forerunners, they said, of a set-up of 75 men calling themselves the Essex Paramilitary Special Forces. The Russians must have pissed their pants laughing. Discretion and operational security were obviously not on their training syllabus. The first place they visited was the American Club in Islamabad, where, after a few drinks, they held a press conference. The commandant of this group claimed on Russian and East German radio stations to have killed Russian and Cuban soldiers in Angola and to have served with Mike Hoare's notorious 5 Commando mercenaries in the Congo in the '60s. The guy was obviously a compassionate man, as he said he had left the (non-existent) 'Rhodesian Foreign Legion' because he had been expected to kill kids. The group announced that they had come to 'kill Russians' with 'M66 shoulder-fired surface-to-air missiles'. I expect the Russian pilots were thumbing through their missile lists and scratching their heads, as no such weapon existed.

The papers and radio carried the story to the Khyber Pass and beyond. After that, I suppose it was bound to happen: the next morning, the men in dark glasses came knocking on my door. Pakistani Special Branch very politely requested that I pack my bag and go with them. With Sessarego hiding behind the shower curtain, I did as requested. At their headquarters, the commanding officer told me that he had orders to deport me. He was very apologetic about the whole affair. My claim to be a tourist raised a smile from him and he told me that he knew why I was there.

With a two-cop escort, I was taken to Peshawar bus station. It was jammed with people, some with livestock, and, feeling my dignity was now at stake, I informed the cops that I was not getting on a bus to be deported. Having arrived by car, I expected to leave in the same way. This caused minor pandemonium, lots of shouting between cops and waiting travellers, who were presumably being told the story so far. A small riot appeared to be developing but this was narrowly averted when a police Land Rover was requested and, dignity intact, we headed for Islamabad.

The escort and driver were very polite. None spoke English but they smiled a lot and showed no hostility towards me. We stopped occasionally for refreshments at roadside eateries and to show my appreciation I paid each time. On arrival in Islamabad, I was taken to a small police station somewhere in the suburbs, handed over and signed for before my escorts departed. My detention seemed a very informal affair. Two police officers armed with old 303 Lee–Enfield rifles sat opposite me in what appeared to be the main room of the station, with an open door that led to the street. A small crowd of local residents and children gathered outside, all wanting to see this foreigner under arrest. This performance went on for some time, until, getting very bored, I requested to know why the procedure was taking so long. An English-speaking officer showed up and told me that the papers had only deported me from the North-West Frontier Province to Islamabad. They were now awaiting further documentation advising them what the next step was.

Things don't move very fast in Pakistan, so I asked that they take me to a hotel where I could clean up. Several hours later, however, nothing had happened and my patience was wearing thin. The brain went into neutral and the mouth went into overdrive. I told all and sundry that this was no way to treat a visitor to their country. I didn't suppose anyone understood what I was saying, so I got up and walked out into the street. This got their attention very quickly; the poor sods with the 303s came hurtling out of the door after me. They got in front of me and were walking backwards with their rifles half-heartedly raised, pointing at knee level. This comic scene carried on for a while, with all the people on the street joining in the parade.

Having now got their attention, I decided it was time to stop, just in case the shouts from the crowd were 'shoot him'. Reversing tracks, we headed back to the police station, with me still ranting at the cops. By the looks on their faces, they hadn't a clue what the madman was saying. Back inside, the English speaker informed me that the delay had been caused by difficulties getting me a flight out of Pakistan. Having read a load of legal bullshit, he told me that the documentation ordered them to put me on the first available flight out of the country. This should have made me feel a lot better, but life is a real bitch at times, and when he told me that this meant I was being deported to Jordan, I hit the fucking roof. I explained that my return ticket was to London on a British Airways flight and that that was the only flight I would leave on. I said that if they put me on the flight to Jordan, I would hijack the plane and crash it into Islamabad. Many phone calls later, another decision was made. As it was now nearly midnight and the flight to London had departed, I would be taken to the local prison to await the next departure. Once again, I'd managed to talk myself into prison. It was Monday and the next flight wasn't till Friday.

Next stop was jail. The prison governor was awoken from his bed and I was taken into his personal living quarters for more paper signing. The governor was an absolute gentleman, ordering his houseboy to make me bacon, eggs and toast with a pot of tea while he sorted out my accommodation for the next few days. After I'd eaten, he told me that he'd cleared a cell so that I had it to myself and that he didn't believe for one moment that I was a spy. My home for the next few days was a cell with barred door leading to a long outdoor courtyard. It was about ten feet by ten feet and had a very high ceiling with a barred grille set into it allowing a view of the sky. There was no furniture of any description. The bed was a pile of filthy, smelly remnants of old blankets lying on the floor. The toilet was a corner with a three-foot-high breeze-block partition behind which was a bucket of water and a hole in the ground, presumably leading to a sewage pipe. To compensate for the smell there was a holder attached to the wall in which joss sticks were burned. My cell door had an integral lock, which was apparently insufficient for a spy of my calibre, as a thick chain and padlock were added. Two chairs were positioned opposite my cell and guards with 303 rifles were ordered to sit and make sure I didn't disappear.

The governor came to see me the next day and asked if I would like to eat something. Fearing the hygiene standards in the prison kitchen, I requested only hard-boiled eggs and oranges. The houseboy brought me a regular supply of coffee, delivered in an attractive silver pot on a tray with a bone-china cup and saucer. No one seemed to have the authority to open my cell door, so I sat cross-legged at the bars, put the cup sideways to enable it to pass through and poured the coffee from the pot outside in through the bars. There was nothing to break the monotony, only the odd sparrow that would come in from the ceiling grille and then get in a panic to escape again.

Friday eventually came and I was given a bucket of water to wash with. In the evening, I was taken with two Land Rovers full of cops to the airport. Seated in the airport terminal surrounded by police, I attracted the attention of the other passengers, including small children who wandered up to me to scrutinise my tattoos. The police were very friendly and throughout the experience I was treated with courtesy and respect. Should you ever get arrested abroad and thrown in prison, I would recommend Pakistan.

The airport shuttle bus took my police entourage and me to the steps of the aircraft. I was the only passenger on the bus; I felt like Carlos the Jackal. My passport was handed to the aircraft purser with instructions to give it to the authorities in London. After take-off, I growled a bit at the purser and told him he shouldn't take orders from a Pakistani regarding my property. He promptly gave it back to me. There was no problem at customs or passport control at Heathrow. The press were trying to find me but they must have discounted the smelly, scruffy bastard who walked out of arrivals – obviously not their idea of what a mercenary should look like. One astute bugger from the *Sunday Times* did get me as I left the terminal.

Sessarego returned a few days later, very pissed off with the Essex Paramilitary Special Forces for making the North-West Frontier a no-go zone for us. He was not exactly enamoured of the Americans at this point either and decided, very unwisely in my view, to earn a few dollars by exposing the operation through the news media. This did not go down well in London or Washington. The revelations, with supporting documentation, showed that weapons, ammunition and rockets had been transported concealed in baggage on commercial aircraft. They had been cleared through British customs with the assistance of MI6 and, after evaluation by British experts, had been turned around and transported to America on commercial Pan Am flights.

This exposure did not suit my agenda. As far as I was concerned, there was still an opportunity to salvage something of my credibility and make a profit. I headed back to Pakistan. Prior to my ignominious exit from the country, I had arranged a collection date with Haji for an AGS 30-mm grenade launcher. Disguised in a baseball cap and dark glasses, I sailed through the formalities at the airport without a hitch. But luck was about to elude me again. I met with Haji and he gave me another cup of tea and berated me for being late before advising me that the AGS launcher had been 'sold to my friend'! As Sessarego had not mentioned any purchase of this weapon, I asked for a description of the buyer. I was told that he was an Englishman. I requested a name if he had one and Haji produced a business card. You know, sometimes you wonder if you should change your profession. It seemed this game was full of devious people. The buyer of 'my' AGS-30 was the British Embassy. Well, you win some and you lose some; at least the thing found a good home. I went back to my desk in Mayfair, where I was certain another deal or adventure would be lurking around the corner looking for me.

CHAPTER 17

AGENTS PROVOCATEURS

BY SPRING OF 1981, I WAS BACK IN THE GROSVENOR HOUSE HOTEL
apartments. A businessman had visited me while I had been acting as
caretaker of Benham Nodjoumi's offices and had been impressed with
the facilities. He had suggested a speculative deal whereby he would
sponsor an office if I would operate from it and I was now ensconced
in Suite 52, Grosvenor House. The situation was very flexible and
it allowed me to come and go at will, freelancing my way around
the arms and security circuit, acting as a consultant for others who
required my services.

The problem in the defence-equipment business is that you cannot
sell anything to anyone who doesn't want to buy it in the first place.
The arms market is as much about who you know as what you know.
With this in mind, the principal remit of our new company, Euro-
Gulf Trading, was selling more ordinary commodities such as rice,
textiles and anything that was sought after in places such as Ghana,
Nigeria and Sierra Leone. This put the company in touch with
overseas government purchasing agents, who often requested that we
quote for military equipment. In my correspondence with numerous
weapons and munitions manufacturers, I explained our situation and
the new approach brought rapid results.

DIRTY COMBAT

To be in the arms trade as a broker, you must have certain assets and attributes, the first being enough money to sustain yourself through long periods of drought. Secondly, you need the patience of a saint, as negotiations can be extremely protracted. As the defence business in general deals in very large sums of money, the profits and commissions can be very high but the cost of arriving at such success can also be great. Travel and hospitality costs can be significant, as it is essential in most cases that the broker has met the buyer's agent in person. The agent may visit you. This will usually be at your expense and will not be cheap, as he will sometimes bring others with him, maybe even his family. Transport must be laid on for the visitors, as well as private apartments or five-star hotels. Money will be given to their wives or girlfriends for a shopping trip to Harrods or the like. Woolworths will definitely be out of the question. Your overseas guests may have limited knowledge of and interest in London's tourist attractions but they will be fully conversant with Louis Vuitton, Cartier and other such emporiums. If your visitors are unaccompanied by wives or girlfriends, then you may be expected to provide pretty ladies on top of everything else.

Getting the right deals was not always easy, either. While the government of Nigeria, say, might spend over a billion dollars on defence every year, a major portion of that would be used to buy aircraft or armoured vehicles. Items such as these were not in the province of a broker like me because this type of weaponry is monitored very closely by the governments whose defence industries offer to sell such equipment. Certain equipment, if sold to a particular country, might create a significant military imbalance in a region and the sale of such items will be undertaken on a government-to-government basis, perhaps requiring approval by the countries' politicians. At this level, there are few opportunities for the small broker; the big players will always win such contracts. What's more, a tank or aircraft may stay in service for years if not damaged or destroyed in war but ammunition and small arms are a constant 'consumable' requirement. Even in peacetime, vast quantities of munitions are expended in training and on live-fire exercises. These are the bread and butter of the arms broker. If a country is at war and/or embargoed, the competition gets hotter and the risks get greater but the potential profits gets bigger, too.

If you're a small fish in a big pond, perseverance and the ability to stay afloat financially when others around sink can pay dividends. One such success for me came out of adversity suffered by two other British brokers, who were seeking weapons for the embargoed regime of South Africa. John Parks and Peter Towers had combined their talents and connections after Peter, a former purchasing director for a naval shipbuilders, left that position when the company was nationalised. He teamed up with Parks, an entrepreneur, and they started by selling Land Rovers to African countries. Towers had good contacts in the arms industry, in particular with Oerlikon and Bofors, whose guns were used on many naval vessels. The two were reasonably successful in their endeavours and were approached by agents of Armscor, the South African Defence Force manufacturing and purchasing agency. They were looking for the right connections to help them to purchase weapons for South Africa's military, which was fighting a counter-insurgency war against guerrillas on the border with Angola. A UN embargo on selling weapons and munitions to South Africa's apartheid regime was in place. The country's arms-manufacturing industry was self-sufficient as far as basic ammunition went but many items still had to be sourced from outside its borders.

In the course of a successful early start in their alliance with Armscor, Parks and Towers were given a shopping list of weapons that were of US manufacture. The list named various models of handguns, ammunition, M16 assault rifles and M203 grenade launchers. In the grey world of arms brokers, there were many who would promise much and deliver little. When a confirmed buyer with real money was on the loose and word got out, everyone wanted to be the supplier. Peter Towers and John Parks had proof of funds – the magic wand that would convince a potential seller that they were for real. The downside was that the weapons they required were manufactured in the USA. In most countries, particularly the Warsaw Pact nations, which were desperate at that time to earn hard currency, it was possible, with enough money, the right connections and a false 'end-user certificate' (EUC) to satisfy the export-licensing authorities, to achieve a great deal. However, this did not apply to the United States. Many who did not fully understand the US government's arms-export verification system had fallen foul of it and ended up in prison. Several dealers and brokers were passing Parks' and Towers' requirements around, trying to resolve the issue, but, with no legitimate EUC, most were either afraid to touch it or couldn't produce proof that they could fulfil the requirement. The deal had passed over my desk and I'd had several meetings with Parks and Towers but I could not resolve the situation. Then they found the solution to their problem, or so it seemed.

They were introduced to two arms brokers from Texas, Gary Howard and Ray 'Ronnie' Tucker, who claimed they could deliver the goods. They impressed everyone with their background – among other adventures, they had been US border guards, patrolling the US–Mexico frontier – and their knowledge of the equipment. They were not, however, all they professed to be, or, rather they were something more. The two men were in fact informers for US customs – snitches, in other words. It is bad enough to come up against undercover agents trying to prevent illegal shipments of arms but it was real bad luck to find a pair like them. As far as I was concerned, they were not trying to save the world from the effects of weapons of death; they just saw an opportunity to make money.

The prices they offered for the goods were competitive, so Peter Towers flew to the USA for further negotiations with the supposed dealers. This trip was not strictly necessary but it was insisted on because Howard and Tucker wanted Towers to commit a federal offence on US soil. In a hotel room fitted out with covert cameras and recording equipment, courtesy of the technical-support unit of US customs, negotiations were repeated and duly recorded. Transport arrangements were made by Parks and Towers, the funds were transferred to a company operated by Howard and Tucker, and inspection of the equipment at the point of aircraft loading was agreed upon.

John Parks brought me up to date with the situation before he joined Towers in Houston for the weapons inspection. I told him that it was a very bad idea and they were taking a big risk – the deal did not smell right. On the evening of 12 May, Parks and Towers went to Houston airport to meet with the crew of a Boeing 707 cargo jet.

Servotech, a company controlled by them, registered in Liechtenstein and Khartoum, Sudan, had chartered the plane to fly the consignment to South Africa. The flight plan registered with the Federal Aviation Authority gave the destination as Khartoum. Two semi-trailer trucks arrived from the Colt arms factory in Hartford, Connecticut, loaded with cases containing 2,200 guns and grenade launchers. Parks and Towers boarded the trucks to check the cargo. Suddenly, much to their surprise, all the aircraft maintenance staff and truck drivers turned into federal agents and customs officers, all pointing guns at them and the crew. Meanwhile, the two Texas cowboys did a quick runner.

Charged with 26 counts of conspiracy, false documentation and violation of the Neutrality Act, Parks and Towers were remanded in custody unless they could post bail of $5,000,000 each. Parks' tearful wife called to tell me what had happened, having received most of her information through the news media. I made enquiries as to who had made the introductions between the British brokers and the Texans. It turned out that the referee for the bounty hunters was Mike Comber, former secretary of KMS Ltd, often referred to as 24 SAS (21, 22 and 23 are the regiments that make up the real SAS), a security company linked with former special-forces and SAS personnel, which had been contracted to quell rebels in the Dhofar region of Oman for Sultan Qaboos in the '70s. I arranged a meeting with Comber and asked him bluntly whose side he would be on when the case came to court. There was no need to growl at Mike Comber, however. He was mortified at having made the introduction based on a casual acquaintance with Howard and Tucker. He turned out to be a nice guy and could not have been more helpful in the days and months ahead.

Shortly after their arrest, Parks and Towers made another court appearance, during which, to the annoyance of the prosecutor, they posted bail. There was furious objection to this and the District Attorney's office demanded to know where the bail money had come from. Their defence attorney told the court that he did not know and that it had appeared in his account the day before. As bail terms had been met, the defendants were back out on the street, although they were confined to the United States until their trial.

DIRTY COMBAT

On 26 August, I flew to Houston to meet with Parks, Towers and their legal team to see if I could help. Comber had agreed to give evidence for the defence. As Howard and Tucker had presented the deal to him, it was a legitimate authorised sale. The problem was that Michael was adamant that he would not travel to the United States. Depositions sworn under oath were not permissible unless taken on US territory, where the prosecution would have the opportunity to cross-examine the witness. This problem was resolved when the defence team argued that a hearing could be held in the American Embassy in London, classified as US territory. Many of the 26 counts in the indictment revolved around the use of false documentation to obtain an export licence from the US Department of Defense. Because I had a good knowledge of the subject, the defendants' team took me on board as a 'technical consultant' for the hearing at the US Embassy in London.

On 4 September, I travelled to Houston again for further discussions regarding the case. On my previous visit, I had had no problems with customs or immigration at the airport. This trip did not go quite so smoothly. At the passport desk, I knew straight away that I'd been flagged up as a potential problem. The computer operator tried to remain impassive but there were a few warning signs, almost imperceptible, in her demeanour. She let me pass and I proceeded to the point where they ask you if you're carrying any plants or vegetables. As soon as I'd moved on, the woman at the passport desk reached for the phone. Before long, I found myself standing in line at the immigration desk with a bunch of dodgy-looking characters waiting for further vetting.

When my turn came, I was requested to accompany two uniformed officers into a quiet room, where they left me after asking for my briefcase. An hour or more passed. Outside my detention room, which was not locked, I could see the customs and immigration officials reading the contents of my briefcase. These seemed to have created some interest and the officers were animatedly passing documents to each other as they discovered some new titbit. There was nothing in the briefcase that could have got me locked up but it did contain promotional material for various weapons. There were glossy brochures on rifles, grenade launchers and mortar bombs, as well as a copy of a $50,000,000 letter of credit issued by the Iranian Ministry of Defence.

Eventually, the FBI arrived. One of the agents leaned against the wall, reading my passport intently. After a while, he said, 'You have a very interesting passport. It appears that in the last few years you have been to every country where there is a war going on. What is it exactly that you do for a living?'

I told him that I worked for a food commodities company but that in the course of our sales to foreign governments they often requested quotations for military equipment.

'I see,' he replied. 'Guns and butter.'

'Something along those lines,' I said.

They asked me if I'd ever been to Iran. The response was in the negative. Enquiring if I'd been to Iraq got the same reply, with the proviso that I might be going soon. I didn't think I'd get away with saying otherwise, given that one whole page of my passport was taken up with a newly issued visa for Iraq.

They didn't seem to want to know what the purpose of my visit to Texas was. After my briefcase had been X-rayed, my passport was stamped 'Paroled subject to [section] 222 of I&N [Immigration and Nationality] Act'. They wished me an enjoyable stay in Houston. I thought it was about time I got a new passport again.

As I entered the arrivals lounge, I could see John and Peter waiting for me. I walked right past them, not wishing to draw undue attention to our liaison. Try as you might, sometimes you just can't win. In true clandestine fashion, they noisily chased after me as if I hadn't seen them. My concern for their well-being was unnecessary as they had already been given chapter and verse on my detention by other federal agents at the airport. They were now quite famous in Houston as the biggest gunrunners the US had ever captured.

In the autumn of 1981, it was put to me that I might want to continue the project that Parks and Towers had been working on at the time of their arrest. A proposal had been submitted to the parties concerned recommending that the next phase of the procurement operation be under my control. At a meeting with two Armscor agents at Heathrow Airport, they gave me a final vetting and approval to take over where the others had left off. Before I could start, however, I had another appointment to keep.

On October 20, I flew to Baghdad with another arms dealer, who had introduced me to the cultural attaché to the Iraqi Embassy in London. Major Husseini was not really interested in culture of any sort; he was a military-intelligence officer in the Iraqi army. His superiors had a crazy plan they wanted to discuss with me. We passed very indiscreetly through Baghdad's customs and passport control in a phalanx of military and security muscle, which shoved all the queuing passengers out of the way to ensure our entry was dealt with quickly. Our accommodation – a small hotel near the banks of the River Tigris that was usually reserved for army officers – was the only discreet thing about the visit. It was not the best hotel in town by a long shot. Its windows were criss-crossed with tape to protect against a bomb blast in case the Iranian air force ever got that close. Bright-yellow barrage balloons floated above the banks of the Tigris.

Maybe if I had had nothing else in the pipeline, I might have been more enthusiastic about the project but it seemed to me to be downright insane. Two meetings were held with military officers, both late at night in some place where there was lots of security and I had no idea where we were. The basic idea was that cutting off shipping to Iran would severely hurt the enemy's war effort and cause civil unrest when shortages of imported goods took their toll on the populace. Trade had already suffered because of insurance restrictions on vessels sailing to Iranian waters and the Iraqis wanted to put another nail in Iran's coffin. They proposed purchasing a cargo vessel (or vessels) that would contract freight through normal commercial channels to Iranian shipping ports. When the vessel arrived in Iran, it would have to wait its turn to unload in the 'roads' to the harbour along with the other ships. The crew of the vessel would be experienced military divers who would plant limpet mines on the other ships' hulls. When these exploded, the stricken vessels would sink and block the entrance to the harbour. This would not only create considerable chaos, it would deprive Iran of what cargo was still being shipped by sea. I was beginning to get the feeling that my phone number was listed under 'Dick Head' in the directory. No one could give me a satisfactory explanation as to how the sabotage team would get away, so I left them to work it out and returned home.

In the UK, I got back to business with Armscor. I planned to source the weapons they required not from the United States but from South Korea. On 3 November, I travelled to Seoul for negotiations with Golden Bell Trading, the marketing arm of Korea Explosives Company (KEC). When you try to bend the rules in the arms game, nothing is ever easy and this deal wasn't going to be an exception. Everything that could go wrong did. The first problem was that banks do not like to be seen handling money for weapons of war, as it may offend their shareholders and major clients. An arms dealer must therefore perform a balancing act, protecting the purchasing client from fraud while maintaining their anonymity and also satisfying the selling company that the conditions of their government's export-licensing procedure will be met. The bank's letter of credit could not name the goods as what they actually were, which was 100,000 M406 high-explosive grenades. In the end, the goods' description and destination were given as 'agricultural percussion units' to Portugal. The consignee was Berg Nurseries (Pty) Ltd. As far as the bank was concerned, we were purchasing 100,000 bird scarers.

To satisfy the Korean government, the documentation would have to give a precise account of what the goods actually were, so another compromise was reached. In Golden Bell's sales catalogue all the items had a code following a description. In the case of the grenades, this read '40mm HE grenades model K801'. These also have a fuse number of KM777. The description on the documentation read 'Percussion units: Part No. 40MMK801KM777', which was ambiguous but included all the relevant details.

For the end-user certificate, I had to do some creative paperwork. I managed to purchase a copy of an EUC as issued by the Portuguese air force. What the air force would be doing with 40-mm grenades, I could not imagine, so I invented a special Para Commando Unit. A printer produced some outstanding headed paper with the blue air-force logo, complete with HQ address. I purchased a Portuguese-made 'golf ball' component for an IBM typewriter, so that the letter would be written in the correct typeface, and hired a Portuguese interpreter who could type. The finished article was duplicated in English. I had forged the signature of a Brigadier Francisco Jose de Q. de Azevedo e Bourbon from a genuine EUC. I passed the certificate to the Koreans, in the back of a limousine going around Hyde Park Corner, and they seemed very impressed by the signatory's position. The document duly sailed through the export-licensing department.

Several weeks later, I made the return trip to Korea to await our air-freight carrier's arrival and sign off on all the paperwork. The next setback was that we had no plane. The cargo plane that was due to collect was supposed to be flying in from an Oman-based company, who refused the charter at the last moment. I think they lost their bottle. This screwed everything up. A military escort that was scheduled to move the grenades from stores to airport had to be cancelled. I went into damage-limitation mode, talking a load of crap about the carrier being grounded for safety checks. It took several weeks of waiting in the Seoul Plaza Hotel before a new carrier was found and a collection date agreed.

The Koreans were very formal to do business with. Every morning at nine all the many foreign businessmen staying at the hotel would assemble in the hotel lobby to be collected by company cars that would whisk us off to offices for meetings. The KEC offices were open-plan on every floor and only the most senior directors had offices to themselves. Every day at 10 a.m. on the dot, the PA system would squawk and everyone would stand by the side of their desks. Then the tannoy would proceed to guide the workers through five minutes of callisthenic exercises. I felt quite embarrassed by this the first time it happened and wondered whether I was committing some faux pas by not joining in.

At that time, a curfew that had been in operation since the Korean war in the '50s was still in place. No one was allowed to go anywhere between midnight and five in the morning. Once a month, an air-raid drill was held. Seoul was a teeming city, crowded with people constantly on the move, so I was really impressed by how disciplined these millions of people were. The air was suddenly full of the wail of sirens and hotel alarms sounded, along with warnings that guests should draw the curtains and stay clear of the windows. I watched from my window, of course, and was amazed at the transformation, which took less than a minute. Buses and taxis pulled in to the side of the roads and passengers got out and disappeared with pedestrians into the nearest underpass or building. Suddenly, there was no movement down below, as if a wand had been waved and everyone had magically vanished. Several minutes passed during which police sirens were heard, along with the rumble and clatter of tank treads as armoured vehicles moved through the city. The sirens wailed again after 15 minutes to sound the all-clear and the hordes carried on where they left off, on the move again.

Finally, another aircraft was on its way to pick up the cargo. I was going to get to go home at last, or so I thought. I was summoned to a meeting at KEC's offices and introduced to Mr Song and Mr Song, both representatives of Korean Air Lines. At this eleventh hour, I was informed that my inbound aircraft would not be given permission to land and collect its cargo. Korea was very protectionist when it came to its economy and third-party charters were not allowed. Korean Air Lines would quite happily take my cargo to Lisbon for me! I explained that it was too late to change carriers and that the plane was on its way. When I demanded to know why KEC had not advised me of this months ago, I got a humble-apology routine. I explained to the two Songs that this fuck-up would cost me my job and that the people I worked for would do no further business with any Korean company. The Songs took their leave and promised they would look favourably upon my situation and do their best to rectify the matter. Within hours, however, I received a further rejection.

An emergency meeting took place at KEC's offices. There are always difficulties to overcome when conducting business of this kind – if it were easy, everyone would be doing it – but problems are there to be solved and obstacles can usually be circumvented. This, however was not the usual type of problem. Money is the solution to most difficulties but buying off the Korean flag-carrier airline was not really an option. There was one avenue open to us, according to KEC, and this was the Ministry of Aviation; they made the rules and they could change them or make an exception. My hosts and I would appeal to the minister in charge, stressing that national honour and Korea's business reputation were at stake, not to mention several million dollars. A meeting was set up with the junior minister for aviation. We would have to speak to him before we reached the man at the top.

Corruption in Korea is not as blatant as in many other countries but a 'small token of respect' wouldn't go amiss, so the meeting at the ministry was preceded by a shopping expedition. First, I purchased a solid-gold key that cost several thousand dollars, a fancy object that looked similar to the kind you might see decorating a 21st-birthday cake. The next stop was a cake shop, where we bought large bags of traditional cakes and what looked like a giant chocolate Swiss roll. At the ministry, also open plan, the cakes were distributed to all the staff, to bows and nods in my direction; I felt like bloody Santa Claus. We sat down with the junior minister and related our tale of woe. I could not understand a damn word of what was said. I just nodded now and then. After a while, the meeting was adjourned to a more private venue – the staff canteen! In the lift, I saw my golden key discreetly slipped to the minister, wrapped up, appropriately enough, in an airmail envelope. Meeting over, we departed, not before I'd done some grovelling, translated by my associate from KEC.

The following morning, I was instructed to purchase another golden key and told that this time it should be a little larger than the previous one. Rank obviously has its privileges in Korea, too. We were granted an audience with the minister for aviation. I had no clue as to how we were doing but at the end I thanked the minister as if he'd just saved my life. KEC would be advised of the final decision later in the day. I spent the day wandering around Seoul, unable to stand the tension waiting in my room. When I returned to the hotel, the reception desk handed me a message slip. The landing permit had been approved.

The Boeing 707 arrived from its parking place in Tel Aviv; the military escort arrived with the cargo; and then the next hiccup occurred. The 707 was a passenger aircraft with its seats removed, which meant the cargo had to be loaded through the side doors by hand. Also, carpenters had to be found and chipboard fitted throughout the plane to strengthen the floor, as the cargo of 1,390 wooden cases weighed 33,364 kg. While all this was done, an armed security detail surrounded the aircraft, along with the Korean equivalent of the CIA.

When loading was complete, the crew and KEC representatives met in my hotel room to sign off on paperwork. Loading manifest, packing list and commercial invoices were exchanged but one final document needed for the Koreans to cash the letter of credit was not in evidence. The airway bill was absent. The skipper said, 'No one said anything about an airway bill.' This was a critical document that the bank required as proof that the goods had been loaded free on board and were now the responsibility of the purchaser. I replied, 'How can you *not* have an airway bill? You're a fucking airline company.' To which the pilot responded, 'You're fucking joking! Last week, this plane had "Nefertiti Airways" painted on it and was delivering guns to some strip in Uganda. If it rains hard, the registration number'll probably wash off.' This issue was resolved by a visit to the offices of Malaysian Airlines. While engaging staff in airway banter, the flight engineer stole a whole pad of bills. Problem solved. I paid $25,000 for a refuel, said my goodbyes at the airport and went back to my room to wait for a call letting me know that the aircraft's wheels had left the runway.

Several hours went by and the call didn't come. In frustration, I phoned KEC. The flight was delayed; aviation inspectors were saying that a side cockpit window was cracked and there was a typhoon over the South China Sea, so the plane could not fly until it was replaced. What fucking next? At last the phone call came: take-off. For me, it was over: whatever happened now I would get paid. From start to finish, the deal had taken eight months.

In the air, the original manifest documents would be torn up, to be replaced by new ones describing a cargo of oil-drilling equipment for Brazil. This would make the direction of flight seem a bit more convincing for the benefit of customs officials dealt with en route. When the flight engineer arrived home, we went for a night out and he said to me, 'I thought that trip was a secret.'

I replied, 'Well, I never told anyone. Was there a problem?'

He said that there had been no problem per se but they had refuelled at Hong Kong, Mauritius and Namibia before landing in Johannesburg and at each stop, although customs accepted their load manifest without checking the cargo, they were parked as far away from the terminal as possible and surrounded by fire tenders until take-off. Amazing, the pull some people have!

As the year came to an end, I accompanied Parks' and Towers' legal team to Mike Comber's deposition hearing at the US Embassy in Grosvenor Square. The Assistant District Attorney didn't improve his case by his examination of Comber and at the trial in Houston, all charges relating to the documentation were dropped. Parks and Towers pled guilty to violation of the Neutrality Act. They received a $110,000 fine and 5 years' probation and came home.

CHAPTER 18

DEADLY NIGHTSHADE

DURING THE FIRST HALF OF THE 1980S, THROUGH MY WORK IN THE security business, I was presented with a lot of unusual opportunities and met a great many people. Few, however, were as memorable as Monzer al-Kassar. He was a Syrian-born arms dealer known by the sobriquet 'the Prince of Marbella'. The intelligence communities referred to him as 'Deadly Nightshade'. He spoke eight or nine languages, travelled by private Lear jet on a diplomatic passport and had accumulated a colossal fortune by nefarious means. I first encountered him one evening in 1984, over dinner at Danny's Bar in Marbella on the Costa del Sol. Danny's was a steakhouse on the quayside at Puerto Banús, popular with the local glitterati. Danny was Lebanese. He had a very fast Scarab boat moored right out front. Danny welcomed Monzer al-Kassar like a long-lost friend and we were shown upstairs to the best table, with a view over the harbour. The lights were twinkling and yacht rigging was tinkling in the gentle breeze. Danny's buzzed with conversation and laughter; it was a perfect setting for a clandestine meeting. I liked hiding in plain sight.

DIRTY COMBAT

I sat next to Monzer. We were accompanied by Frank Conlan, an arms broker and mutual acquaintance who had first introduced me to Monzer, while already sitting at the table were a number of sophisticated-looking Middle Eastern men. Monzer leaned closer and quietly asked me about the tattoos on my hands. I suspected that Frank had given him the low-down on me, so I admitted I had been in the slammer. I looked at his face, which, with its large nose and fleshy chin, had the appearance of having been sculpted from clay. He certainly didn't seem fazed by the admission.

'Do you know Johnny the Bosh?' he asked.

Johnny was a well-known 'face' in the criminal underworld of the '60s and '70s; he had been able to make a 'twirl', or skeleton key, for just about any high-security lock. 'I know of him,' I said, 'but don't know him personally.'

Monzer rattled off the names of more English criminals.

'How do you know those names?' I asked.

'I was in Brixton Prison for two years on remand, in the maximum-security wing. I got to know quite a few people.' Monzer mimicked a cockney accent and proved his familiarity with rhyming slang. Later, he said I should come to his home for lunch the next day so we could talk some more.

The next day, Frank drove me to Monzer's Renaissance palace, Palacio Mifadil, from Villa Alkassar, another of his homes, where he had put us up. Frank then headed off for the airport. Palacio Mifadil was set in several acres of gardens surrounded by high walls. Two 60-mm mortar tubes decorated the entrance. I stepped through double doors and into a hallway illuminated by a domed skylight. Later, Monzer would show me an article from *Paris Match* magazine on his home, headlined 'The Palace of a Thousand Intrigues'. Over traditional mezze served at an octagonal table in his opulent dining room, I was introduced to Monzer's very attractive wife Raghda, the mother of his two young daughters. She was related to the Syrian president, Hafez al-Assad.

After dinner, we adjourned to the lounge, with its enormous matching three-piece suites and ornamental Moorish figures in turbans and traditional dress, for coffee. Through wide windows hung with drapes I saw a swimming pool in the shape of a four-leaf clover.

238

I stood at the mantelpiece inspecting the family photographs as I waited for Monzer. One picture was of an older gentleman inspecting a parade of guards. He told me that it was his father, who had been a diplomat, being honoured on his retirement.

When we were alone, he asked, 'Who do you know in Israel?'

'No one,' I replied.

'Are you sure?'

'Course I'm sure, why wouldn't I be?' I answered firmly.

'You have Israeli phone numbers in your address book.'

I felt I was being accused of something. 'I think I would know if I knew an Israeli,' I said.

Monzer produced a photocopy of a page that I recognised as being from the address book that I kept in my briefcase, which was always locked.

'Where the fuck did you get that from?'

'From your briefcase. I like to be sure about people who I do business with.'

I knew my briefcase had been locked when we had met for dinner the previous evening. Somebody had opened the combination locks on my case and relocked it again without my knowing.

'Let me see the number,' I said abruptly. Monzer passed me the piece of paper. 'The number doesn't mean anything to me. Why don't you ring it and maybe we'll have a clue?'

I guessed Monzer had probably rung the number already. Nevertheless, he agreed. He listened for a moment before hanging up. 'It is a hotel in Tel Aviv,' he said, giving me an inquisitive look.

'OK, now I know. It's a number Frank gave me some time ago when he was on one of his trips. I've probably never called it, which is why the country code meant nothing to me. And by the way, I don't like people snooping around in my private papers.'

Monzer's apology lacked sincerity but he then told me, 'I have several jobs in mind for you. They should be of interest to you. Can you get a man and woman, a husband and wife, whom you can trust absolutely?'

I considered this for a moment. As a rule, women were only called upon to act in a surveillance capacity. 'I know a couple who are trustworthy but it would depend on what they have to do.'

'I need them to book into a block of apartments in Madrid and live like normal people on a long holiday. They have one objective: to move into another apartment that is currently occupied. They could be there for days, weeks or months but they must get this particular apartment. I will give you the address. OK?'

I nodded. It all sounded pretty straightforward to me at this stage. 'What happens when they get into the new apartment?'

'One step at a time,' Monzer replied.

I flew back to the UK and contacted the two people I had in mind. They weren't married but they knew each other very well. It transpired that Anne and Geoff were both looking for a new challenge and a change of scenery. I was to advise Frank that I needed funds. It appeared that I was a mere subcontractor. I briefed the couple and put them on a flight to Madrid. Their destination was a block called Apartamentos Recoletos. Weeks passed with no new instructions received. My guess was the pair would be required to recover some kind of electronic surveillance equipment. By this time, Anne and Geoff had made friends with the concierge and told him that, as Anne suffered from claustrophobia and was frightened by the lift, she wanted to move to a suite on the ground floor. Eventually the call came: they were in.

I flew to Marbella and told Monzer the good news.

'Tell your husband and wife they should purchase whatever tools they need to dismantle the kitchen units without damaging them. When the units are removed, they will find a hiding place that contains a large black briefcase. If the case is there, they are to remove it and rebuild the units, leaving no trace that they have been tampered with.'

I passed on these instructions and returned to Britain. At a prearranged time the following evening, I was waiting in a phone box for a call from Madrid.

Geoff said, 'We have the item in our possession as described.'

I told him the combinations. 'What I want you to do is open the case. Inside are some items. Please do not describe the items on the phone. Just count the items and tell me the number.' We were playing the game by pre-agreed rules.

'There are five items plus a small bag containing other items.'

'OK. Wait for further instructions.'

I made a phone call from a different booth, received my next set of instructions from Marbella and then called Geoff back. 'You are to check out of the apartment, paying the bills and any surcharge for short-notice cancellation. Make some excuse about someone dying or having an accident. Take a train to Benalmádena on the Costa del Sol. Under no circumstances should you take a plane. When you are checked in to a hotel, phone me at home. I will call you back for the location and meet you there.'

Two days later, I got the call and flew to Spain. I met Geoff and Anne at the Benalmádena Hotel. I opened the case to find three semi-automatic pistols, two revolvers and a brown drawstring bag with dozens of rounds of different calibres. The revolvers were Star stainless-steel .38s. The pistols were a tiny little .25 Baby Browning, a Tokarev 7.62-mm TT-33 and a 9-mm SIG Sauer with a monster of a custom-built silencer attached to the muzzle. I noticed that the serial numbers had been drilled out very professionally. I took possession of these items and left Geoff and Anne to decide whether they wanted to stay in Spain or go home. I took the case to a motel, where I photographed the contents for my own records before heading off to see Monzer. He returned to the motel with me, took possession of the guns and left.

I took it that I had passed Monzer's test. Several days later, we had lunch at Palacio Mifadil again and he told me he had some work for me. The first offer was a job liberating two people from a courtroom, the location of which was not imparted, nor would it be until closer to the time. Unknown parties were to make an appearance at a special hearing, which was yet to be arranged. Advance notice would be given. My task was to take the defendants from the courtroom to a vehicle parked a few miles away. I would also travel by car. One added proviso was that I was not to hurt the judge, as he was 'our man'. I wondered whether the recovery of the bag of guns was related to a professional hit team who had been apprehended, the tools of their trade undiscovered.

Driving a Mercedes 500 saloon (courtesy of Monzer), I spent several days familiarising myself with the Costa del Sol. Like all his vehicles, it carried a green Cedars of Lebanon sticker.

One evening, after having dinner with Monzer and his family, I retired to the television room with Raghda and Abud, a close associate of Monzer's. I skimmed through a copy of *Harper's Bazaar*, gazing at an advertisement for a diamond and ruby necklace. The advert didn't say how much it cost. I guessed if you needed to ask then you couldn't afford it. Pointing to the necklace I enquired, 'Raghda, do you like this? It's very beautiful, yes?'

She glanced at the picture and her face lit up. 'I have this one, also this,' she said, putting her fingers and thumbs to her earlobes to indicate earrings, then clasping her wrist to suggest a bangle. 'All the same, from London. Monzer gets for me.'

'A lot of money, I think?' I replied.

'I do not know but must be, I think. Monzer makes call and man from bank come.'

He had to have a serious fortune if the bank came to him rather than the other way around. One night, we went out to dinner and ended up at the casino in the Andalucía Plaza Hotel. Monzer played blackjack at a private table. It was one on one, him against the dealer. When I asked him if he had won, he proudly showed me a worn cheque made out to the casino. 'I play only blackjack. This cheque they have to give me back with profit every time I play.' Evidently, he knew to quit when he was ahead.

My next tasks were to obtain office space in Amsterdam, set up a company and assemble a team to await instructions in Marbella. Frank and I returned to Britain to hire six guys, three of whom flew in from South Africa. I rented a villa in nearby San Pedro from an agency in Puerto Banús, a company that also ran a travel agent's from the same premises. With an arms-broker friend called Phil, I set about locating the Amsterdam office space. We were hampered by Monzer's precise requirements. He insisted that the office should be on the ground floor with direct access to a canal. No reasons for these conditions were offered. While we headed to Amsterdam, the rest of the team moved into the villa and awaited instructions.

Several weeks passed before Phil and I found an office that we believed fitted Monzer's requirements. But when he came to see it, he took one look around and said, 'No good. It must have no one else on the ground floor.'

Now I was pissed off. 'What's wrong with this? It has everything. The other offices next door won't bother us.'

Monzer was immovable. 'It must have nobody on your floor but you, even if you have to take whole floor.'

'It's not easy to find a place on the ground floor. We've turned down so many of the offices we've been shown around. The agencies might get suspicious. We're finding it hard to turn down perfectly good offices that aren't on the ground floor.'

'Keep looking. You will find something.'

Eventually, we did. The office was no more than 20 ft from the canal and we were the only ground-floor tenants. We rented it by the month under the name of a company registered in Sierra Leone. It existed, although it had nothing to do with Monzer or me. I chose the name having collected a few of the firm's business cards while on a gold run from Africa. Monzer arrived for an inspection and approved the office. Then he gave me a telephone number and handed me a piece of paper with a long list of artillery and mortar ammunition. He told me to phone the number and request a telex number to send the list for the recipient's consideration. Monzer knew that my call would receive a wary response and questions would be asked as to how I had got the telephone number. I was instructed to say that an unnamed person in a Swiss bank had given it to me. I was told to ask the person if he might be interested in purchasing some items we had for sale. This seemed a very strange way to do business.

Monzer added that the recipients would be interested in only one item. 'They want ammunition for a Russian T-72 tank. They will not come for gold or diamonds but they will come for these.'

Monzer departed. I looked at the international telephone number. Something about it seemed strangely familiar. A call to directory enquiries revealed that the recipient was in Tel Aviv. 'What are we into here?' I remarked to Phil. 'There's something very wrong about an Arab selling arms to Israelis . . .'

Phil rang the number, as his telephone manner was better than mine. The conversation went as Monzer had predicted and the unnamed party gave a telex number. I sent the list to the number provided but there was no immediate response.

At this stage, Frank was put into play by Monzer. He turned up in Amsterdam as I left for Marbella. Frank would run the office with a secretary. Phil was paid off and went home. The next news I heard was that we finally had a response to our list. The buyers wanted to come to Amsterdam to discuss the tank ammunition. The ammo was bait. The mice had taken their time but now they were coming out of their hole to inspect the cheese.

A week or so went by and I heard nothing more. Meanwhile, the phone line into our villa at San Pedro had stopped working. Monzer raised this issue when I went to see him. I told him that it had been reported to the rental agency in Puerto Banús, run by a guy called José, and that we were waiting for him to fix it.

'They will take weeks to do anything. I will send someone to the phone company. I know the boss there.'

As I was visiting Puerto Banús myself, I stopped at the office to drop José a friendly reminder. When I arrived, the receptionist, who handled the travel side of the business, looked very upset.

'Are you OK?' I asked.

She glanced towards the stairs (property rentals were handled on the first floor) and nearly burst into tears.

'What's the matter? Has José upset you?'

'No, no. Please, we cannot speak here. I am not to speak about it.'

'Tell me . . .'

'Please please, do not see José now. I will meet you outside when I go for lunch in one hour.'

I didn't want to get involved in some lovers' quarrel but, as she had always been very helpful, I agreed to see her. We met in a coffee shop. She looked very apprehensive.

'The police were with José in the office. I was questioned by them about you.' Her lips were quivering and the tears were welling up in her eyes.

I attempted the innocent-tourist routine. 'What could they want with me? I have done nothing wrong. I am not wanted by anyone for any crime. What did they want to know?'

'They want to know where you have travelled to,' she told me. 'They want to know about anybody else who is with you, too. If you come in for travel tickets, we must give them the details.'

I continued to act innocent. 'Why don't the police come and ask me? I haven't committed any crime.'

'I will get into very much trouble for telling you.'

'I will never tell anyone that we have spoken about this, I promise you.'

'These are not ordinary police from here. They are from Madrid.'

'I haven't been in Madrid, so why are they concerned about me?' For some reason, I sensed she knew more than she was telling me. I continued to question her gently. 'But why the Madrid police?'

'These are special police. They are the anti-terrorist police.'

With that admission, she slumped in her chair. Acting suitably shocked, I reassured her that I would never mention the conversation again and advised her that neither should she. 'This is all a big mistake,' I said, pressing two hundred-dollar bills into her palm. On the return journey to San Pedro, I noticed I was being followed.

I briefed the team on these developments. A couple of the guys went for a run; nothing unusual there, but this time they were looking for vans or cars on surveillance duty. I reckoned it would be difficult for a surveillance team to keep tabs on us without blowing their own cover. In those days, the Costa del Sol had no motorways and there was only one route between Malaga and Gibraltar, the N1 coastal road. It would be obvious if we were being tailed.

I could not phone Monzer under the circumstances and I thought it best not to go straight round to the palace. I was having dinner with him at Danny's that night, so it was a question of patience.

I was outside the restaurant when Monzer and his entourage arrived. We entered and climbed the stairs. 'Everything OK?' he asked me. 'No problems?'

'No. I have a problem.'

'Well, I have some news for you, as well.'

When we were seated, the buzz of the place making conversation more private, I related the day's events. Monzer's story fitted in with mine. 'The head of the telephone company came to see me after I sent someone about getting your phone fixed. The problem is not with the line; it is with the rental-agency meter that monitors the time on the line for billing. There are two government tape recorders hooked up to your number, with no conversation on them.'

'So what do you want me to do?'

'Do nothing. They cannot know anything. Their investigations must have only just started. Everything will be OK. Everything is in motion.'

It was pointless asking what the fuck that was supposed to mean. I knew that 'one step at a time' would be the answer.

The following day, we spotted our surveillance team. They had parked at the end of our road in dark saloon cars. We must have caught them by surprise, as, when we passed their position, one of them was outside his vehicle. He should have stayed still. Instead, he raised a mobile radio to his mouth. He must have realised that this was a bad move, as he panicked and dropped down behind his car door. He was so obvious he might as well have held up a sign that read 'cop'. We cruised into Marbella centre, where the traffic was thicker, to see if they handed us over to another team. The car in front of us tried to anticipate every turn-off we made. They seemed to be under the illusion that we had not 'made' them. We decided to keep it that way and just ignored them.

I had to go to the palace that evening to talk with Monzer. Frank was already there when I arrived. It had been a flying visit and he was preparing to leave. He beckoned me to follow him to his room, where he was packing his suitcase. He looked anxious.

'What's the problem, mate?' I asked.

Frank put his finger to his lips and then circled it around to indicate that the room might be bugged. In a very low voice, he said, 'We are in the shit.'

I did not like the sound of that 'we'.

'How?'

'I've been arrested,' he whispered in his low Irish brogue.

'By whom?'

'Some international anti-terrorist unit. I was flown to Belgium and plugged into lie detectors. We are in trouble big time.'

'What nationality are they?' I whispered.

'The fucking lot: MI6, CIA, Mossad and a few others. I can't explain here. Get to London. I'll meet you at the airport. It's very important. For fuck's sake don't tell Monzer.'

With that, Frank departed, leaving me to act as if nothing was amiss. I told Monzer I had to return home the next day on personal business and would come back the day after that. When I met Frank at Gatwick Airport, he looked very worried. We found a quiet place to talk.

'What the fuck is all this about, Frank? What's this about being arrested?'

'I was picked up several days ago by the Dutch police. They handed me over to a bunch of spooks who flew me by helicopter to Belgium. They questioned me for hour after hour about Monzer. What are we doing with him? Why have we got offices in Amsterdam that are obviously being set up for him?'

'So what did you tell them?'

'I lied, of course. I told them it was just another trading company.'

'How could they just pick you up and fly you out of the country? The Old Bill doesn't perform like that.'

'This fucking lot can do whatever they want. This isn't the local plod. This is a whole fucking intelligence unit. Believe me, they know everything.'

'And what is "everything", Frank?' I demanded.

'That I've been coming into Amsterdam by train carrying bags full of weapons. Pistols, Uzi sub-machine guns and a load of ammunition. The secretary is a fucking terrorist from Lebanon. The telex you sent about the ammunition was bait to get two particular Jews to come over from Israel. A hit squad from the PFLP or PLO is going to make sure they don't go back.'

'Is this what you know or what you think?'

'I fucking know,' he said angrily, 'and so do they. Mossad monitored the calls from the moment the number was dialled. It was their people we were getting in touch with.'

I only partly believed Frank's story. It seemed a little fantastical. There were a thousand questions that required answers.

'So where are the weapons now?'

'In the office. They're in the hollow table stand.'

The office had a circular wood-and-glass-topped table supported by a hollow ornamental pedestal.

'So if they know all this, why are you out on the street?'

'They want to let the operation continue. Then they can capture the hit squad, or kill them if they put up a fight.'

This did worry me. 'When these guys come to Amsterdam, you know I'm supposed to meet them and take them to the office? What chance have I got in a fucking firefight? Monzer's people will think I've set them up and the other side won't give a fuck who they shoot. What happens if they arrest everyone?'

'They say they'll get us out of it at the court stage.'

'If you believe that, you must be completely fucking mental. If we abort this thing now they'll have nothing but the weapons. Then what are they going to do?'

'They told me that if we didn't go along with it, they would make our lives unbearable in future.'

'Well, Frank, you go back and tell them from me to get fucked. I have never put anyone in jail in my life and I'm not about to start now. I know this is bad and you're in a worse position than me at the moment. I'm going to mark Monzer's card and tell him to abort this operation. I'll give you until tomorrow to do whatever you have to do to protect yourself. I'll tell him that we met late tomorrow and you told me this story. I'll just bring your arrest forward a few days so that he doesn't know you had this information when you were at the palace. I'm sorry, mate, but whatever happens after that is up to them. I can't do what they want. I eat at his table and I cannot and will not be part of anything that knowingly puts someone in the slammer. I'll take my chances but I don't expect you to tell this spook outfit what I'm going to do.'

Frank knew I was not going down the road that he, or rather they, proposed. He looked concerned and so was I, even if I had my doubts about the veracity of his story. My personal code of ethics forbade me to call anyone a snitch without convincing proof but, at the same time, I had to consider the possibility that Frank might have more of a role here than mere victim.

I sweated out another day before telling Phil most of Frank's story.

I suggested that if he was collared by the police he should admit only that he had set up an office. Phil was Jewish and was particularly angry to discover that he had been part of a sting against Israeli interests.

I called Monzer late the following evening from a safe phone. 'Whatever is planned for the Amsterdam office must be aborted now. The law knows what's going to happen, so stop anyone from going there.'

'How do you know this?' he replied.

'Frank was arrested. I can't explain on the phone.'

'Get back here and explain now.' This was not a polite request.

After catching an early flight the next morning, I entered the palace with trepidation. Monzer and I went to the basement, where there was a recreation area with a swimming pool, sauna and seating areas. The walls were decorated with beach scenes. Monzer probed me about my story. I could only fall back on what I had already told him. I kept to my version of events, not telling the true date of Frank's arrest. He sat very quietly for a long while, staring at me. He looked angry. I noticed that the tiled bottom of the swimming pool was decorated with a picture of a shark.

The silence was finally broken when he asked, 'You believe this shit you just told me?'

'Now you hold up a minute. Don't get fucking angry with me. I didn't say I believed any of it. I'm just telling you what I was told. Don't shoot the messenger. I'm in the shit here as well.'

'That fucking Irish cunt has done this, I can feel it.'

I was not about to become Frank's defence counsel. I sat quietly.

'You know I sent Abud to Amsterdam to meet some people coming in? I have called him back, so they will have nobody to arrest now. I will find out the true story. But this Irish bastard isn't telling the truth. Why isn't he here with you?'

I shrugged, figuring it was a rhetorical question. 'How are you going to find out the truth?' I asked.

'I will go to Madrid and ask contacts in the anti-terrorist unit. They will find out everything.'

I had a couple of questions. 'If Frank is telling the truth, what do you think will happen next?'

'Nothing. What have they got? Only whatever Frank told them.'

'What about the guns in the office?'

'If Frank hasn't told them, they won't know, will they? If they find them, they must have been there all the time before you rented the office. Why should you know they were there? You wouldn't take a table apart, would you?'

'If the Israelis believe you were involved, will they come after you?'

'No, never.' Monzer sounded confident of this.

'Why not?'

'They know better. None of their people have been killed.' His next remark was chilling. He spat it out in frustration. 'If they do anything to me, thousands will die, their children's fucking children will die, and they know this.'

When he had calmed down slightly, Monzer told me that he was going on a trip. I hoped this was not a case of a rat leaving a sinking ship. He said he would be in touch and told me to send my team home from Marbella, as nothing was going to happen in the near future. I thought it seemed a bad time to discuss fees. The guys took it philosophically. I told them only what they needed to know. Some stayed behind until the rental agreement ran out. Others went home.

Monzer called a couple of weeks later, having left Spain, to request that I return to Amsterdam and check if the guns were in the table support. Being reluctant to take on this task, I was relieved to have a copper-bottomed excuse. 'I don't have the keys to get in.'

'Come to Vienna, then. I have them.'

He fucking well would, I thought. Always one step ahead of the game.

'Let me know your flight schedule and I'll meet you at the Hilton.'

I evaded the surveillance team and travelled to Austria via London. As planned, I met Monzer at the Hilton. I agreed to return to Amsterdam only because I figured I owed him something and I thought he would be a useful man to keep in with. Two hours later, I flew back to Marbella, where two tickets were purchased for me and Alex Lennox, a close friend and former soldier, to travel to Amsterdam. I thought it best to have someone with me to watch my back. At Schiphol Airport, I let Alex go through passport control first, as I figured if I was going to get lifted anywhere, it was going to be here. If that happened, I wanted a witness to see the arrest. However, I sailed through and, walking around the city, it seemed we were clean; I saw no sign of a surveillance team in pursuit. We checked in to the Holiday Inn and I explained the game plan to Alex.

We headed down to the office, Alex following me at a distance to look out for anything untoward. I clutched the keys in my hand, ready to dump them in the canal if things went pear-shaped. Ambling along like a sightseer, I stayed alert to the possibility of a surveillance operation. Even if no one was watching me, someone might be keeping an eye on the office. I had told Alex that when he got halfway down the street, I would be halfway back up the other side, having crossed the canal bridge. If there were any vans or suspicious cars parked up, I would abort and keep walking.

A couple of weeks had passed since Frank's arrest and helicopter trip. I reckoned the opposition would have pulled out by now, assuming we had abandoned our operation. I was very nervous as I approached. I scanned doorways and alleyways for danger. I really did not want to do it and I was a heartbeat away from just walking on by. But I knew that if did, I would not turn around and make a second run. I stopped thinking and went for it. I was up the steps, key in lock, turn and push, and I was in the hallway, door closed behind me. I don't think David Copperfield could make someone disappear off a street as fast as I did. I would never get to use the other key. Four security padlocks had been attached to hasps drilled into the framework of the door. There was also tape across the door with the word 'sealed' on it. I took one look and was out the front door immediately. Moving rapidly away from the building, I turned left at the first junction, hit the next turn and made tracks away from the area, throwing the keys into the canal. When my heartbeat slowed, I headed for the hotel, showered and waited for Alex, who was not back.

Three hours passed. Then came a knock on the door. I looked through the peephole.

'Where the fuck have you been?' I demanded.

Alex replied defensively, 'I saw you go in but I didn't see you come out. I moved on a few yards and kept watching the door. When you didn't show again, I figured something had happened inside. I couldn't stay in the area any longer. I'd been hanging around too long.'

I couldn't have been inside the door for more than ten seconds. Alex would only have had to glance away for a few moments and I'd have been back out and gone again.

'We're heading out of here right now,' I said.

At Schiphol Airport, I let Alex go through first once again, watching him take a seat on the other side of the passport desk. I waited my turn and presented my passport, knowing that my name would be checked against a computer record of those wanted for offences. I knew straight away the flag had come up. The passport checker's body stiffened as she looked at a screen I could not see. Then she requested my ticket and attempted to disguise the fact that she was writing down my details on a pad out of my line of vision. She returned my passport and ticket and ushered me through. I kept away from Alex until our flight was called. As we boarded, security guards rubbed down every passenger. This was to see if I had others with me who might be carrying something. I sighed with relief when we took off.

When we disembarked, I joined Alex. 'Fuck! I didn't think we were going to make it out of there,' he said, adding, 'As soon as you were out of sight, the woman at the desk left her station in a hurry. She went into an office and came out with a few men who looked like cops. They went to her computer and then they got all excited.'

Monzer did not believe I had returned to the office in accordance with his request. He asked me to give back the keys and I had to tell him they were in the bottom of the canal. 'I will find out everything in the end,' he said. 'I will be in touch.' It sounded more like a threat than a promise.

POSTSCRIPT

In June 2007, Monzer al-Kassar was arrested in Spain on an extradition warrant from the US government, charged with plotting to supply millions of dollars' worth of weapons to Colombian rebels and with conspiracy to kill American citizens.

A spokesperson for the US Attorney's Office told a press conference: 'Where others see suffering, chaos and conflict, al-Kassar sees opportunity and dollar signs . . . [His] arrest on complex conspiracy and money laundering charges halfway around the world is a tremendous feat . . . al-Kassar is no stranger to guns. But yesterday he and his henchman found themselves in an unfamiliar position – looking down the barrel of a gun, the very tool of their trade turned against them.'

Held in custody in a maximum-security prison in Madrid, he lodged an appeal against extradition, but on 13 July 2008 he was flown to New York, where he is scheduled to face trial on 3 November.

CHAPTER 19

OPERATION PHOENIX

IN MY EXPERIENCE, TROUBLE NEARLY ALWAYS STARTS WITH a phone call, and it arrived with a capital T when I picked up the telephone one day in May 1988. My ear registered the Irish brogue and I guessed it would be something out of the ordinary. Frank Conlan's calls were always full of promise but they usually brought their fair share of problems, too. He told me he was in Bogotá, Colombia, and had a job offer for me. I had to fax to a certain number a proposal outlining what services I could provide of a military nature. The emphasis was to be on counter-revolutionary warfare and anti-terrorist capabilities. I drafted a letter on headed paper from an old company of mine, Technical Support Services. It pretty much claimed that the services I offered were a cross between the SAS, the CIA and MI6. The fax was transmitted to a retired brigadier general, Jorge Salcedo Victoria. Within the week, I received a reply, in which the general stated that he still maintained close relations with the highest commands of the Colombian army, air force and navy and that his son was in the army, and specialised in counter-terrorism work.

On 19 June, I went to the mansion in Norfolk where Frank lived with his wife, Yoko. The second houseguest was Jorge Salcedo, son of the brigadier. Jorge was of medium height with a paunch, dark hair and moustache. He spoke perfect English. Throughout our relationship, in the two years that followed, he retained the same pleasant, amiable attitude. Jorge had a proposal that would fire my imagination and put the adrenalin on overtime. I knew little about Colombia, but, as we walked the grounds of Frank's house, he gave me a thumbnail sketch of its troubled and violent history. Colombia's problems revolved around two major issues, which had become interrelated to some degree. Those two issues were cocaine and guerrillas, and both had taken their toll on a nation branded the most violent country on earth and the world's biggest supplier of narcotics.

The guerrillas, numbering many thousands, were Marxist revolutionaries. There were many different organisations, known by abbreviations such as M-19, ELN and FARC. These groups portrayed themselves as resistance armies dedicated to overthrowing the imperialist government that subjugated the masses. Armed with automatic rifles and other military weapons, they used terrorist tactics, including murder and kidnapping, in a hit-and-run war against the state. Colombia was a land consumed by violence. There were at least 15,000 murders every year, most of them drug related. The rebel movement FARC (Fuerzas Armadas Revolucionarias de Colombia, or Armed Revolutionary Forces of Colombia), by far the largest guerrilla army, had killed or kidnapped for ransom hundreds of Colombian soldiers and police over the years. Despite this, the government's policy was one of negotiation, a situation that frustrated military leaders.

Jorge brought with him news videos and recent papers. One carried as its lead story an open letter from the charismatic and highly respected General Raphael Pena Rios, who had resigned in protest against what he saw as President Virgilio Barco Vargas's appeasement of the guerrillas. He gave facts and figures to demonstrate that the growing numbers of guerrillas were undermining the democratic government.

According to Jorge, all this was about to change. Senior military officers had decided that they had had enough of being hamstrung by Vargas's policies. Various options had been discussed in top-secret military meetings. Most of these were discounted. An overthrow of the democratic government by *coup d'état* had been seriously discussed but it was decided that this drastic step was almost unthinkable. The consequence would have been civil war. The history of Colombia was already steeped in blood. The last civil war, known as La Violencia, had cost hundreds of thousands of lives in the 1950s.

Who came up with the final plan? I've no idea. Someone at those secret meetings knew more than the general public did and proposed a radical solution that might solve the problem. It seemed that President Barco had initiated highly classified talks with FARC leaders (known as *el secretariado*, the secretariat). Secret meetings between senior government ministers and the guerrilla leadership were being held high in the Andes Mountains at a place known as Casa Verde. This building, the venue for the talks, was nothing more than a way station on the trail leading from the nearest village up the mountain to the complex of buildings that made up FARC headquarters. There was a constant presence of some four to six hundred guerrillas at FARC HQ, in an area of approximately twenty square miles, which contained a training ground for fighters, and a school for communications. The original plan was that, at a time when government negotiators were meeting with the secretariat at Casa Verde, a unit dressed as Colombian soldiers would attack and kill the FARC leaders. The attack would be captured on video and released to the media for broadcasting to the public, thus exposing the government's secret meetings with the guerrillas. Of course, there would be a backlash from left-wing FARC sympathisers but the plotters believed that most people, not to mention the media, would be horrified at the revelation of the government's cooperation with terrorists and that it would be forced to adopt a hard-line policy against members of FARC. Thus, the guerrilla group would never recover from the blow it had been dealt. Any attempt to discover the perpetrators of this attack would hit a brick wall, because, of course, it would have been committed not by Colombian soldiers but by foreign mercenaries.

I had spent several days with Jorge learning about Colombia and the plan. Now it was time to start looking for men capable of and willing to execute it. I got in touch with Peter McAleese and drove to Hereford to see him. Things were not going well for Peter and he was staying in the Booth Hall, a run-down pub and lodging house. He had come full circle, having left the SAS years ago, he was back in Hereford, shovelling concrete on a construction site. Having returned from ten years fighting in Africa, his soldiering career was at an end. There were no more wars to fight. He had also smashed his legs when his parachute malfunctioned and had had to have several operations. He was back on his feet but was finding it difficult to get work in security. You might expect the circuit to jump at the opportunity to employ such an experienced ex-soldier but the commercial security market is as much about corporate image as actual security. Many companies like to employ former soldiers, however inexperienced, who have only ever served in Her Majesty's Forces. I discreetly slipped Peter £200; if he thought the proposition was bullshit, at least he was getting paid to listen to it. I told him about the scheme and he agreed in principle to be the team leader if it all turned out to be for real and if I could negotiate finances.

On 1 July, Peter, Jorge and I flew to Bogotá to review the mission, code-named Operation Phoenix, with our sponsors. With hindsight, I would hazard a guess that the intelligence services began to gather the information they would build up about our operations over the next couple of years from that very first visit to Heathrow Airport. We had gone through passport control and were about to board a direct flight to Bogotá when a breathless uniformed customs officer intercepted us and requested our passports and tickets. 'Where are you going?' got a polite but sarcastic reply. The flag watcher at the computer must have been in the toilet when our names popped up. Special Branch policemen can sometimes be shy and retiring creatures. They must have dispatched the out-of-puff customs officer to make sure we hadn't switched flights or routes in true spy-novel fashion.

At the other end, Jorge cleared us through Bogotá's Eldorado Airport, reassuringly wandering in and out of areas designated off-limits to non-official personnel. The drive to the Plaza Hotel downtown was fume-filled and chaotic. The traffic was horrendous. Multicoloured buses painted with religious slogans did battle with the teeming throng of cars and bikes. During the stop–start journey, children thrust cartons of Marlboro cigarettes at the car windows, imploring with big brown eyes set in dirty faces as they slalomed their way in and out of the traffic.

Bogotá is 8,600 ft above sea level, set against the backdrop of the Andes Mountains; it was invariably cold and wet because of the proximity of the fog-shrouded peaks. Roads were congested, sidewalks crowded with people. Street vendors abounded, working from small shacks that sold everything from sweets to hardcore pornography. Colombian Indians sat cross-legged on the pavements displaying their handmade crafts as barefoot street children in ragged clothes begged in small gangs, pointing to their mouths to indicate their hunger.

Peter and I checked in to the Plaza Hotel and for three days we heard zilch from anyone. The chambermaids would always giggle a lot when they saw us; we had the impression that, since we spent most of our time together in the room, they figured we were on honeymoon. On the evening of day three, Jorge came to see us, apologising for the delay but with no more news. We would get used to this *mañana* factor. On the fifth day, Jorge returned in company with three other men. Two of them were army officers from the 3rd Infantry Battalion's HQ in Bogotá and the third was a representative of our financial backers. The army officers supplied maps and aerial photographs of the location of Casa Verde and we planned overflights of the Sumapaz Valley. We flew in a small Cessna from Bogotá's old airport to the area. As we flew alongside the mighty Andes Mountains, it was possible to see how a determined guerrilla army could stay undefeated for years in the spectacular, inhospitable landscape.

There were many hours of discussions and poring over maps with Jorge and others. From a financial viewpoint, it was in my interests to get as many men as possible on this mission; from an operational standpoint, however, that decision was left to Peter. The final figure was agreed at 12 men. A plan of sorts was formulated, requiring our insertion by helicopter to a particular spot. Equipment lists were drawn up and presented to our hosts, along with an outline of our initial planning. This was well received. Then, what the Americans call 'mission creep' began, when they asked us if we could take out the convoy that supplied food and stores to the guerrillas. This was a train of 100-plus mules and their drivers, which travelled from the village of San Juan to FARC HQ every few weeks with supplies.

We told our hosts that we would do it as long as it didn't conflict with the main operation. We requested Claymore anti-personnel mines. With only 12 men, we would not have enough strength in depth for such an ambush and we would need the mines to supplement our personnel shortfall. Our equipment list was scrutinised and debated in Spanish. We didn't need to speak the language to know that something was wrong; the words '*no possible*' kept coming up. We couldn't have 66-mm anti-tank rockets or the Claymore mines. Various reasons were given depending on who was talking at the time. We were told the operation was so secret that removing these items from military stores would compromise the mission. I confronted Jorge in private. I wanted to know what the fuck was going on if the military couldn't supply us equipment that was in their stores. It was difficult to get angry with Jorge but several repetitions of 'that's a load of bollocks' finally elicited a bit more information.

Several of our meetings had been attended by Armando Vargas, boss of Comerandes Ltda, an agricultural land sales company. It turned out that all the finances for the mission were being paid through him because the military were so determined to keep their involvement untraceable. Vargas worked for José Gonzalo Rodriguez Gacha, known to Colombians as 'El Mejicano' because of his fondness for Mexican music. Wealthy landowners in rural areas had formed their own local groups of fighters, *autodefensas*, to defend against the guerrillas. The Mexican, wealthy beyond most people's wildest dreams, owned vast tracts of land and farms and supported one of the largest autodefensas, ACDEGAM. This was an association of cattlemen, ranchers and farmers in the Middle Magdalena Valley region of Colombia. As funds could not be taken from the military budget to pay for our operation, the Mexican had been approached to fund the mission, as he was violently opposed to FARC.

On 9 July, I parted company with Peter, leaving him to continue overflights while I tried to purchase the military equipment we needed from outside sources. With a contract agreed and funds in the bank to pay personnel for several months, I passed the equipment requirements on to Frank Conlan, with the approval of Jorge. Later that month, Peter flew to South Africa to recruit more men for the team. At the end of the month, Peter and I met in Hereford for a mutual debriefing. The personnel we'd selected were on standby in England and South Africa. Various routes had been chosen for their travel, with staggered arrival times. On 4 August, Peter went back to South Africa to confirm travel arrangements with the others. The next day, I flew to Colombia with two team members, Dean Shelley and Roy Kaulback, both of whom had previously served under Peter in 44 Para Brigade of the South African Defence Force.

After more meetings with the officers at their battalion HQ, we were driven 200 km through the winding roads of the Cordilleras Mountains to the small town of Puerto Boyacá, a few kilometres from the banks of the Magdalena River. On a previous trip, Jorge and I had travelled for miles in the area around Bogotá looking for a suitable training area. We had not found anywhere suitable but foremost in our minds had been the fact that we planned on fighting in freezing cold at a height of over 14,000 ft, where the oxygen content of the air diminishes significantly. The journey to the Magdalena Valley had dropped us almost to sea level and had a subtropical climate, so the area that had been chosen in the end was not particularly appropriate.

The town was very quiet when we arrived, a spaghetti-Western set with a few chickens wandering around. We stopped at a small bar and went in for a drink and so that Jorge could ask for directions. Our arrival had not gone unnoticed. Toyota Land Cruisers and Nissan Patrols drove slowly past and took up positions at either end of the street. The vehicles were bristling with radio antennas and full of armed men. Jorge made a phone call and we went back to our car. The four-wheel drives closed on us and indicated that we should follow. They led us to a shabby two-storey office building with a large sign over the door that read ACDEGAM.

From these offices, we drove off-road until we reached the Laguna de Palagua. Half a mile off the shore of the lake was Isla de la Fantasia, Fantasy Island. Our escorts made a radio call and a speedboat came hurtling across the water to the jetty in front of us. Marcos, our boatman, and his wife, Fenix, were caretakers of the island. The main house there would serve as a base for our team. It had eight bedrooms, whitewashed walls and a terracotta-tiled roof. There was a thatched outdoor dining area and a small bar. A bungalow a short way off housed Marcos and his family. Chickens and a pig roamed freely among the trees and shrubs of the three-acre site.

Peter and the team were all *in situ* by mid-August and fitness training began. At dawn each day, we crossed the lagoon and ran three miles on rough roads, passing nodding-donkey oil pumps and swampy fields where Brahman cattle grazed. We repeated the run in the afternoons and when our endurance improved we started to carry weighted Bergen rucksacks over the same route. As we were still without weapons, military training consisted of map-reading lessons and learning emergency medical procedures. We constructed a model of our island hideaway and took it in turns to formulate detailed plans for its attack as if we were the enemy.

So we played fantasy war games on Fantasy Island until the first batch of rifles showed up. What a disappointment they were: six well-used Heckler & Koch G3 rifles, courtesy of the Colombian army's Bárbula Battalion, based on the outskirts of Puerto Boyacá. Everyone was pretty well versed in using the G3; it had been much used in Rhodesia and we'd all spent some time out there. Nevertheless, we all went through Peter's retraining programme. More G3s were delivered in early September. Better armed now, we went ashore to conduct patrols and counter-ambush drills. Live firing was restricted in case the locals thought guerrillas were attacking the area.

To little avail, Peter and I pestered Jorge about the missing equipment. He said it was 'being taken care of'. We did not see that much of Jorge, as he preferred the creature comforts of Bogotá. Our conduit to Rodriguez Gacha was ACDEGAM's chairman, a prominent landowner called Henry de Jesús Pérez. Peter got on well with Pérez and asked him repeatedly about the helicopters we had requested for the Casa Verde mission.

As I learned, ACDEGAM was originally formed as a vigilante group to protect peasants and cattlemen from marauding bands of guerrillas. But as time went by, the horizons of Henry's little band expanded. Perhaps due to the element of machismo always present in South America, the band got bigger and more violently anti-Communist. By the time our little group of warriors arrived, Henry Pérez controlled a peasant militia. This fact was not lost on the drug lords of the Medellín cocaine cartel, being the largest landowners in the country. So Henry's army had lost its way a bit or found a more profitable route, depending on how you look at it. His men were now soldiers – not well trained, but soldiers nevertheless. When they weren't killing guerrillas, they protected the cocaine laboratories of Medellín head honcho Pablo Escobar and of Gonzalo Rodriguez Gacha, our paymaster. The region we trained in was known throughout the country as the Paramilitary Republic of Colombia. Even the military had to get permission from the drug barons to go in there.

More requests for helicopters and equipment fell on deaf ears. By this time, we were the most highly trained team in the world for an assault on Fantasy Island. Then that phrase 'mission creep' popped up again. In company with Jorge and a small army of bodyguards, Rodriguez Gacha, a cold-eyed man in a white Panama hat, paid us a surprise visit one day and must have liked what he'd seen. Peter informed the team that the original Casa Verde mission had been superseded. The prime target now was FARC headquarters itself, and a few more recruits would be joining us for training, as we were going to war.

The first batch of 13 men included Rodriguez Gacha's son Fredy Rodriguez Celades. He was so fat that he looked significantly older than his 16 years and struggled to complete our training runs. The recruits were better armed than us, bringing with them their own FN rifles, Chinese-manufactured AK-47s and side arms. They were a friendly bunch and keen to learn. Not that they lacked experience in killing people; what they needed was cohesion and discipline.

Dean Shelley's shooting prowess, or luck, raised our collective status as instructors to great heights. The recruits had been taking potshots at the cormorants on the lagoon. Most of the cormorant's body sits underwater, leaving only its head and neck as a target, too small for the locals to hit from 30 metres. Dean wandered over to study the Colombians' firing technique and they invited him to participate in the shoot. Shelley drew his nickel-plated Smith & Wesson pistol, casually took aim and fired. To collective amazement, his 9-mm round struck a bird's head, which exploded instantly. Shelley tucked the pistol back in his belt and sauntered away to the cheers of the highly impressed Colombians. When he was out their earshot, he whispered, 'Fucking hell, how did I manage that?' Needless to say, he refused to make a second attempt and basked in the admiring glances of our new recruits.

We now had a new contact in the Bárbula Battalion, a dapper little man called Major Julio. He was a demolitions officer, so I requested that he acquire some explosives and other necessary kit for me. He brought commercial gelignite (not the C-4 plastic explosives I had asked for) along with American-made detonators, fuse, trap switches and det-cord. At least I finally had some of the stuff I'd asked for.

Mainland training was still confined to patrols and ambush drills. We kept up the long runs, too. Fredy always finished in last place, soaked in sweat, with his breasts bobbing up and down like those of a well-endowed woman, everyone cheering him to the end. The new recruits didn't speak English and our Spanish was limited, so we now had a language barrier to contend with. When Jorge was absent, which was often, things progressed slowly. I started a demolitions class and managed to put together a Spanish–English dictionary on the subject. I might not have been able to hold a long social conversation but I could blow things up in Spanish. As more recruits arrived, Fantasy Island became overcrowded. Meals were taken in shifts.

For intelligence purposes, Peter and I watched FARC propaganda videos. Our prime target was now its two-man leadership cell: Jacobo Arenas, FARC's 55-year-old ideological leader, and 63-year-old legendary guerrilla fighter Manuel Marulanda. Secondary targets were propaganda director Alfonso Cano and recruiting chief Raúl Reyes. We watched these videos carefully but not with as much enthusiasm as the Colombians studied Al Pacino in *Scarface*, cheering loudly at its violent climax.

The Colombian magazine *Cromos* carried an in-depth article by two left-wing journalists who, with a photographer in tow, had visited FARC's headquarters. We were interested to learn how they had travelled to and from the camp on horseback and on foot. The writers were a potential intelligence goldmine and we approached them in the hope of getting them to spill the contents of their notebooks for our benefit. Royston Kaulback and I returned to Bogotá and, posing as British journalists with FARC sympathies, arranged a meeting with them at the Hotel Dann. Not even Hollywood could invent a more incongruous mercenary than Royston. His father, a highly respected former colonel, had hoped that, after leaving Cambridge University, his son would continue the family's military tradition. Roy spent as short a time as he could get away with in the British Army before going to fight in Rhodesia, after which he joined Peter's para brigade in South Africa. Roy came across as an unashamed racist and snob. He spoke with a plum in his mouth and his conversation was punctuated with terms like 'gook', 'dink', 'kaffir' and 'floppy'. He would claim, perhaps to wind us up, that Hitler had been a kind, compassionate man. Fortunately, there was a softer side of his character and he could be incredibly charming, particularly towards women. Roy did most of the talking when we met the hacks, one of whom was female. What did we get from it at the end of the day? Well, we sure as hell weren't going to be walking there to fight. The journey sounded like a nightmare; without helicopters, we were going nowhere.

After returning to the island, Kaulback, Shelley and I transferred to a remote farmhouse on the banks of the Magdalena River. Two former FARC guerrillas were brought to us for interrogation. Both were women, no more than girls, really, who now worked as radio operators for Henry Pérez's organisation. Most guerrillas captured by the autodefensa units were tortured and executed. Occasionally, they succeeded in convincing their captors that they had been with the rebels under duress; sometimes this was true. Shelley and I were only there as minders for Kaulback, who spoke a little Spanish and was to conduct the interviews. We were hoping to confirm the information we had about the target. It was interesting to listen to Roy's methods in debriefing them. From what I could gather, he was as smarmy as he had been during our meeting with the journalists. Kaulback's job wasn't made easier by Shelley taking the piss out of his gentle interrogation techniques with comments such as: 'Stop fucking around, you wanker. Shoot one of them in the head. The other one will tell you everything.'

By the time we'd been on the island for about three weeks, more recruits were coming our way, so we moved location, heading several hours north into the hills. Our destination was a camp at Al Arisa, known to ACDEGAM's fighters as Escuela Almaguer Cincuenta, or 'Combat Camp 50'. The journey was mostly over rough, unmade roads, punctuated by small shacks that sold refreshments and cigarettes. These cottage industries must hardly have been viable, as traffic was almost non-existent. We soon learned that not everything was as it appeared on the surface. Every innocuous-looking little pit-stop or old lady on a donkey had a radio transceiver and would report our presence in the area. Nothing moved without the drug barons and paramilitaries knowing about it in this neck of the woods.

Camp 50 was spread over several mountainous square kilometres. There was only one flat piece of land in sight and that was used as a football pitch cum parade ground. Our new home was a wooden shack converted into a bunkhouse, a sorry state of affairs after the relative comfort of Fantasy Island. We had seen bunkers strategically placed on the hilltops as we arrived. The whole area had these sited all round and manned by armed men. A stream ran through the edge of the camp at its lowest point and when it rained this flooded and turned our football pitch into a lake. We now numbered more than 60 and training went into full swing. Parades were held in the morning and drill instruction was the first order of the day. Most of the Colombians had two left feet; they might have rhythm on the dance floor but they were useless at marching. Peter was very patient with them and injected a great deal of humour into the training, which the recruits responded to enthusiastically. Some of the trainees had received professional instruction before, as an Israeli training team had run a close-protection bodyguard course at the camp before we arrived.

The men were split into groups and instructors were allocated. The men worked long days moving round the training syllabus. Patrol formations were explained on blackboards in Spanish and English. One of our guys taught a class explaining hand signals and gun groups; after a while, he reckoned he could speak Spanish fluently by just adding an 'o' to the end of every English word. Roy Kaulback, along with Dave Borland and Terry Tagney, two Australians, took weapons drills and field stripping. In time, the trainees could take apart and reassemble several different weapons blindfolded. Dean Shelley, Alex Lennox and Mark Griffiths set up a 'jungle lane'. As they progressed through the lane shooting at the targets that would suddenly appear, the trainees did not know how many rounds they had in their magazines, or sometimes the propellant would have been removed from a bullet. This taught them to react quickly, to hit the deck or find cover and change magazines when they found they had no bullet up the spout, instead of standing there trying to figure out why the gun didn't go bang. A lack of explosives limited the amount of demolitions training I could give. The meagre supply we had was used to turn cut-down beer cans into bunker-clearance charges. Weapons aiming and sighting was the responsibility of a guy called Gordon Brindley; as a former member of the famous shooting club at Bisley, he was an excellent sniper. The long days ended with the inevitable football match, which helped bonding between instructors and trainees. Fredy was always in goal because of his weight. There was always plenty of after-game banter, with accusations rife that Fredy had nobbled players when easy goals had been missed.

Peter and I would wander for miles checking on groups sent out to set mock ambushes for other patrols. Scanning the treeline with binoculars one day, Peter spotted something irregular. As we approached, we found that a section of trees had been cut back and a Bell JetRanger helicopter hidden beneath the canopy of trees. It would have been invisible from the air. Peter and I looked at each other. So much for the lack of helicopters around here. Jorge had always dismissed our requests for choppers with a shrug. Later, he explained to us that this aircraft belonged to a local cocaine laboratory and was used to transport the German chemists who worked there.

When we'd been there for about two weeks, we left Camp 50 abruptly at four o'clock in the morning. We were told that even this larger camp was no longer big enough to train the required numbers of troops. We were schooling ever-increasing numbers to fight FARC for Rodriguez Gacha's purposes. We boarded long wooden pirogues to cross the Magdalena River and were relieved simply to reach the opposite bank. The fast-flowing, turbulent river was awash with debris and trees swept down from the mountains. We were then led through the forest to a grassy airstrip, where, with perfect timing, a Dakota passenger plane landed. We flew 1,200 km that day. The first stop was a grass runway at Inmarco Airport. This was nothing more than a field with a covered waiting area without seating. The last leg of our journey was made in three Cessnas, which flew us across more jungle. En route, we stopped to refuel. In the vast expanse of trees below, a tiny patch of grass appeared and coded messages were sent over the radio. We circled above until several people briefly emerged from the jungle to remove the steel cables, invisible from the air, that stretched across the runway. Uninvited landing here would probably cost your life. A quick refuel and a piss and we were off again, catching fleeting glimpses of the armed men at the jungle's edge. When we reached our destination, our little craft swooped and turned at treetop height before we suddenly dropped onto another airstrip. This time the watchers in the jungle didn't hide. Without delay, they ushered us towards a riverbank, where fibreglass dories waited to take us up the San Miguel River. The channel of water, about 600 ft across, was the border between Colombia and Ecuador. We were now deep in the Amazon Basin.

Forty minutes upstream, after passing several rough timber homes from which small Indian children waved, we came to a two-storey wooden house, painted blue with a concrete patio to the riverbank. Our living conditions were certainly not improving. The couple who lived there with their young daughter had only one windowless spare room, so most of us bunked down on the first-floor veranda. By the following day, everyone had arrived, except Fredy and his bodyguards. I think the whole thing was all a bit too strenuous for him. A cook was hired to cater for us, an Indian whom we called 'Typhoid Mary'. She was fat and wore a battered trilby hat and her cooking was disgusting, although an excess of hot chillies partially disguised the taste. Poor Jorge. He hated every moment we were there. He was so used to indulging in the finest eating places of Bogotá that Typhoid Mary was his worst nightmare. We got fresh meat one day when a large dug-out canoe delivered us a live cow, which had been towed along behind the boat and seemed very distressed. When the sorry-looking beast was finally dragged up the bank, one of the guards who'd come with us from the airstrip shot it in the head with his FN. The Colombians cut its throat, bleeding it into a bowl so they could make their version of black pudding.

The food might have been bad but the communications system was good. The radio set (by which Jorge would sit for hours, as if it was his last, desperate link with civilisation) could patch into the Colombian telephone network. I asked Jorge again about the equipment we had ordered and he told me that Frank was having it shipped to Antigua, from where it would be collected in small planes and smuggled into Colombia. The list of equipment we had originally requested was relatively modest; the goods would have filled only half a ship's container and should have taken no more than 90 days to reach Antigua. The problem was that when Rodriguez Gacha found we could supply our own equipment, he had attached a list of materiel he wanted for his own fighters. The stuff Frank was now trying to ship to Antigua weighed 58 tons. The number of aircraft required to bring in our gear was now enough to run an airline.

There wasn't a lot of open ground around us, so much of the training we did was in the jungle. We set up night camp attacks, which proved very realistic. God only knows what the local Indians made of the gunfire and explosions those nights. One day, some unexpected and unwelcome visitors came to have a look at us. A few of us were in the river, which served as exercise for those who felt like swimming across to Ecuador. The previous day, a demonstration had been arranged for the trainees on how to fire Zulu grenades from the FN rifle. The trainees had been impressed as Shelley fired them over the river and they exploded in Ecuador. As we bathed leisurely, without warning, two helicopter gunships, complete with rocket pods and nose cannons, popped up from the Ecuador treeline. They hovered low above us for a few moments, the water rippling with the down-draught, before spinning away and disappearing as quickly as they had come.

Were they just curious or were they offering us a polite warning?

Who knew? As a result, however, we moved camp again. The owner must have been pleased to see us go. She had a fighting cock that crowed at ridiculous hours of the night. One morning, it was found dead in its cage. I don't think she bought our suggestion that it might have died of a heart attack. No one admitted to its killing. We headed downstream this time, in long wooden canoes with outboard motors. Our pleasure at leaving that dump quickly turned to dismay when Typhoid Mary got in the boat with us. About 40 minutes downstream, we pulled in to a steep bank. In a clearing cut from the surrounding jungle was a large, partially completed timber shack on stilts. There were no facilities of any description. Light was provided by a little generator, latrines had to be dug and washing was done in the river. Sleeping was not so easy either. The insects that inhabited the night were the size of small helicopters and made about as much noise. Occasionally, they'd whack into your head. The Colombians slept in hammocks slung under the hut, and the floor would creak and move as they rocked down below.

The fun to be had exploring the vicinity was the camp's only redeeming feature. Following a track through a banana grove, we found another wooden shack. This one sold beer and was used as a bar by the region's cocaine guards. Further exploring the surrounding jungle, we came across a path made from tree bark, presumably to facilitate the movement of the drums and equipment that had been required for the disused cocaine laboratory to which it led. The lab was housed in two buildings about half a mile apart. The first place had a corrugated-iron roof, painted green to fade into the canopy of trees that surrounded it. There was a large precipitation table, with powerful overhead lighting to generate heat to dry the moist cocaine during the last stages of production. The first stage in the process had taken place in the next facility, which was deeper in the jungle. Here there were many empty 45-gallon drums that had once contained ether. The labels showed that the ether had been sourced from German chemical companies. All the paraphernalia required for production of the drug from the coca plant was there: washing machines, spin dryers, microwave ovens, all just abandoned; the jungle reclaimed the sites. When we asked about the lab, we were told that it was an old

Communist guerrilla one, that the goodies had chased the baddies away: another load of old bollocks. I reckoned it had been abandoned by ACDEGAM when they'd found a more convenient site.

Our training programme was still limited in its scope. Now, the problem was lack of ammunition. Long patrols were organised to pass the time and there was more classroom work for me. A demolitions class was set up under the hut. Booby trapping and bomb making were what the Colombians wanted to learn about. The lessons were mainly confined to theory, as we had little equipment, but the practical lessons indicated that unless the trainees improved quickly, they would be the first victims of their own devices.

For one lesson, I showed them how to use a wristwatch to time a detonation. The trainees watched carefully as I removed the second hand and bored a small hole in the glass front, inserting a cut-down drawing pin through the hole, making sure the pin made no contact with the face of the dial. Pushing a detonator into the ground close by, I severed one of its flying leads, connecting one cut end to the watch's metal winder and the other to the head of the drawing pin on the outside of the watch glass. The minute hand was set for several minutes before it would make contact with the pin. We connected both free ends of the flying leads to a battery and waited. As the seconds ticked away, the trainees counted down the last few loudly in anticipation and gave shouts of glee as the detonator exploded, showering them with earth.

After I'd explained the theory, each member of the class came forward to reassemble the now dismantled watch and connect it to a new detonator. They understood the principle but the practice eluded them. Given a new drawing pin, they would fail to cut it short enough, or they would strip too much insulation from the flying leads and short-circuit the switch on the watch's outer casing. Every attempt resulted in a premature explosion that made everyone jump. To the delight of the class, I would then pronounce the bomb maker *morte* and make him sit at the back. When everyone in the class was theoretically dead, we carried on to something else.

Gordon Brindley came in one day and added the 'ice bomb' to the syllabus. This crude time bomb was supposed to add a touch of humour but it was simple enough for the trainees to try for real at some time – and pretty nasty, too. Take one hand grenade and place in a receptacle containing water up to just below the ring-pull. Place in the freezer until solid, remove from container, remove pin. The ice prevents the trigger's spring lever flying off until it melts.

As time went on and we didn't see any active duty, the explosives were gradually used up on making abatis charges (designed to fell trees), on rapid excavations for defensive trenches and for fishing – not that we ever managed to get one single fish. The last of the detonating cord was used by Peter to make grenade necklaces as improvised Claymore-style mines for an ambush lesson. When there were no more explosives to produce bangs, the recruits lost interest in demolitions lessons.

These lessons of ours might be considered controversial. We would be accused later of causing an escalation in the violence between the government and the narco-paramilitaries. I would argue, though, that we did not go to Colombia to train killers. The fighters we taught were already perfectly proficient in murder. If we were guilty of anything, it was making them more efficient. A few statistics on the situation prior to our arrival might help to put our role into perspective. Between 1982 and 1988, there were over 92,000 killings in Colombia. The guerrilla groups and the cartels' paramilitary organisations had killed 6,000 police, 70,000 civilians, over 1,500 politicians, 173 judges and many more soldiers. In 1988, there were 88 verified massacres (the official definition being more than 5 persons killed simultaneously). Most of our trainees were men wanted for one crime or another. Many had graduated to organised combat from the streets of Medellín, where some had undertaken contract killings from their early teens, working as *sicarios*, drive-by assassins. The sheer level of violence in Colombia was astonishing. Paramilitary organisations controlled rural Colombia with an iron fist and violent death was an everyday fact of life – one that we did not introduce to the country.

With ammunition down to protection levels only, no explosives and shit food, morale was at rock bottom. Everyone was drinking more and sporadic bursts of gunfire from trainees on their way back from the jungle bar were becoming more common. It was time for

272

Rodriguez Gacha and his associates to shit or get off the pot. We waited for a decision from their end but Peter was losing patience. We were ready to do battle in the Andes . . . or fuck off home.

We might not have been spending our time very productively, but we did meet some interesting people, although we didn't really know it at the time. One of the guys we were training was Diego Viafára Salinas, known to most of our team as 'Mia Farrow', in reference to his middle name, or 'Doc'. He was no more a doctor than he was a film star, although he had trained in medicine for five years. Viafára was ACDEGAM's chief medic. He had played an instrumental part in forming the organisation and establishing its rules and regulations. There was more to him than met the eye. It would later emerge that he was a Communist guerrilla with the M-19 group. He had handed himself in to the Bárbula Battalion at Puerto Boyacá during an amnesty but not from lack of commitment to the cause – in fact quite the opposite. He had been asked by M-19 to infiltrate the narco-paramilitary organisation of Henry Pérez and the Medellín cartel. Amnesty seekers were inevitably handed over to the ACDEGAM by the army, who operated hand in hand with them. Far from being protected, they were usually murdered after interrogation, their bodies cut up with a chainsaw and disposed of in the river. Two who handed themselves in at the same time as Viafára had ended up feeding the fish. But Pérez saw potential in keeping Viafára alive. Over five years, he became as trusted as anyone could be and was privy to the secrets of the organisation's leaders. Doc supplied information to his controller, Dr Carlos Toledo Plata, for nearly two years, until, as a known member of M-19, Toledo was assassinated by the organisation Viafára now worked for. The Doc was not the most enthusiastic or proficient trainee we had. I would have thought that the chances of him affecting my life in the future were practically zero, but then life has a habit of proving me wrong.

The weapons that Rodriguez Gacha had ordered had not arrived yet, we hadn't been given any helicopters and no further ammunition was sent down to us. Finally, we decided that enough was enough and called it a day. Even the Colombians were pleased. They too were sick of Typhoid Mary's cooking. I flew back to Bogotá with Jorge in one of the Cessnas, while Peter and the team went by boat upstream to Puerto Asís. Renamed by all Port Hashish, it was a small jungle town full of drug dealers and loose women. For a couple of days, until their transportation was arranged, the guys could 'escape and evade' the unwelcome attention of all those females!

After meetings with Armando Vargas, arrangements regarding the last of our pay were sorted out. The lads flew in and were paid off. Shortly after our departure, several men dressed as policemen entered the offices of Comerandes Ltda and machine-gunned Armando Vargas to death. It seems we had only just got paid in time.

Before we left, Peter and I had a final discussion with Jorge, who was as disappointed as us by the end result of the project. FARC would live to fight another day. Was the whole thing for real or were we conned? I think that it started off with the best intentions but these got lost along the way; the gangsters took control and used us for their ends. Nonetheless, I wouldn't have missed it for the world. On 2 November, Peter and I said *adios* to Jorge and farewell to Colombia; it was a pleasure knowing him and a pleasure to have been there.

CHAPTER 20

TILTING AT WINDMILLS

IN FEBRUARY 1989, I GOT A PHONE CALL FROM JORGE SALCEDO AND it all started again. Would I be prepared to come back for another mission? 'Yes, subject to terms and conditions.' On the 13th, I met Jorge and Mario off a flight from Bogotá. I hadn't seen Mario since the early days of the last contract, when he had supplied intelligence reports and maps from his battalion HQ. Jorge and Mario told me that they had resigned from the army and were now civilians. They brought me up to date on events in Colombia. FARC were still going strong and kidnappings were on the increase. Rodriguez Gacha had declared war on the government over mooted extradition treaties with the United States for drug runners. Paramilitaries were bombing newspaper offices, police headquarters and anyone who pissed them off.

Jorge and Mario were very careful to cloak their paymasters in a veil of respectability. Not that I believed much of it, but, in this game, ethics tend to take a back seat when the alternative is shovelling concrete. My prospective clients, according to Jorge, were a group of 'businessmen' whom Pablo Escobar had sworn to kill. The Medellín cartel had mounted a bombing campaign against their business interests. These businessmen lived in Cali, the third-largest city in Colombia. More than 30 bombs had exploded in stores in the group's Drogas La Rebaja chain of mini-supermarkets, of which there were 350. When asked why they were being targeted, Jorge could not give a satisfactory explanation. After the last episode, I demanded to know the truth before I would commit to any sort of contract.

Jorge told me as much as he thought was prudent, bearing in mind that I had not yet accepted the job. The businessmen were the Cali cocaine cartel. The Cali cartel did not receive the same degree of publicity as the Medellín cartel, whose violent exploits were much reported. How Jorge had got involved with the Cali cartel was never explained to me. The mission on offer had one aim: to kill Pablo Escobar. This time, there was no suggestion that our business had government or military backing, although he stressed that we would have no problems with the authorities. It was always difficult to fully understand the role of the so-called authorities when it came to dealing with the cartels. Alliances were often motivated by fear, corruption and expediency.

On 15 February, I went to Hereford to visit Peter McAleese. I brought him up to speed and invited him to join negotiations with the principals in Cali. We decided to take Dean Shelley and Alex Lennox along with us; they were the benchmark for the types we would need for an operation of this kind. Jorge and Mario set off several days before us and on 24 February, we flew to Colombia via Panama. We passed through Cali airport's security checks, with Jorge monitoring our progress like a mother hen. The city, the prosperous capital of the Valle de Cauca district of Colombia, has an almost tropical climate and is renowned throughout South America for its beautiful women. We deposited our luggage in a luxurious apartment block that had armed security in the lobby. There were no worries about nosy neighbours, as we had the whole building to ourselves. The accommodation was five-star, with our own bar and en-suite bathrooms. In my walk-in dressing room were electronic money-counting machines. I hoped I might have use for them.

When we were unpacked and showered, Land Cruisers took us to Jamundi, a small town on the outskirts of Cali. We were going to meet the four powerful bosses who controlled the region. I knew very little about any of them, as Jorge always simply described them as businessmen, and their names meant nothing to me. The meeting place turned out to be a private sports complex, complete with running tracks, swimming pool, gymnasium, sauna and thatch-roofed open-air lounge area. The complex was surrounded by sheet-steel fencing and entered through steel gates manned by security guards. The four men were relaxing with drinks. I would have to convince them that we were capable of achieving their aim. Jorge made the introductions, translating for us, and we were given beers. Jorge's speech was punctuated with '*si señor*' and '*patron*', all very subservient stuff. The four men were two brothers, Gilberto Rodriguez Orejuela (aka 'the Chess Player') and Miguel Rodriguez Orejuela ('El Señor'), plus Helmer Herrera Buitrago ('Pacho') and José Santacruz Londoño ('Don Chepe' or 'El Gordo'). They were dressed casually but expensively in designer slacks, handmade shirts and Gucci-style loafers. 'Pacho' Herrera the youngest of the quartet was dressed in a Sergio Tachini tracksuit and trainers and had designer stubble. All wore expensive but conservative jewellery and Cartier or Rolex watches. There was a surprising lack of bodyguards on show but there were other buildings nearby and I had no doubt that we were being watched.

During lunch, the front gates opened and a three-ton open-back truck drove in with maybe fifteen policemen in the back. Any remaining concerns about the authorities were dispelled, as the cops had come in for lunch. Before we got down to business, a call was made on a walkie-talkie radio and several men appeared carrying equipment for us to look at. There were night-vision sights and goggles, cheap bugging equipment, Desert Eagle pistols, crossbows and a 50-calibre Barrett sniper rifle in a five-foot-long carry case. I hoped this wasn't going to be the full extent of our armoury. While Dean and Alex played with the toys and used the swimming pool, I got down to the business of negotiation. We had drawn up a comprehensive list of questions intended to gauge our chances of achieving the aim. It was obvious they had no idea where Escobar was at any given time of the day or week. All their intelligence as to his whereabouts was historical. I pointed out that we were entirely dependent on them for information about his location and that it had to be in 'real time' or close, otherwise we would be pissing in the wind.

Their lack of understanding was highlighted when they asked how long I thought it might take. I turned the question around and asked them, with what they knew, how long did they think it should take. The response was 'a couple of weeks'! There is a lot more to putting together an operation like that than meets the eye and, as a result, negotiations with the client are more often than not frustrating. They rarely grasp the complexities involved and see everything in very simplistic terms. Usually, many problems that a client will not have considered have to be factored into the equation. An operation that requires the contractor to supply the equipment and weapons can take many months to put together successfully.

I went into my sales pitch about our capabilities and how far we were prepared to go. We would bring a team whose backgrounds encompassed all the military skills required to facilitate such an operation. At this point, it was in my interests, financially speaking, to have the largest number of personnel on the ground that the clients would stand. I wanted to secure personnel who were engaged in lucrative paying positions in various parts of the world. This would require a salary commensurate with the risk – and at this point it was not possible to quantify the risk. As I had no way of knowing how long it would take to complete the mission, I required a three-month advance payment for an initial twelve-man team. Regardless of the time taken, all payments would be for a minimum of three months, in advance, with an operational bonus payment to be discussed when a clearer idea of the mission plan was formulated. This offer was accepted.

We returned to the apartment. That night, we took delivery of several pistols, an Ingram Mac-10 sub-machine gun and a 12-gauge Mossberg shotgun in case we had unwelcome visitors. The next day, Peter and I flew over Escobar's principal residence, Hacienda Napoles, in the province of Antioquia to the north of the country. We were in a 12-seat Cessna armed with cameras and zoom lenses. The pilot maintained a height that would give us a good view of the 7,000-acre estate without alarming anyone on the ground. It was

278

impressive to say the least. From an arched entrance with a full-size Cessna mounted on the top, a driveway several kilometres long led to a gatehouse, beyond which was the main living area, which covered dozens of acres and was surrounded by steel fencing punctuated by thatch-roofed guard towers. The living complex was thick with trees and shrubs. Outside one edge of the fencing was a long airstrip; inside was a large lake, stretching the full length of the fence. The main house had a terracotta-tiled roof, one large swimming pool to the front of the house and another, smaller one off a side wing, presumably for guests or bodyguards. To the rear of the house there were more trees and another lake acted as a barrier to entry on foot. In the main grounds were a football pitch, a tennis court and two helipads. A large L-shape building of modern design housed the bodyguards' quarters, we were told, as well as a museum that contained a bullet-riddled car that had supposedly belonged to Al Capone. Across the rest of the estate were scattered other large buildings, aircraft hangars and an equestrian centre/bullring. A huge satellite dish glistened in the sunlight. My first impression was that this was going to be a hell of a job.

Financed for three months, I departed Colombia to organise the team. Manpower is not as easy to acquire as you might think, at least not the type that would be prepared to take on this mission. There are many good ex-soldiers available for high-risk work but in general those risks are cloaked in respectability, undertaken for private military companies (PMCs) with government blessing. While danger is always present, there are certain comforts, such as insurance against death or injury, guaranteed casevac to medical assistance and an infrastructure geared towards maximising your chances of survival. Some of the team that I had on standby I had worked with before. Four from the previous Colombian venture had declined for various reasons or were deemed unsuitable. They were replaced by Don Milton, Stuart McVicar and Andy Gibson, all ex-SAS, and former marine Billy Chambers. Two former South African Reconnaissance Commandos who had served in Rhodesia and elsewhere also went to make up our dirty dozen.

Advance payments were made to some and air flights coordinated. Medical equipment was purchased: sutures, inflatable splints and tracheotomy sets. I purchased portable searchlights with infrared lenses, Firefly infrared markers that used strobe lights, which could be seen only with night-vision equipment, to be used as 'friendly' identification at night. We had no clear plan at this stage; Haçienda Napoles was just the most obvious possibility. I therefore tried to cover as many eventualities as possible, buying electronic bugging kits, frequency counters, radio scanners and direction-finding equipment.

We were set, so the members of the team began to fly out to Colombia. I travelled with the British contingent to Heathrow. I had an enormous amount of luggage, about which I was likely to be questioned when it went through the luggage scanner. It was a bank holiday so I had taken some precautions to ensure we got through the queues quickly. A friend, Chris Holah, who worked for the Transport Security Directorate at Heathrow, smoothed our passage through the formalities. At Cali, we were met by Jorge and cleared through the airport.

Finally, the team was in place. No one except Peter and I knew who our intended target was; they had been told only that the operation was high risk. I guess it says a lot for Peter's leadership qualities that he was able to bring these men on a blind mission. Once everyone had settled in, a pep talk was given about safety and keeping a low profile. Security was a major issue, as kidnapping of tourists seemed to be a full-time occupation for some Colombians. We had security drills for accessing the apartments we were staying in. All personnel had weapons available but it was thought prudent to forbid the carrying of arms outside the premises, since tourists don't usually carry Mac-10s or Mini-Uzis.

The first few days were set aside for R&R and acclimatisation after the long flight. Cali has many sleazy bars and discos, which were investigated by all concerned. We had an early problem with that old demon booze. The miscreants were chewed out at Peter's morning briefing and a fine was imposed, not that I'd ever remember to deduct it from their salaries. The team was finally told officially what our aim was, although by this point the rumour mill had guessed it. I produced a picture of Escobar, torn from the *Sunday Times Magazine*. The aerial photographs we'd taken were enlarged and a photomontage of Haçienda Napoles was constructed. Maps of the region were pored over as we searched for the best possible route in to undertake a close-target reconnaissance. Jorge and Mario assured us that this was out of the question; any stranger moving in that area would be spotted by some yokel and reported directly to Escobar's security. We set up our radio equipment and listened to numerous coded conversations between drug dealers and producers. Our Spanish was not up to much but we had added to the group a Colombian raised in New York. Omar, known as 'Flaco', meaning 'skinny', worked for Chepe Santacruz; having been arrested on money-laundering charges in the USA, he had jumped a million-dollar bond and was now our interpreter.

The city lifestyle was not conducive to work. We needed a place to train and get fit, so we moved out of our penthouse apartments, to the annoyance of some who would have preferred to continue their nightly forays into the Sixth Avenue clubs and bars. Our next move, however, was not much more in keeping with our training requirements. We went to stay in a hilltop complex outside of the city. It was a weekend retreat for Miguel Rodriguez's wife and children. Beyond the white-walled armoured gatehouse complete with armed security guards, was a leisure complex set in some 30 acres of landscaped gardens. The grounds were surrounded by two layers of wire fencing separated by a dog run. The facilities included a weight-training room, sauna and swimming pool, not to mention the riding stables, tennis and volleyball courts, indoor bowling alley and quad bikes. Our quarters were of the standard we had become accustomed to downtown. We had a black cook called Bertha, who catered our excellent meals. Gardeners and maintenance men maintained the property and tended the Japanese garden, complete with ornamental stream and bridge. They tactfully avoided contact with us.

This was not exactly what we had had in mind for our team, who thought they had died and gone to heaven. A regime of training was soon put in place. At six every morning, we mustered for a multi-kilometre run around the track. This was always led by Dean and Alex, who were the fittest. No distance was ever stipulated and they seemed to be in competition to see how far they could push each other and consequently the rest of us. Breakfast was followed by weight training, volleyball and anything else of a strenuous nature.

Section leaders had to be selected and Peter went about this in his customary way: we were each told to put the name of the person we would want next to us in a foxhole if the shit hit the fan on a slip of paper. This was a way of gauging the team's collective opinion of its members. The ballot was secret, so no one knew who had specified whom. The men who had the most votes were made section leaders. We were not in the army and no ranks were allocated to individuals but there had to be some form of structure to maintain a sense of military order and discipline. Peter, of course, was the team leader. I would fit in where I was needed. My background was not a formal military one, so I had to earn the respect of those who had not worked with me before. A measure of authority came with the cheque book and the fact that I could hire and fire at will.

When we'd been in Colombia for about a month, I was summoned to the cartel's offices, situated in a suburb of Cali called Ciudad Jardín (Garden City). Rodriguez ran his business from a walled complex of single-storey terracotta-tiled buildings. The Rodriguez empire was multifaceted: the Drogas La Rebaja chain, radio stations, property companies, banking, import–export, car dealerships, even the local football team. The office suite was typical of a successful corporation: secretaries and typists working, phones and telex machines, the bustle of everyday commerce. I was taken to a large workshop where a consignment of refrigerators and other white goods was being unpacked. The back panels were removed to reveal dismantled weapons taped inside, each part numbered: our equipment had arrived from the USA via Mexico. The consignment was made up of Colt AR-15s, M16s, spare magazines, handguns and night-vision sights.

The following day, a van arrived at our accommodation, with our weapons hidden in an ingenious false floor accessed by tilting the body of the van to one side. Now that we had something concrete to show them, the team's mood lifted. They were like kids in a toyshop. We took an inventory of what we had. Along with the guns from the day before there were many thousands of rounds of ammo, a couple of Heckler & Koch G3 rifles, some Smith & Wesson pistols, some

.357 revolvers, an Italian sub-machine gun, M72 anti-tank rocket launchers and dozens of C-4 demolition charges.

Boredom vanished like smoke in the wind. Now that the team had their guns, they were acting more like soldiers. We spent over a week on stripping, assembly and stoppage drills, until we could do it blindfolded. On the volleyball court, we ran mock assaults and room-clearance drills, entry and exit, with all-round defence from imaginary helicopters represented by chairs. We held night drills against attack by enemy gunmen on our compound, having the floodlights turned off to practise defending against an invisible enemy in the dark. Then it was time for live-firing drills. We chose our weapons and the equipment was loaded onto a van. We drove to a hilltop farm where we could fire away to our hearts' delight.

Satisfied with our equipment, we were returning to base when we stopped at a dusty little village bar for a beer. This stop would provide another example of the corruption prevalent in Colombia at that time. We were quietly drinking beers and lounging around our vehicles when a lone police officer on a patrol bike cruised past. He gave us the once over and turned around before parking the bike and strolling towards us. In his motorcycle leathers and Ray-Ban glasses, he was straight out of a Hollywood movie. We wore civilian clothes but his attention seemed to be on our footwear; most of us had on black combat boots, which we were breaking in. I had to give him points for observation. We did not reply when he waffled something in Spanish at us. We had no idea what he said but it was probably something along the lines of 'What the fuck are you lot up to?' Mario intervened, producing his military ID, which did not impress the cop one little bit. From his tone of voice and finger pointing, it seemed he wanted to know why a dozen men who would not talk to him were hanging about in this quiet little village wearing combat boots.

A heated argument ensued between Mario and the cop. Mario had a Mac-10 in a shoulder bag and it was beginning to look as if he might just pull it out. Jorge kept out of the row and told us to not do anything rash, as he could see some of the guys casually manoeuvring towards the weapons truck. The two antagonists seemed to have reached an impasse and Mario made a call on his radio. A short while later, another motorcycle turned up. This time it was one of our guys. The rider gave a bag to Mario, who passed it to the cop. I'm pretty certain it wasn't a bag of doughnuts. The cop went on his way and we learned another lesson.

Another spanner went in the works when Terry Tagney asked for a private meeting with Peter and me. He told us straight out that his nerve had gone. He was terrified at the thought of what we were contemplating and wanted to pull out and go home. As we could not keep him against his will, after he'd assured us he would not breach our operational security, we sent him back to South Africa. We saved him any embarrassment by telling the team that his wife was ill and needed him home. I flew to England to find a replacement.

The weeks passed. Peter, Jorge and I would go for lunch meetings with the four businessmen, who would tell us that Pablo Escobar had been seen here, there and everywhere. The information was always days old and of no possible use to us. Escobar was elusive. Haçienda Napoles was the jewel in his crown but he very rarely spent any time there. He held meetings there when he wanted to impress or intimidate someone of importance. The estate had been subject to raids by police and military before. Always informed in advance of these visits, Escobar made himself absent. He knew it was the most vulnerable of his many bolt-holes; large as the place was, it was not as easy to get lost in as a city.

Finally, in April, we decided that without a specific target to train for, we were just blowing smoke. We chose to focus on Haçienda Napoles. Efforts to get Escobar there would be our sponsors' responsibility. Jorge and Mario supplied us with all the information they could source about the house and grounds. We received copies of military and police reports on government attempts to apprehend Escobar. Our photomontage went under the microscope and the more we studied, the less we liked. We had initially chosen the football pitch as our landing zone but it was ruled out. Under magnification, we could just make out anti-helicopter wires criss-crossing the field. Another overflight confirmed it; the helipads were also wired and it looked like we might have to find a pilot with the balls to squeeze us into the tennis court.

Our next step was to find an operational base. Peter and I were taken to a sugar-cane field on the outskirts of the city, where we boarded a Bell JetRanger helicopter. It flew us through the gorges and over the peaks of the Cordilleras Mountains to a jungle hideaway about 50 miles west of Cali. We landed on a pebbled beach on the banks of the Manguido River. Our destination was a large cabin built on wooden piles, with a veranda of red and white planks. Inside, it was one large room, with a tiled kitchen area and a toilet and shower room at the rear. The furnishings consisted of a large table and benches, and a few wall decorations, notably several animal skulls fixed to the back wall. There were no beds but the toilet actually flushed. The water for this and the shower was pumped from the river, powered by an electric generator. We briefly met the owner, a Colombian who spoke with an American accent and lived in Chicago. The cabin, surrounded by dense jungle, was called La Guagua and it was soon to become our base camp.

A few days later, the JetRanger and a new addition to our mini-air force, a Hughes 500 helicopter, ferried in the team. A lot of work must have taken place before we arrived, as mattresses, mosquito nets, cooking utensils, food, soft drinks and other provisions were on hand. We spent some time sorting our kit and a guard-duty roster for night-time security. We were in the middle of nowhere and in Colombia the middle of nowhere is where guerrilla groups and cocaine bandits roam. The cook was a very old black man who performed wonders on a Heath Robinson barbecue contraption.

Another helicopter was on order, as the JetRanger was unsuitable for troop transport and the Hughes 500 was earmarked to be our gunship. After a week or so, it arrived. In the jungle across the river, a clearing had been cut and a log-and-tarpaulin-covered hangar had been built beneath the tree canopy. Sleepers and planks had been laid to form a landing place that allowed us to slide the aircraft under cover. Our new toy was a Huey, the model that had staked its claim to fame in the Vietnam War. Wherever it had come from, it must have been a long way away, as the passenger compartment was occupied by a long-range fuel tank. Our aircraft mechanic removed the tank and went about the task of a complete service. The Huey arrived decked out in blue-and-white livery, which did not suit our plans, so we decided to respray it in the livery of the Colombian police, with 'Policia Nacional' on the sides and the Colombian flag.

While we were waiting for paint and spray equipment to arrive, deluges of rain completely drenched our beach and marooned us indoors for days at a time. We were flown back to Cali for R&R. I phoned home to make sure my wife and kids were all right. Mary did give me one piece of bad news: our mission was about to have a hole punched in it by James Adams, the defence correspondent of the *Sunday Times*. During my trip back to England to replace Terry Tagney, a news article that had originated in Colombia and America had been picked up by the British press. A member of the Medellín cartel had surrendered and claimed to *El Espectador* newspaper that he had undergone a military training course in bombing techniques taught by foreign mercenaries, specifically former members of Israeli and British special forces. There was no clue as to his identity and he was flown to the USA, where he was entered into the Witness Protection Program and was to testify at US Senate hearings. As was usual when the rumour mill about mercenary operations was on the go, various journalists rang me to ask me about the story. I pled ignorance, telling them that I'd heard nothing about it but thought the guy's claims sounded like rubbish. This seemed to satisfy them and no follow-up stories were printed.

Since then, James Adams, whom I had never spoken to, had investigated the story further. He had found out that there had been a British mercenary presence in Colombia the previous year, perhaps through connections in intelligence. My wife told me that Adams was about to publish his article and wanted us to comment before it went to print. Peter and I were certain that Adams could not have details of our latest venture because the team had not been briefed until they arrived. Our first reaction was to ignore him but the story might create the kind of interest and speculation we wanted to avoid. I decided to call him.

Adams read us his story, most of it speculation based on what he had learned regarding the secret witness now in US custody. Most of it was nothing much to worry about, especially as the mission discussed was all in the past. However, his story stated that Peter McAleese, Dean Shelley, Alex Lennox and I had flown to Cali this year. I assume Adams had accessed a flight manifest, as we had all travelled on the same British Airways flight to Panama. If the story made its way into the Colombian press, this would jeopardise our mission. Our previous paymaster, Gonzalo Rodriguez Gacha, was an associate of Pablo Escobar's Medellín cartel and was one of the most dangerous men in Colombia. It would not be rocket science to work out that if we were in Cali, we were operating for the Cali cartel. We promised to call Adams after we had digested the story. We arranged a meeting with our sponsors and told them the position regarding this security breach. The first suggestion was to pay him off. I explained that the *Sunday Times* was a prestigious newspaper that prided itself on its integrity and that we were unlikely to stand a chance of succeeding.

I called Adams again and explained to him that by publishing the article, he would put at risk the lives of the men who were currently with us. He wanted to know what we were up to this time, which, of course, I was not about to reveal. I offered him a deal: if he would hold off, we would give him the true facts of our previous trip when we returned. How was he to know that we would not renege on the deal if he agreed? I told him I would instruct my wife to give him photographs of Peter and I that would prove conclusively that we had operated in Colombia the previous year. If we did not honour our deal, he could publish his story complete with pictures. We invited him to Cali but he declined. He didn't trust us that much! However, the offer of the photographs obviously intrigued him and he wanted more information for his story, so he agreed to meet us in Panama City.

On 11 May, Peter and I met James Adams at the Riande Continental Hotel. We sat at a table by the swimming pool as the day drew to a close. Adams was in his 40s and dressed *Miami Vice* style in linen jacket with rolled-up sleeves, loafers and no socks. We ordered drinks and got down to a verbal fencing match, having to parry questions regarding the aim of our current mission. We told him that if we completed our programme without media intervention, we would give him the full story of our previous trip when everyone had returned home. He pressed hard for clues about our new objective but we responded that if we succeeded, he would be able to connect the dots and would have a better handle on the facts than anyone else. He agreed to hold the article for as long as possible, although if other media outlets got hold of the story, he would publish.

We collected the team and headed for La Guagua, where the paint and spraying equipment had arrived. It took several days before the job was finished and our chopper was white and emerald green, with 'Policia Nacional' stencilled on either side of its fuselage and the Colombian flag painted under the tail rotor. The atmosphere was great, with tremendous camaraderie among the lads, who all mucked in to help. I was quite proud of the finished article and felt certain that should all else fail, we could all get jobs ringing cars in a 'chop shop'.

Our training was somewhat constrained with our mini-air force not yet ready but we had daily briefings on all phases of the intended operation, used the beach and river as a firing range, tossed grenades and fired rockets. We ran through the plan aloud, with volleys of abuse from section leaders if we made an error. We had formation walk throughs, killing imaginary wounded up to our limit of exploitation, a pre-agreed boundary past which it wasn't worth chasing an escapee. We had additional aircraft in support roles for the day we attacked Napoles and we had to know all the call signs. We rehearsed bringing in the choppers with different smoke colours. Yellow indicated a clear landing zone, while red warned the pilot that he would be coming under hostile fire. Maps of the area were studied and emergency rendezvous points (ERVs) selected in case some of us had to bomb-burst out on foot if one or more of the helicopters sustained damage and was unable to pick us up. We had emergency radio call times and Firefly light-up times at our ERVs, so that friendly overflights would know we were at our pick-up points.

When the Huey was ready, we started work on the Hughes 500, which was sprayed military matt olive green. Work was done to accommodate a pintle-mounted general-purpose machine gun (GPMG, or 'gimpy') in the doorway. The police- and army-liveried helicopters were designed to give us a tactical advantage. Escobar's estate had been raided by government operations in the past and these visits had always been conducted without a shooting match; instead his staff would apologise for his absence and offer refreshments. If all went well, we should be allowed to approach the estate and be on top of them when we opened up with the guns. The gunship would be zigzagging forward directly above the house, at hover speed and rooftop height, out of range of blast debris and ground fire from the immediate vicinity. Peter would man the gimpy and I was going to be riding the skid bar, wearing a harness so that I could lean out and drop satchel charges, portable explosive devices, along the front of the house.

Our camouflage arrived along with black ski masks and purpose-made combat vests with various pockets to hold spare magazines, radios and grenades. They had built-in backpacks for emergency civilian clothing and 'shock packs' (intravenous saline drip bags, syringes, morphine ampoules and shell dressings). We got our explosives and I started work on the satchel charges, constructing them with C-4 explosive and instantaneous detonating cord, rigged with 15-second-delay time pencils. I equipped the house-clearance team with 'knock-knocks', small explosive devices with double-sided sticky tape attached. When they came to a locked door, they could simply slap a knock-knock over the lock and blow the door in. We rigged the beach with poles and hessian sacking to create 'rooms' so that the team could practise.

Elsewhere in Colombia, other work was being carried out. Electronic engineers were working on a small Cessna, fitting it with re-broadcast and repeater equipment. This would be circling the air above us, boosting our communication capabilities. The Cessna was referred to as 'Telstar', while the JetRanger and Hughes 500 were 'Taxi 1' and 'Taxi 2'. Our helicopter pilots were both Colombian. The guy who flew the Huey was code-named 'Toyco' and was a former air-force major. The Hughes pilot, 'Tiger' was a serving police captain in the anti-narcotics squad. I would learn his real name only when I took the dog tags from his dead body.

There was still no information on Escobar's location on any given day. The delay didn't worry me; the longer he stayed alive, the longer we got paid for playing war games. Besides, we weren't quite ready yet.

DIRTY COMBAT

We were now heading for our fourth month in Colombia. So much for the cartel's guesstimate of two weeks to completion. The days and nights in camp were hot and muggy. Humidity was high and when we weren't soaked in sweat, we were marooned in the cabin by torrential rain. The beach would disappear and our home would be sitting above the water on its wooden piles as the river invaded the ground around us. We would have to travel to the helicopter workshop by dug-out canoe until the waters receded again.

We took another break. Peter and I gave a situation report to our sponsors at the ranch home of Chepe Santacruz. The driveway was flanked by fields and stock pens filled with Brahman cattle. The house was brand new; the windows still had protective sheeting over the glass. It was a mansion, complete with enormous Doric columns and huge front doors straight out of *Scarface*. There were about 20 Nissan Patrols and Land Cruisers parked outside. About 60 armed bodyguards, the combined muscle of our four paymasters, were hanging around, some engaged in a friendly football match. There had still been no positive sightings of Escobar, but they knew he was going to hold a party on the estate to celebrate some sort of family occasion. We were told it would be a big event and Escobar would definitely be present. This was the first time that we had come close to getting any positive warning of Escobar's whereabouts at a specific time. Nonetheless, we declined to mount the operation. The problem was that many women and children would also be attending. Our planning and training was not geared towards surgical precision and the mission would end in a bloodbath with lots of innocent victims. Fortunately, our sponsors were not cast in the same mould as our previous paymaster, who would have slaughtered indiscriminately to get to the person he was pissed off with.

Fun-and-games time was over for the team and back at La Guagua training was relentless. We had two additional members of the team in Mario and Omar, who insisted, with the blessing of their bosses, that they were coming on the actual operation. They were playing catch-up, having been missing for the earlier training sessions, and it showed. Full dress rehearsals were begun. Clad in camouflage and ski masks (marked with dayglo yellow crosses to identify us to our own side in the air), we performed our mock assaults as if they were the real thing. We lived in a cacophony of sound and the smell of gun smoke was always in our nostrils. As helicopters swooped from the skies with guns blazing from the doorways, men leapt out firing machine guns and rockets. Explosions ripped through the air as satchel charges and grenades detonated. We performed our walk through, making sure there were no enemy survivors as the helicopters were called in by our smoke. Escobar always went to the cocaine lab in the sky. Job well done. The only problem in our game, of course, was that the cowboys would always win, as the Indians were non-existent.

The dress rehearsals were vital, however, in finding out flaws in our reaction times and exposing shortcomings in some of our equipment. The craftsmanship of our combat vests left something to be desired. They had to take quite a lot of abuse and they began to fall apart; a pistol or radio that was in your pocket one minute could be gone the next. We made adjustments to the equipment until we were satisfied with what we had. Our lives might depend on it.

There came a time when the novelty wore off. For us, all the gun smoke and testosterone needed to be going somewhere. We were fast using up materiel that would be required on the job in training. The more we trained, the greater was the likelihood that someone would receive an injury that would set us back. We had been working for so long that the guys had thousands in their bank accounts. I would never question their courage or commitment but when you've got money in the bank and a hard-on, why play games in the jungle that might get you killed? If any team member had pulled out at this stage, it would have been a serious problem. We had reached our peak and were pretty sick of training. We couldn't afford to hit a flat spot because of boredom. We had to be better than good on the day or Escobar's gunmen would iron us out. We flew the team, with Jorge, to Panama for a complete break from the whole operation. Peter and I stayed behind; we felt they deserved to do their own thing without us monitoring their every move. Jorge would keep them in check. The team took a scuba-diving course and did whatever else took their fancy in the clubs and bars of Panama City.

On one of my trips back to England, I had bought children's toy sets that included model farmyard buildings, fences, houses, trees, planes and helicopters. Taking advantage of the team's absence, I arranged a meeting with our sponsors at one of their many luxurious homes. Peter and I built what is referred to as a 'sandbox model' of our target in the living room. We spent several hours constructing the model, which was complete with support aircraft suspended on threads from the ceiling. The model helicopters were attached to short poles so that we could simulate flight. We rehearsed our little scenario until we had it all off pat.

When we were ready, eight people entered the room and seated themselves opposite the model. We went into our introduction to the forthcoming show, with a translator relaying it to the audience. We took them through the operation step by step. The last act ended with the villain of the piece getting his just deserts. The team flew off into the setting sun and everybody lived happily ever after. This went down a storm. We actually got a standing ovation; they absolutely loved it. It's always nice to know you've made someone's day.

Chepe Santacruz approached me after the show and, in broken English, offered me a million dollars if I brought him Pablo's head. I have read several accounts of the mission since suggesting that we were going to kidnap Escobar and throw him from the helicopter. We were not being paid for excess baggage. However, at that price, I would have made room for a part of him.

When the team returned from Panama without spending a day in jail or causing any diplomatic incidents, we breathed a sigh of relief. All back in our jungle hideaway, we cleaned and checked equipment – and waited. We sunbathed and swam in the river, never more than a few yards from our weapons. The choppers were checked over, aviation gas was filtered and fuel tanks were filled, and still we waited.

CHAPTER 21

DEATH IN THE CLOUDS

SATURDAY, 3 JUNE STARTED OFF NICE AND SUNNY, WITH ONLY THE occasional cloud in a clear blue sky. The camp came to life with the usual noises and comments of an all-male group, most of it profane and unprintable. The camp sex maniacs fantasised out loud about some centrefold model sitting on their face or performing some other sexual act. The camp psycho was mumbling aloud, 'fucking' this and 'fucking' that, about anything and everything. I should have charged extra for him, as, given the amount he talked, you could be forgiven for thinking he was more than one person. Everyone drifted down to the river's edge to perform their ablutions. It would have seemed quite a sight to an outsider, these men of different ages, shapes and sizes, some naked and others draped in towels, all carrying guns. Some were built like brick shithouses. The younger ones lean and muscular, pumped iron like it was a religion and could run for miles, revelling in their youth and masculinity. Several were stocky without the muscle definition of the younger guys; age and booze, a combination that would take its toll on most of the men in time, had wreaked havoc on their bodies. They were all fit, certainly fitter than most, whatever their age or physical shape implied. Some bore jagged or puckered scars left by bullets or shrapnel, pale marks on their suntanned skin. One limped slightly; closer scrutiny would reveal long scars running from knee to ankle, the legacy of a parachute drop that had gone wrong.

It was mid-morning when the radio burst into life. The operator listened for a while to the coded Spanish transmission. The message was our signal to go. Escobar was sitting by his swimming pool at Haçienda Napoles. Peter gave the order and the team went about their tasks in readiness for departure. Within the hour, the metamorphosis was complete. Dressed in full battle gear, each team member checked his equipment, which was then double-checked by another man. Radio tests were completed; the support group and house-clearance teams had good comms with the team leader.

Peter gave a last briefing. For operational purposes, he had colour-coded the areas of the mansion and divided it into three numbered sections. The rear of the house was 'Black', the right of the house was 'Red', left was 'Blue' and the front was 'White'. The support group's position would be in front of the house, so this system was required to allow the house-clearance teams to tell us to switch fire into White 2, say, keeping us informed of areas that needed to be targeted. Once inside, the house team would advise Peter, in the gunship, which section they were in and as they moved they would call out their position. As they fought their way through, the support group would target the area one section ahead of their position. The gunship would act as an aerial 'stop group', picking off runners into or out of the building as it circled above.

The two house-clearance groups comprised Billy Chambers, Pete Donnelly, Rob Moore, Dave Borland, Don Milton, Dean Shelley, Alex Lennox and Ned Owen. The support group consisted of Stuart McVicar, Andy Gibson, Mario Delbasco, Omar Ospina and me. We each received 300,000 pesos emergency money, in case we had to make our own way to an ERV point.

The pilots left the cabin as soon as the briefing was finished. Preflight checks were completed and we heard the distinctive 'whoomp whoomp' of the Huey as it cleared the treetops, followed closely by the angry-bee sound of the smaller, more manoeuvrable Hughes 500.

Peter said a few chosen words, ending with 'Let's do it.' It was going to be cramped all the way as the Huey had been fitted with internal long-range fuel tanks, while the Hughes had had its rear seats removed and we had to sit on the belts of linked ammunition for the gimpy. The choppers took off just before noon, bound for a covert refuel site code-named 'Kiko', which was two hours' flying time away. Kiko was ten minutes from target. There, the doors would be removed and the machine guns mounted. Three other aircraft were also making for the patch of sky above our target. With our helicopters in the livery of the police and army, our pilots were equipped with a code word indicating that we were on a classified operation in case we came into contact with the real thing in the air. In the back of the Hughes, the support group sat, surrounded by ammunition belts and 45 kg of explosives, with nothing to say, each immersed in his private thoughts. We had passed the point of no return.

Eighty miles from Kiko, the weather changed and we had to climb above low cloud. It began to rain and gusts of wind buffeted our machines as we flew towards a ridge known as 'Cuchillo Silencio', meaning 'silent knife'. The two aircraft moved further apart as each pilot searched for his own path over the green-clad peaks. The cloud was like acres of dirty cotton wool, the mountain peaks appearing and vanishing as it rolled over them. The Hughes sounded as if it didn't like what it was being asked to do. It rose ever higher, still enveloped in cloud, as Tiger searched for a clear line of sight. I looked over at the altimeter; it was showing 8,200 ft. Our little craft bucked and twisted its way through the increasingly wild wind and rain, which swirled off the saw-tooth ridges, whipping at the fuselage. Tiger spotted a space between the peaks and went for it. At that moment, the rolling clouds slid silently across the gap, like the last piece of a puzzle completed by some malevolent god.

There was no warning, no horrified screams anticipating imminent disaster, just a perceptible drop in the noise from the whirling rotor blades, perhaps because of the silencing effect of the clouds wrapped around us like a shroud. The next thing I remember is being upside down, then the pain in my head. For a few moments, nothing made any sense and then I realised that Mario and Omar were not in the cabin with me. Foliage was partially filling the doorway and the door was gone. It took a few stunned seconds for me to grasp that we had crashed. Panic set in briefly before the survival instinct took over. I knew I had to get away from the helicopter; a helicopter crash in a film is almost always followed by a ball of fire as the gas tank explodes. My mind was racing, anticipating the explosion, as I clawed my way through the foliage in the doorway on my hands and knees. Out on the forested mountainside, I had no bearings. I was completely panicked and disorientated. Heading downhill, I came to a clearing where I stopped and attempted to regain the power of rational thought. I didn't think of the others at this stage; I had heard nothing and seen no one since the crash.

Looking back up the incline that I had just scrambled down, I could see the wreck of the Hughes. Lying on its side, it steamed and sizzled in the wet and broken trees. My mind racing, I wondered how long had it been since we'd crashed. Had 15 seconds gone by? Was I far enough away if the satchel charges exploded? I didn't move for several minutes, trying to calm down and assess the situation. Then I saw Peter McAleese stagger out of the undergrowth further up the slope. He was obviously in pain and was having difficulty walking on the wet ground. I left my refuge and climbed up to meet him. I was still concerned about the satchel charges and proceeded to search among the wreckage and debris until I found them. I cut the fuse trains and removed the detonators and time-delay pencils.

From out of the foliage staggered Omar and Mario. Omar was bleeding from numerous small wounds to his face but Mario appeared to be relatively unscathed. Calmer now, I realised that there had been no Hollywood-style explosion because we were nearly out of fuel. We tried to assess the full extent of the damage. The Hughes was partially embedded in the undergrowth and the centuries of decayed material beneath, which had cushioned the impact of the crash. Our equipment was scattered for yards around; machine-gun ammo belts were hanging from the doorway, draped down the craft's sides. The contents of Omar's and Mario's lost combat vests were spread around and hanging from branches.

We didn't say much, only asking about each other's injuries. Peter was obviously in pain. He was having trouble walking and seemed to have broken ribs. My head hurt very badly and was bleeding profusely, my face a mask of blood. My rifle was probably the cause of the injury. It had been propped in front of me prior to the crash. I didn't want to put my hand on my head to feel the extent of the damage. I was convinced that my skull was split and I would feel my brains. I do not know how Peter got out. It would have been impossible for him to have escaped from the front seat after the helicopter had landed. I believe he was thrown out as it turned a somersault and the doors were torn off by the trees. This was probably what had happened to Mario and Omar, too, as when I had made my scramble for freedom the vegetation blocking the doorway had been virtually solid, as if undisturbed.

Suddenly, we realised that Tiger wasn't with us. We glanced around but saw no sign of him. We couldn't see into the cockpit because smashed trees obscured the windscreen and nose section. I burrowed my way through the branches and crawled into the cockpit. As the helicopter had landed on its side, everything was at an angle. I saw Tiger lying in an awkward, twisted position, with the control stick still between his legs. His skin looked grey and when I spoke to him, he opened his eyes but remained expressionless. He was mumbling '*mi pierna*', which I knew meant 'my leg'. I examined him to try to find the source of the pain. His legs felt unbroken but when I looked around the back of his hips I saw a massive wound. He was ripped open from his spine to his stomach; his liver was exposed and nearly hanging out of his body. Looking to the others in the doorway, I drew my hand across my throat and shook my head. He was dying and would be dead shortly but I told him reassuringly that he was going to be OK.

We scrambled around to find our shock packs among the scattered equipment. Frustratingly, much of the medical equipment was damaged when we found it. Eventually, an intact syringe was discovered and I went back in to put Tiger on a saline drip and give him a morphine jab. I could not get a vein in his right arm, as they had collapsed with the shock of his injuries. The body's defence mechanisms had gone to work, minimising the blood supply to uninjured areas. I turned my attention to his left arm and saw something I hadn't noticed before. A gaping wound stretched from shoulder to hand, as though a butcher had filleted his arm. It was just one wide flap of flesh with the bone exposed. The Perspex bubble of the windscreen was smashed, only jagged shards remaining. His arm had probably been sliced through when he was catapulted into the windscreen. Given how terrible his injuries were, there was remarkably little blood.

Tiger was mumbling in Spanish; I think he was praying. I asked Omar and Mario to talk to him and give him what comfort they could in his last few minutes. I injected several morphine ampoules directly into his neck. Within minutes, Tiger was dead. I removed the dog tags from around his neck; it was the first time we ever knew his real name. The body of Gustavo Gonsalves would lie in the helicopter until it was recovered some time later. Eventually he was given a military-style funeral. His obituary stated that he had died while on active service, taking part in an anti-narcotics operation.

We couldn't dwell on Tiger's loss; we were in the shit ourselves. Peter struggled in vain not to go into shock, recognising his own symptoms. I tried to connect him to one of the saline drips but his veins had collapsed and I couldn't get the cannula into his arm. Instead, I cut the drip bag open and he drank from it as we moved him to cover. With Peter made as comfortable as possible, we hunted around for a radio. About 40 minutes had passed since the crash and the team in the Huey must have known something was wrong, as both choppers should have reached Kiko at the same time. Calling on Telstar's frequency, we raised Jorge and advised him that the Hughes was down and Tiger dead. As I was talking to Jorge, I saw the Huey searching above the mountains in the distance. Taking a compass bearing on it, I told Jorge that we had a visual on the others and gave a compass bearing that would bring them towards us. We draped a red towel over a shrub, as the remains of our chopper blended with the green around us.

The Huey spotted us and hovered above our position. Ironically, we were only a few feet from the summit; if we'd been a fraction higher, it would have been only a close shave. There was not much the occupants of the Huey could do for us, as the pilot could not land. The wind buffeted it about, side draughts from the mountain catching it. However, they informed us that they could see a stream that started west of our position. One of us was to follow the stream down and they would land and follow it up until we met. Peter was now in real pain but would not use his morphine. I stripped a satchel charge and lit a fire using the C-4 to give him some warmth, as he was shivering with cold. We ripped open shell dressings from the shock packs and wrapped them inside Peter's bulletproof jacket to insulate him from the cold. Then, leaving the other three, I set off to find the stream. I took no radio with me. Only one worked anyway and the signal would probably not get through the jungle canopy. I didn't take a weapon, either, as I had lost my pistol in the crash; my rifle was no use because I would need both hands free.

The journey was not easy. The trees and foliage were dense, almost like rainforest. Fallen trees and decaying vegetation created a false floor in many places, so that often I thought I was walking on solid ground when in reality I was on a crazy scaffold of rotting timber. Daylight appeared through the greenery and, thinking I must be making progress, I headed towards it, only to find myself on the edge of a sheer drop. After a while, I located the stream and tried to follow it down the mountain. It had no banks that you could amble along; its serpentine path took it under dense vegetation and I made slow progress. As the stream became wider and deeper, I waded into its bitterly cold waters in an attempt to take the easier path under rather than through the vegetation. The stream was not deep, but I had to crawl on hands and knees in places and became drenched. Then, suddenly, I came to a several-hundred-foot drop to another level. I had to traverse the ridge again in search of another path downward. The light was not good, as the canopy was dense, and time was also against me. Late afternoon was now turning to dusk, which meant a long, cold night ahead. About an hour had passed since I'd left the others and the dim light, fading fast, was beginning to make movement dangerous. Then I heard branches breaking from behind and above me, and a voice called out asking for my position. A few minutes later, Omar and Mario appeared.

This was not a pleasant surprise. One would have been a relief but both meant Peter was now alone. I registered my disapproval but

DIRTY COMBAT

Mario insisted we would make better time with three of us. He said that Peter had agreed to them both following me. Mario had taken the only workable radio but it was no damn good to us and left Peter without comms of any kind. Within fifteen minutes, we reached another sheer drop and had to back off. Visibility was down to zero, so we settled down not far from the edge to wait for dawn. It was a very long night and we did not sleep. We were soaking wet, as was everything around us. As dawn started to filter its way through, we attempted to light a fire to warm ourselves but nothing would burn. We heard the sound of a Bell helicopter starting up and taking off and assumed it was our Huey, which had spent the night at the bottom of the mountain. With all the effort expended so far, we were probably only 500 vertical feet down the mountain from the crash site. We still had hopes that some of the team were making their way up towards us, though, so we decided to make tracks to meet them.

Our progress was slow. We had been on the move for about four hours when we heard branches breaking below us. Whoever it was must have heard us as we crashed and crunched along. We tucked ourselves into cover and waited. Mario had brought along an Uzi sub-machine gun, which was the only weapon we had between us. We listened to our visitors climbing up towards us and knew it wasn't our team, because they were speaking Spanish. As they came into view, we could see only two men, who appeared to be unarmed. Mario called out to them, Omar and I remaining under cover. The men quickly explained that they were friends, sent by our people to help us. This satisfied Mario and we broke our cover. The two men were short and stocky, dressed like *campesinos* (peasant farmers).

We told our two-man search-and-rescue team that we were part of some kind of military operation and needed assistance because a man was injured. They had a rope with them, which they had used on the climb up. This was a godsend, as the route we took downhill was not one we could have managed without it. The two Colombian guys could climb like mountain goats and we spent a lot of time hanging off trees or moss-covered rock faces as they took us the short way, straight down. Even this direct route took about six hours. At last, we arrived at a sandy clearing with a stream running through it. Several hundred yards away was a small scruffy-looking shack. It was surrounded by a rough fence made from tree branches. The campesinos made us hot chocolate on an open fire, which we drank from tin mugs.

There is little flat ground in rural Colombia and from the shack you could not see more than 50 yards at ground level, due to the undulating terrain. This lack of visibility probably saved our lives. One of the farmers came over the rise, telling us happily that our military friends had arrived. A Colombian army patrol was sweeping the area, presumably looking for us, he explained. Our hosts got a bit of a shock when Mario ordered them to leave with us as we headed for the mountain. He was holding the Uzi in a manner that left them in no doubt it was more than a polite invitation. We melted rapidly back into the jungle and began climbing upward and round the edge of the mountain, so that we would be under cover but have a view of what was happening below.

We could see about a dozen soldiers. They didn't seem particularly purposeful and were casually wandering around, as if looking for anything untoward. As their patrolling was not focused on the mountain itself, I assumed that they did not know that a helicopter had crashed at the summit. Presumably, the Huey, or our support aircraft, which were circling the area, had been spotted and aroused someone's curiosity. This was Escobar's back yard and he had the influence to instigate the search patrol. We stayed out of the way until very late afternoon. Then, the farmers took us to a small valley, where we came to a shack with a wooden corral around it. This was obviously for cattle, by the looks of the cowpats everywhere.

Mario and our farmers were now firm friends. God only knows what inducements he had offered them. Mario and the two campesinos left to find somewhere he could communicate with his bosses and to bring back some food. Omar and I found a hiding place and lay in the last rays of the sun as it fell rapidly towards the horizon. I took stock of my condition and was somewhat worried. My head still hurt, my camouflage was smeared with blood, and my knee had swollen considerably – another legacy of the crash, which I hadn't noticed before. As dusk fell, Mario and the farm boys returned with food and large bottles of soft drinks. We took refuge in the shed and lit a fire outside the doorway, using the dried cowpats as fuel. It was another long, cold night but our conditions were luxurious compared with what Peter must be enduring alone up in the clouds on the freezing, wet mountain-top. Mario seemed impervious to the cold and slept all night. Omar and I ventured out in the dark to collect more cowpats to feed the fire as we shivered the night away. The next morning, it rained and when the rain ceased a heavy mist came rolling into the valley. It reminded me of the eerie special effects in the movie *The Fog*.

Late in the afternoon, the wind picked up and the fog dissipated. Just when we had given up hope of being picked up, the noise of the Huey's rotors broke the silence. The wind and uneven terrain made it difficult to land. The chopper hovered a few feet from the ground, the pilot trying to keep it steady. When he was satisfied, a rescue team leapt out, carrying ropes and machetes. As they cleared the aircraft, we scrambled aboard and the pilot pulled up and away. We landed at a ranch airstrip and transferred to a small fixed-wing Cessna, which flew us to a private airfield on the outskirts of Cali, where vehicles were waiting to collect us. We were taken to an apartment where Gilberto Rodriguez and a doctor were waiting to check us over. None of us had injuries that required anything more than basic first aid. We showered and changed out of our camouflage into civilian clothes provided for us.

I was driven to the apartments we'd stayed in when we first arrived in Cali. There, the team was awaiting news on Peter. Another night passed. The rescue team, with our two campesinos, had made their way back up the mountain to the crash site. Peter later told me that they had reached him that night and attempted to bring him down in the dark with the aid of torches. This, apparently, was a painful experience and only a partial success, so another night was spent halfway down the mountain. The following afternoon, a car came to take me to the apartment where I had been checked over by the doctor. Peter was on his way back, expected at any moment. When he arrived, he looked absolutely awful: smeared with mud, in pain and exhausted. He did not have the mobility or strength to undress, so I helped him strip off and washed him down in the shower. The doctor recommended that he be taken to a hospital for X-rays, as he suspected broken ribs and broken bones in his hand.

That night, Peter arrived at the apartments, having been to some private hospital for a complete physical and X-rays. Diagnosed with severely bruised and broken ribs, he was not going to be doing anything strenuous for a while. After some lively debate about whether the team should be paid the operations bonus, it was agreed that our failed operation was a risk taken with best intentions. I paid the bonus and everyone was happy again. We had a meeting to decide what the next step would be, assuming there was going to be one. It appeared that our disaster had not alerted Escobar to our operation, so we went back to the drawing board. Our sponsors were keen to carry on as planned and viewed this as only a minor setback. We made one proviso: we would recruit our own combat helicopter pilots to fly the assault teams in, although Toyco would still fly with us. Now, there were going to be three Hueys and two more were ordered.

On 18 June, I flew back to the UK to meet with two female Colombian money couriers, who flew in separately, one from Miami and one from New York, both carrying large sums of US dollars, money owed to me for salaries, equipment and expenses. Our first pilot, Dick, joined me in London from Cape Town. I recruited a second pilot, who could not join us for several weeks, as he was under contract, flying some executive around. Peter's recovery was progressing slowly. Dave Borland, our medic, had been keeping an eye on him. In the early days, he had administered small quantities of morphine to dull the pain so that Peter could sleep properly. Dick was taken to La Guagua and put through his paces in the Huey by Toyco who gave him the thumbs up to our paymasters. We moved the team back to the hilltop retreat on the outskirts of Cali and went back to playing volleyball and running.

A further three months' salary was due. This time, I was paid in cash in Colombia. Arrangements were made for me to board a flight to Panama without my hand luggage being searched. My connecting flight was with KLM to Schiphol Airport, from where I would travel on to London. About an hour or so after take-off from Panama, the pilot announced that we had slight generator problem and were going to make a stopover at Aruba in the Dutch Antilles to fit a replacement part. The part would take a while to arrive, so we were put up for the night in a hotel. The following afternoon, we departed Aruba for Schiphol. The timing of our departure could not have been worse for me. The scheduled arrival of the original flight would have allowed me to transit Schiphol without going through passport control or Dutch customs. Now our flight would reach Amsterdam after the airport had shut down for the night. KLM were putting us up in a hotel again. This meant that I would have to enter Holland. I had never had any problems with the Dutch authorities before but they were aware of my involvement in an incident in Amsterdam and I knew I would be on their watch list.

Sure enough, they came for me. They were very polite. While my fellow passengers went off to board a courtesy bus, I was taken to an office. Then came the usual banal questions that officials ask, already knowing most of the answers. Of course, when they searched my luggage, they could not help but notice several kilos of $100 bills. Asked if I was going to spend it in Amsterdam, I replied that I wasn't. They photocopied my passport and some of the money, asking no questions about where it came from or where it might be going. It's at times like these that you get the feeling your secret really isn't a secret after all. You wonder whether they're letting you run with the ball to see how the game ends. I was free to go but it was a racing certainty that I wouldn't make it through Heathrow without a pull by someone.

I cleared passport control and retrieved my luggage, but customs were waiting for me in the 'nothing to declare' lane. There were about five officers. Reading their body language, I knew I was not going to get past them. I headed straight for them and with a cheery 'good morning', told them that what they wanted to see was in my hand luggage. They feigned surprise but addressed me as 'Dave' before looking at my passport. They seemed impressed by the amount of money and asked what it was for. I really didn't want to fuck about with more silly word games, so I told them that it was to purchase radio direction-finding equipment. They asked what that was for, so I said it was for tracking specific radio signals to locate the party that is transmitting on them. They enquired as to what happened then and I told them, 'When we locate the source, we go and kill them.' This got a few laughs and seemed to make sense to them. They zipped up my bag, wished me good luck and let me through.

While I was in London, I met with the other helicopter pilot and shipped him to Cali to meet the rest of the crew and undergo his flight test with Toyco. When I headed back to Colombia, Peter had recovered most of his mobility and would have liked to go back into the jungle but our helicopters had not yet arrived. I guess it would be fair to say that we were beginning to realise that this venture was coming apart at the seams. The original impetus had gone, discipline was slowly being eroded and cliques were forming. I would never question the team's skill or courage in the face of danger. Put them in a bar with money in their pockets, however, and anything could happen. It was during this period that we lost a second team member, when Ned Owen decided it was time to go home. I gave him my videotapes of some of our time in Colombia and asked him to post them to my wife.

During August, we moved the men to Panama again. They were billeted in the Tower House Suites, a luxury self-catering hotel. Peter and I, along with Dick, remained behind in Cali, planning to join the team later. On 18 August 1989, the wheels finally fell off our mission. On that day, Luis Carlos Galán, a charismatic politician who had set himself up in opposition to the cartels and who was the red-hot favourite to win the forthcoming presidential elections, was gunned down at an election rally near Bogotá. The public outcry was enormous and the fallout from the assassination would eventually bring down the two most powerful drug cartels in the country.

That same day, President Barco issued an emergency decree bringing into force the extradition treaty with the United States. The army and police were ordered to arrest all known drug dealers and confiscate their assets and property. The news media had a field day. In a country where assassinations of police, judges and politicians were everyday occurrences, this was, for the moment at least, one killing too far. Domestic pressure to curb the power of the drug gangs was added to by the world's largest consumer of Colombia's cocaine: the United States.

Peter, Dick and I were transferred from the downtown apartments to a residential area outside the city centre. For the next week, we stayed behind closed doors as military patrols sealed off streets and police conducted house-to-house searches for known drug dealers. Arrangements were made for Dick to leave for South Africa; it was unlikely that anyone had connected him with our operation at that point. Omar came for Peter and me late one evening. A police raid was imminent on our apartment block. Unbeknown to us, the Rodriguez brothers' mother lived in the same building. The authorities were now searching for our sponsors. We were transported in a Jeep Cherokee to Omar's apartment, taking care to avoid security checkpoints.

It was too risky now for us to stay in Colombia. Terry Tagney and Ned Owen had gone to the media and James Adams had published the story of our planned raid on Haçienda Napoles. We were front-page news all over the world. The article had the basic plan of attack right but there were some inaccuracies and the piece was accompanied by a fanciful artist's impression of the intended raid. Arrangements were made for Peter and me to join the team in Panama, which would not be so easy now. Security checks at the airport had been doubled. Once again, we got a glimpse of the relationship between the Cali cartel and the authorities. On the day chosen for our departure, we walked through the concourse and down the corridor to the aircraft without catching sight of one single cop, DAS or soldier, without having to check in or go through passport control. We just walked onto the plane. In Panama, we were met by a very pissed-off crew, including two new members, who were awaiting our move back to Colombia.

We would never make it back again. We were now being featured on television news programmes around the world, thanks to Tagney and Owen. Having spent only a couple of weeks with us on the second operation, Tagney had decided to cash in. His lurid version of the events of our first Colombian mission was featured on CNN. Owen, meanwhile, had copied my videotapes and sold them to a British TV company, along with his take on events. We were not supposed to find out who gave the televised interview. In the UK, his features were blacked out and his voice disguised. Owen obviously did not read the TV company's small print, however, because the footage was sold overseas where it was shown without these efforts to disguise him. The last I heard of Tagney, he was in a wheelchair, having been shot in both knees with a .357 Magnum.

It was agreed with the cartel that we should disband the team for now. When the dust settled, we could come back and try for Escobar again. We assembled for the last time in a lobster restaurant in Panama. It was a farewell to a great bunch of guys who lived life to the full, lived it on the edge and loved every minute of it. We said our goodbyes to Jorge and on 3 September we flew back to England. Despite all the media attention now focused on us, we breezed through Heathrow without one team member being stopped by Special Branch or customs. It didn't take long for the media to find out we were back, of course. The tabloids offered me as much as £10,000 for 'Sex in the Jungle' stories. It mattered not that there were none to tell; they would make it up – murder, pillage, rape – as long as I endorsed it.

When the frenzy died down, it wasn't for long. On 13 September, the US government revealed that it had a secret witness who had testified to our activities in Colombia. The TV news showed an extract from a US Senate hearing in Washington. From behind a screen, a Colombian was giving evidence about his years with the Medellín cartel. His name was Diego Viafára Salinas, the ACDEGAM medic known to us as Doc, whom we had trained during the anti-FARC mission. Shown my picture on a large screen, he identified me as David, the explosives instructor and second in command of the mercenary team. Viafára did a real number on us. He claimed that our training programmes were partially responsible for the increasingly violent war being waged by the drug cartel against the Colombian government.

On the same day, two Senate investigators came to my home to request that Peter McAleese and I give testimony at the hearing in Washington. We declined. I was still in touch with Jorge Salcedo and advised him of the situation. Almost a year later, I was again asked by the US government to testify in Washington, at another hearing on arms trafficking, mercenaries and drug cartels. With the knowledge of the Cali cartel, I agreed, and on 27 February 1991 I testified about our role in Colombia. My evidence covered the original mission in 1988 and the 1989 plan to kill Pablo Escobar. I refused to identify any person or persons involved, either as paymasters, recruiters or team members.

Later in 1991, I was requested by an attaché of the US Embassy in London to discuss a subject of interest to them. I met with John William Lee Jr of the DEA (Drug Enforcement Administration). He enquired if I was aware that the US government had a multimillion-dollar reward on the head of Pablo Escobar. Would I consider offering my services to Escobar as a way of getting close to him? I wasn't quite sure how to take this suggestion. Some might consider me a little mad but I'm not stupid. I was certain Escobar would consider it an opportunity not to be missed and send me a first-class ticket. His only concern would be how long he could draw out my death. Lee's response was along the lines of, 'Oh, yes, we hadn't thought of that.' Thanking him for his concern, I declined. The irony of the offer would become apparent only some 12 years later, when I was serving time in a US federal prison, convicted of an offence related to my bid to rid Colombia and the world of Escobar once and for all. Well, shit happens, as they say.

CHAPTER 22

LOCKDOWN

I STARTED ON THE ROAD TO THAT US PRISON IN AUGUST 2003, WHEN I flew from London to Houston. Check-in at Gatwick was uneventful and my main concern was being on time for the connecting flight to El Paso, Texas, where I was heading for a five-day chemical-warfare survival course. On completion, I would receive a Department of Defense ID number, which I needed in order to undertake contract work in Iraq. It would allow me to enter and exit the country through Kuwait without applying for a visa every month.

Visiting the USA had long been a risky business for me. My last trip to America had been in 1991 and it was nearly a disaster. Once again, a phone call from Jorge Salcedo had started the trouble. Jorge phoned in July 1991 to request a meeting with me in Panama City on the 23rd. Since my exit from Colombia, Pablo Escobar had negotiated his surrender, along with his top lieutenants, with the Colombian government, receiving preferential treatment in return for turning himself in. He was ensconced in a prison known as 'Le Catedral', situated in Envigado, the suburb of Medellín where he was born. Escobar dictated the rules of his confinement. The military were not permitted within two kilometres of the prison. The guards were handpicked from among the residents of his home town and were all known by him. Escobar would make no court appearances until his trial, if there ever was one, for security reasons. Needless to say, this cosy arrangement did not suit the Cali cartel, as Escobar was able to continue running his drug empire from the prison. The difficulties we had had before in pinning down Escobar's location at a specific date and time no longer existed and the Cali bosses wanted me to come up with a plan to eliminate Escobar once and for all.

Jorge knew a lot more about the prison and Escobar's circumstances than most. In accordance with Escobar's terms, the prosecutor and judge had to fly into the prison by helicopter when he decided to allow a hearing. Jorge had managed to fly in with them as co-pilot, disguised in a helmet and flight suit. Over the next few days, I debriefed him about everything he had seen at the prison. It was not a very imposing structure, a two-storey building of concrete blocks with asbestos sheeting for the roof. Internally, it was made up of dormitory-style rooms, although Escobar had a private luxury suite, complete with oil paintings and other luxuries.

The Medellín boss was an expert when it came to his own security. Helicopter landings and a frontal assault were out of the question. All landing areas were criss-crossed with anti-helicopter wires, lowered only for the judge. Assault from the roof was also ruled out, as tough cyclone-wire netting had been strung on the inside under the asbestos sheeting. There would be no time to start cutting through that under fire. It was known that the inmates had access to weapons, so a firefight was definitely on the cards if we put boots on the ground. Machine-gun posts were clearly visible. Jorge reassuringly told me that he would perform some magic trick rendering the machine-gun posts inoperative. I took this with a pinch of salt. The whole thing sounded like a bit of a pipe dream to me. Maybe the Cali leaders had been using too much of their own product.

While we were discussing the pros and cons of the operation in Jorge's room, he received a call from Joel Rosenthal, a Miami attorney representing Lucho Echeveria, the half-brother of Cali boss Chepe Santacruz Londoño. The call confirmed that the Attorney General had signed papers allowing Echeveria's sentence to be reduced by 15 years. I asked Jorge about the deal. In 1989, the US government had sent thousands of troops into Panama to depose President Manuel Noriega. Having spent millions of dollars and killed many innocent civilians, they finally captured Noriega and he was flown to the US to be tried on charges including drug trafficking. Now, however, there was a problem: there was not enough evidence to convict him. A deal was struck between the Justice Department and the Cali cartel: if they would supply evidence of Noriega's drug dealing, Echeveria would get credit for it.

One Ricardo Bilonick was the answer to both parties' prayers. A former diplomat and business associate of Escobar, he too was wanted by US justice. The Cali cartel offered to pay him $1,250,000 and look after his family if he surrendered to the US Marshals, who would take him to Miami where he would testify against Noriega. In exchange for his testimony, the Justice Department would ensure that he received no more than three years in prison, after which he would enter the Witness Protection Program. It sounded to me like Noriega didn't stand a chance, and indeed he was convicted in 1992. In the end, he discovered the deal and appealed but his conviction was not overturned.

After my meetings with Jorge, I returned home to ponder how I was going to try and iron out Pablo Escobar again without getting killed or going to prison. I considered the matter until September, when I flew back to Panama. I'd come up with a plan that might just work, with a bit of luck – well, maybe more than a bit.

Most of the more obvious options were ruled out and at first I'd thought that I might have to pass on this one. However, I tried to think of a more unusual method. I made model helicopters out of cardboard and cornflake boxes and realised that if the doors were removed, I could build sloping ramps from either side. Inside the cabin doorways, I could rig three drums per side. Each drum would have a release pin. When this was pulled, the drum would roll down the chute and away from the aircraft. Each of the three drums would be connected with cord to its opposite number on the other side. I practised on my models using cotton reels and it worked very well.

The drums would be filled with C-4, about 35 kg per drum, to be detonated using remote-controlled switches. Two other helicopters would be required, protective gunships that would drop smoke and keep everyone on the ground busy. The chopper with the explosives would hover-hop along a couple of feet above the apex of the prison's sloping roof. At intervals along the roof, the pins on pairs of drums would be pulled, discharging them down the chute so that they rolled down either side of the prison walls. We would need three hops along the roof to space out the charges, releasing a pair of drums at each hop. Then it would be up and away, with our protection joining us. As we pulled clear of the prison, we would detonate the explosives. El Catedral would be the meat in a C-4 sandwich, a couple of hundred kilos exploding at either side.

That was the general idea. I thought it was pretty innovative. If nothing else, it would give Pablo a fright. I explained the concept to Jorge in graphic detail. I think he was impressed but he and his friends had another plan in mind. Since our last meeting, they had met a Costa Rican air-force pilot, who, according to Jorge, could 'drop a bomb in a bucket'. He would, for the bargain price of several million dollars, put a couple of 500-lb bombs through Escobar's cell window. What he could not, or would not, do was steal an aeroplane from his country's armed forces for the mission.

I departed Panama with a new mission: to buy a Cessna A-37B Dragonfly, a ground-attack bomber, designed for low-level counter-insurgency strikes. It was certainly the machine for a job of this sort. It carried an enormous payload and was equipped with a six-barrel GEC Minigun in the nose. It had been used in Vietnam but was now obsolete, although it was still in service with the US National Guard and in various Latin American countries. I put out enquiries to brokers and to friends who were into flying their own planes, but without success. I had another browse through the reference books and noted that the Dominican Republic used to have Dragonflys in service. I remembered a guy I had met when I had been involved with a Surinamese rebel group who were trying to remove the country's military dictator. He was called Frank Castro and he operated a small airfreight company running Dakotas around the Caribbean, so, at the beginning of October, I gave him a call.

Castro had a chequered career, to say the least. Born Eulalio Francisco Castro in Cuba, he was a former contractor for the CIA. He had been involved in gunrunning and training Nicaraguan Contra fighters and had connections with Medellín drug bosses. My call to Castro was a casual enquiry, asking if he knew of a Dragonfly in private ownership for sale, as I had a potential client who needed one for his collection. About a week passed before Castro advised me that he had found a seller prepared to part with his Dragonfly if the price was right. Castro had no idea what this aircraft was going to be used for or where it was going. On the surface, it appeared to be a normal commercial deal. During the next month, a series of faxes and phone calls were exchanged. I set out my requirements as to the condition of the aircraft, its location, the terms and conditions of sale, etc. There was considerable prevarication on the seller's part. Various locations were proposed for inspection, ranging from South Carolina to Puerto Rico. Eventually, Castro invited me to Miami to meet with Fred Lewis, the broker representing the seller. I took Mary with me for a week's holiday. We had friends in Miami and could kill two birds with one stone.

On 1 December 1991, we checked in to the Hyatt Regency, where I met with Castro and Lewis, who reassured me that the deal would close. I told them that I required a decommissioned, privately owned aircraft. I could not and would not offer an end-user certificate. I would not purchase the aircraft in the United States and would take delivery in the Dominican Republic only if Frank Castro could arrange the necessary flight clearances. Castro offered to supply an EUC from the Dominican Republic but Fred Lewis maintained that the plane had been built from three others that had been broken for spares and reassembled into a flying condition. The aircraft would be broken down again for containerisation and reassembled in the Dominican Republic. This would, with his connections, mean that an EUC and export licence would not be required. I was careful not to offer to get involved in the actual export.

As far as I was concerned, logistics were the main problem. The Dominican Republic was more than 1,000 miles from the plane's final destination, an airstrip on the Guajira Peninsula in Colombia, near the Panamanian border. The Dragonfly was a short-mission aircraft with a 450-mile range, so I requested costs for wingtip fuel tanks to be fitted. I was assured that all my conditions were clearly understood. Pricing was agreed and we parted company. We still needed to confirm where and when I would inspect the Dragonfly.

More faxes followed, more time passed and I nearly gave up on them. Then, finally, I got an inspection date. I contacted Jorge and made arrangements to meet him in Miami. After more phone calls, with Lewis whining about the extra cost of flying the plane to Florida, we were told to meet him at Opa-locka Airport, Miami, on Wednesday, 11 December. Lewis had another guy with him, who claimed he was the technical man should we have any questions. We entered a hangar and there it was. They let us wander around it and I couldn't resist sitting in the cockpit. Jorge had brought along a video camera and I had a still camera. Lewis and his sidekick moved outside when we started taking photographs. My first concerns were the presence of a Minigun, which we had not requested, and the lack of ID markings. We took some sneaky pictures of Lewis and his technical friend and decided to buy time while we did some checks. We queried the absence of ID markings and were told it was for commercial reasons, to protect the owner should we fail to purchase.

We called Frank Castro from a payphone and Jorge had a heated discussion in Spanish about the Minigun we hadn't asked for. All in all, the deal smelled of sting, although by whom we were not sure. Jorge and I arranged to meet that evening and he departed with the video and the film from the camera. I told Lewis that I would pay a $25,000 non-returnable option to purchase, to cover his out-of-pocket expenses if we did not close the deal. I advised him that there would be a few days' delay while we made a final decision as to where and when the Dragonfly would be paid for. That evening, I met Lewis in a Dunkin' Donuts shop, parted with $25,000 and agreed to meet at Opa-locka on the Monday, in company with our pilot/inspector.

Within 36 hours, we knew that the second man with Lewis was a former DEA agent and that Lewis was also 'dirty'. Jorge departed for Colombia. I was still being contacted by Lewis several times a day. He was trying to sell me everything in the US military arsenal, presumably for the benefit of a tape recorder. I left on the Sunday and arrived in the UK on the Monday. I faxed Lewis a tongue-in-cheek apology for my hasty exit. A call to a friend in the US confirmed that Lewis was working with US customs in Puerto Rico. He was part of a unit called EXODUS, which mounted undercover operations to prevent the illegal export of defence equipment. I was the target of Operation Dragonfly; it must have taken some thought to come up with that one. Frank Castro was, and perhaps still is, a confidential informer (CI). A CI stands to receive a reward calculated as a percentage of the value of goods confiscated. I wonder how many of Castro's associates have gone to jail never knowing he was a federal snitch. Lewis called me several times, making excuses about why things had gone wrong, offering me another aircraft. Of course, I would have to come back to the USA to inspect it.

I heard no more about the matter until December 1995, when I received in the post notification of the confiscation of $22,000 (I assume that the shortfall of $3,000 went to Castro) by the US Customs Service. I could appeal the decision and the forms required were enclosed. I duly appealed, of course, enclosed all the correspondence between me and the other players, along with my version of events. In due course, my appeal was denied – not that I was surprised.

When I reflect back on the incident, I cannot help but feel disgust at the US justice system. I cannot stand, hand on heart, and plead innocence in the affair. Morally, I was as guilty as sin. I was prepared to let two dealers break the rules as long as I did not actively contribute. But when I phoned Frank Castro and made the first enquiry, he had no idea what the plane was for or where it was going. It could genuinely have been going to a private collector for all he knew. Yet from the moment I hung up the phone, Castro started a chain of events that could have ended up with me in prison. I was set up; there never was a Dragonfly for sale. Also, when I first met Fred Lewis, I made it clear that I could not and would not supply an EUC. At any time, if either one of them had said, 'You must provide an end-user certificate,' I would have walked away.

So, that had been the outcome of my last trip to the US. However, I was still to experience the US justice system at full strength. I didn't know yet how difficult it can be to fight your corner when the deck is stacked against you. As my flight began its approach to George Bush Intercontinental Airport, Houston, in August 2003, I was about to find out. I stepped off the plane door to be met by a group of uniformed officers. They escorted me to an office and told me I was under arrest for conspiracy to violate the Arms Export Control Act. Apparently, there was an outstanding fugitive warrant dating from 1994. As I had not entered the US for over a decade, there was some confusion as to whether this warrant was still valid. I was informed that it pertained to an incident regarding the export of an aircraft. I explained that the plane had never been purchased. To further confuse matters, the indictment had not been brought against me until 1994, although the supposed offence had taken place in late 1991. Several hours later, however, I was transported in handcuffs to the Federal Detention Center in Houston.

By the time I got to the reception unit, the place was on lockdown for the night. I was fingerprinted, photographed and strip-searched. Dressed in a bright-orange jumpsuit, I was about to spend the next few nights in what is commonly referred to by inmates as 'the hole'. The official name is the SHU, or Secure Housing Unit. This is the punishment block and segregation unit for inmates who have behaved violently or others who pose a threat to order. I was given no bedding on that first night, although I did receive a two-inch plastic toothbrush and a bar of soap. The cell contained two bunk beds, a stainless-steel shower unit, toilet and sink, and a concrete table at which to eat. I was cold and did not sleep well, knowing my employment in Iraq had just disappeared down the drain. My future now held nothing but uncertainty. Breakfast in the hole was a culture shock. At 4 a.m., a slot in the bottom of the door was opened and a tray slid through, along with a small polystyrene cup containing ice, to be filled with water from the sink. The tray contained a sandwich and bag of crisps. The food was to be removed and the tray handed back. The slot slammed shut and that was my lot until lunchtime. The shower didn't work well, either. Unless you timed it just right the water was cold. The electric light was controlled from outside by a guard and the only natural light came from a four-inch-wide four-foot-long armoured glass window.

Several days later, I was moved to the general-population cell blocks and made my first court appearance, to be arraigned. This rigmarole is not a pleasant experience. At the crack of dawn I was taken to the 'bullpen', a holding cell crammed with others making court appearances, strip-searched again and given a brown-bag breakfast of a baloney sandwich, crisps and a carton of milk. The guards then handed us over to the US Marshals Service, which is responsible for inmates outside the prison confines. Now dressed in a green jumpsuits, we were shackled in leg irons, waist chains and handcuffs before we shuffled our way to the prison bus to court. Guards armed with shotguns watched us as we loaded up and as we got off and headed for another bullpen under the court. It was a long day and lunch was more baloney and a frozen carton of fruit juice that came as a solid lump of ice.

In turn, groups were taken to court and the charges read out. Bail bond applications were made by those who had legal representation. I did not have an attorney so a public defender named Brent Newton took my case. Newton was great. He argued that the warrant was not valid or suitably stamped and that the case should be dismissed. The judge wanted to confirm that I was the party to whom the warrant applied and demanded that formal ID was made by the agents involved in the case. They were in Puerto Rico or Miami.

The rigmarole was gone through in reverse and we all ended up back in our cells. The inmates were a mixed bunch of characters, in for drug dealing, shootings and every other conceivable offence. I got on with them as well as could be expected under the circumstances. The food remained crap and the days were long and boring. The exercise yard was indoors, so fresh air was in short supply.

My second court appearance came a week after the first. A customs agent named Castillo had flown in to formally identify me. As I was charged with conspiracy with persons unknown to violate the Arms Export Control Act, my attorney asked Agent Castillo who else had been involved in the case. Castillo responded that the only others involved were an undercover customs agent, and a confidential informer. Newton was just about to address the judge when she beat him to it. She said, 'As Mr Tomkins cannot *conspire* with a government agent, he will be acquitted, so I will release him on bond of $100,000 to appear in due course.' She explained to me that I would have to pay bail of 10 per cent, which would be refunded to me if I appeared in court on the agreed date. She then said, 'That is far too much. Make that 5 per cent.'

Unfortunately, I never got the chance to make bail. The system went into overdrive to stop me hitting the streets. Immigration put a 'hold' warrant on me. Castillo flew to Miami and lodged an appeal against the Texas decision. I was unaware that the Miami appeal was taking place and was not represented by counsel. Some months later, I was given a copy of the motion filed by the government. It made interesting reading and was a foretaste of what I could expect to come up against. It made me sound like something akin to Osama bin Laden's right-hand man. Apparently, I was a danger not only to the community but to the international community, as well. I was a major international arms dealer and mercenary, with international connections and the ability to flee justice. I had the knowledge and ability to obtain other passports and identities.

After my second court appearance, the case was covered on the local television news. Shortly afterwards, I was handcuffed by guards wearing black Nomex flameproof gloves, the type worn by combat troops and fighter pilots, and put back in the hole again, this time because I was a high-profile case, under investigation by the SIS (Special Investigative Supervisor) office. This is an internal prison unit that investigates gang activity, inmate killings, stabbings and other serious offences. It also conducts investigations into individuals to assess whether they pose a threat to the system or a danger to others. After a week in the hole, I was interviewed about my experience with weapons. Could I make explosives from items available in the prison? Could I analyse the security in place and organise men to riot? I figured it was wise to reply 'no' to all their questions. Eventually, I got the OK and was sent back to general population.

After about three weeks in Houston, I was moved to Miami, where my case was to be heard. The first leg of my journey took me as far as Oklahoma. We were flown there by JPATS, the Justice Prisoner and Alien Transportation System, otherwise known as Con Air. The plane was not a C-130 as featured in the film of the same name but a Boeing 727 with a rear loading ramp. We filed onboard in shackles and under guard by armed marshals. The marshals were a flash lot and obviously wanted to reinforce the Hollywood tough-guy stereotype. Some wore T-shirts with a screaming eagle emblazoned on the front and the slogan 'Only Bad Boys Fly Con Air' on the back. They chewed tobacco and clearly regarded us with disdain. The aircraft was stripped of tables and other items that could be used as weapons. The in-flight meal came in a brown bag, again. It was none too easy to open and eat with your hands shackled to your waist.

The prison we were headed for was the Federal Transfer Center at the edge of Oklahoma airport. It had its own loading bridge to transfer prisoners straight from the plane to a bullpen inside the prison. There were more searches and walk-through metal detectors, which I kept setting off because of the shrapnel in my body. I had to strip and was made to deep squat, so that if I had been concealing a 'shank' (a crude knife) up my ass, I would have stabbed myself with it. I was put in a cell with a Haitian doing a 12-year sentence and waiting for transfer to the penitentiary at Atlanta. I couldn't use the phones. All calls were made collect but overseas numbers were not permitted. In two weeks, I was on another Con Air flight, destination Miami. We landed at Opa-locka Airport, where I had inspected the Dragonfly. After more than a decade, I had come full circle.

I was incarcerated in the Miami Federal Detention Center, in unit Golf West. As prisons go, it was all right, clean with two-man cells. The majority of the inmates were awaiting trial or transfer to their designated prisons after receiving sentence. Here, I would begin to understand the snitch culture that dominates the criminal-justice system and is utilised to great effect by the federal authorities. When I was arrested in Houston, it had been more than 30 years since I had last walked through the gates of a prison (not including the odd deportation). In my day, it was a matter of honour and professional survival that you never grassed on your associates or indeed anyone. Here in the USA, it was commonplace, as the possibility of a reduced term of imprisonment was used by the authorities to encourage those whose sentences had not yet been decided (a category that included most of the prisoners in FDC Miami) to provide information on others.

Judges in the States have limited discretion when it comes to sentencing, as they must abide by the Federal Sentencing Guidelines. These are subject to variation only by 'upward departure' or 'downward departure', meaning that sentences can be increased or (much less frequently) decreased when there are exceptional circumstances not taken into account by the guidelines. The only other way a criminal might have their sentence decreased is under Section 5K1.1 or Rule 35(b) – the snitches' charter. These allow sentence to be reduced if the defendant gives 'substantial assistance' to the authorities in the investigation or prosecution of another person who has committed an offence.

This loophole allows the government to do deals with criminals when it suits their purposes. A classic example would be the conviction of John Gotti, the Mafia boss once known as 'the Teflon Don'. When he and fellow high-ranking mafioso Sammy 'the Bull' Gravano, were arrested following a major FBI operation, Gravano's testimony convicted Gotti. Meanwhile, Gravano, who had admitted to murdering 19 people, was sentenced to only five years, after which he received a new identity and home courtesy of the Witness Protection Program.

There was, therefore, an atmosphere of suspicious caution between inmates. It is not unknown for a prisoner's cellmate, whom he has never met on the outside, to appear at his trial as a vital witness against him. He will give evidence that the defendant told him incriminating information while they were locked up together. This information might indeed be the defendant's account of his crime – although who's to say he didn't embellish it? On the other hand, it might be information supplied by the authorities or by the witness's vivid imagination.

I was no stranger to prison culture, but I still had a bit to learn about the American rules of the game if I wanted to survive. There are predators and prey, and it doesn't take a genius to figure out that the bottom of the food chain is the wrong place to be. The vast majority of inmates had been in prison more than once in their lives and had friends or associates in the system. I found the main differences between US prisons and British ones were that the American ones were much larger, sometimes housing many thousands, and that there was more racial tension. The prison population included a broad range of nationalities with many Colombians, Mexicans, Haitians and Puerto Ricans, even Russians and Israelis. However, in the six prisons I had the displeasure of spending time in, I met only two other Englishmen. I was a novelty to the other prisoners, many of whom seemed to think I was Australian. There was no animosity, only lots of curiosity, which helped me to break the ice and forge acquaintances.

I made my first Miami court appearance. The feds and customs agents were claiming that in capturing me they'd saved the world from a serious threat, and the media cottoned on. The TV news sent cameras and the case was on the front page of the *Miami Herald* the following day. This enhanced my status with the other inmates, which would be a good thing as long as I wasn't flash about it. The downside was that it made me a high-profile inmate in the eyes of the prison authorities. On paper, conspiracy to violate the Arms Export Control Act is a white-collar crime; this put me in the pussycat category. But suddenly, the media were introducing attack-bomber aircraft, assassination, mercenary, drug cartels, Pablo Escobar and safe-blowing into the equation. My cell-block credibility went up but the Nomex-glove mob came back. Handcuffed again, I was taken back to the hole.

This time, I spent five weeks rotting in that shithole. I had a Haitian preacher as my celly. He spoke no English and was obviously mentally disturbed. He read the Bible all day and prayed aloud for hours until I couldn't hack it any more and read him the riot act. He didn't understand a frigging word but the tone got through to him. After 21 days in the same cell, the system moves you to another for security reasons, just in case you've made friends and are plotting something. My next move got me a view over Miami harbour and I could watch cruise ships come and go in the sunshine. You might have considered it therapeutic if you were half mad.

My new attorney, Hector Flores, eventually came to see me in the hole. He and Jan Smith, another public defender, had been allocated my case by the State of Miami. We met in a small room, separated by a glass partition. The telephone that should have allowed us to talk to each other did not work, however, and Flores went off to protest to the judge or prosecutor about my circumstances being prejudicial to my case. It was about this time that my mental state reached its lowest ebb. I had little to read, could not smoke and none of the cellmates I was assigned was exactly brilliant company. I remember one morning when breakfast came through the door at four in the morning there were peach slices in one of the tray's compartments. Because you had to hand the tray back after taking its contents, I found myself sitting on the floor in the dark, facing the toilet, with peach slices in syrup dripping through my fingers.

Eventually, thanks to my attorney's efforts, I was told that I was to be returned to the general population. The same day, a third con was placed in my two-bunk cell. I thought I'd be leaving before night, so I relinquished my bunk. However, they managed to fuck that up. There had been a mix-up with the dates. I wasn't moved until the next day and had to sleep on the floor next to the stinking toilet, an experience not improved by the Senegalese Muslim getting up at 3 a.m. and praying next to me on the floor. When I returned to my old cell block, I hadn't shaved for weeks and it was several months since my last haircut. I looked like a demented Santa Claus with my white beard.

I was learning all sorts of new tricks. No matches or lighters were allowed in the prison and cigarettes had to be lit from a wall-mounted electric element during the regulated smoking times. Smoking in the cells was forbidden but this rule was broken by many. To light a cigarette, you took a battery from your Walkman radio and a tiny strip of silver paper from the cigarette pack. One end of the silver paper was held to the terminal, the other to the side of the battery, and the silver paper would spark and glow for long enough to light a cigarette. Another piece of inside knowledge was that if you had friends in a unit below the one you were in, you could communicate through the 'toilet telephone'. At a prearranged time, you went to a cell number that corresponded with one on the floor below. Both parties then shoved a tube made from two Pringles containers into the

S-bend. By using your tube alternately as speaker and earpiece, you could communicate through the plumbing. Makeshift tattoo guns were made from ballpoint pens with the ink and ball removed and replaced with a piece of guitar string. This acted as the needle and was attached to a small electric motor gleaned from a hair trimmer purchased from the commissary.

The currency in US prisons was one-dollar postage stamps; these changed hands by the thousands during the course of a week, used for everything from booze and dope to gambling. The inmate population referred to correctional officers, or prison guards, as 'cops', and they were the enemy. They viewed the inmates likewise, as many guards are killed or seriously injured in US prisons. A guard could make life unbearable if he took a dislike to you or if he happened to be a bastard. In the system, I learned a lot of things from a diverse bunch of villains, from the best way to grow marijuana or convert cocaine into crack to how to set up a website to divest the gullible of their money. Many of the cons I met were very clever. Although they had been caught, some had made millions from their schemes and lived in luxury for years.

The weeks dragged into months and several court appearances were made. My attorneys filed a motion to dismiss the case on grounds that I had been denied a speedy trial. Under US law, a defendant should be bought to trial within 70 days of the indictment. This period may overrun for a reasonable period due to certain circumstances. In my case, it was argued that insufficient effort had been made to bring me before the court as a fugitive from justice. The government had had my location for over ten years. In 1995, they had been in communication with me regarding the confiscation of the $25,000 paid to their undercover agent.

To get around this, they flew in a lawyer from the British Crown Prosecution Service to give evidence that my charge was not an extraditable offence and that an English court would not have returned me to the United States if requested to do so. When the other side was asked when they had applied for extradition and discovered that it would not be possible, customs testified that they never made an application, that 'someone' in their office had advised them that the British court would not surrender me on the charge. Instead, an arrest warrant for me had been entered into the computer system.

In due course, we received the court's opinion on this argument, which would be passed on to the judge allocated to my trial. According to the judge, it was quite obvious that I had avoided travelling to the United States for over a decade and that, by entering me into the computer system, the agents involved had exercised due diligence as required. A letter from me dating from 1996 and indicating that I would be prepared to appear in a federal court to challenge the confiscation of the $25,000 was somehow interpreted as a *refusal* to appear.

I had made it clear that I would be prepared to go to trial; without evidence that I had had co-conspirators, it would be hard to prove a charge of conspiracy. Who were these 'persons unknown'? The judge began to question Agent Castillo about the other parties involved. The inspection of the aircraft had been secretly videotaped and Jorge Salcedo was clearly shown. When questioned under oath as to the identity of the party with me, Agent Castillo replied that as far as they could ascertain he was a high-ranking Colombian military-intelligence officer. They had no idea where he was, or whether he was alive or dead. From my point of view, this was bullshit. Jorge had testified against Cali bosses and was in the Witness Protection Program. Castillo might not have known his specific whereabouts but the US Marshals certainly did.

The prosecutor advised the court that they were applying to the Department of Defense for a certificate to show that I had not made an application for an export licence. Now, I had spent years avoiding, circumventing or bending the export regulations of numerous countries and I knew very well, and had known at the time, that under the International Traffic in Arms Regulations, which implement provisions of the Arms Export Control Act, a foreign national *may not* make an application for an export licence for military equipment. An application on behalf of a foreign government or company must be made by a US citizen who is a registered arms dealer or broker. How could it be evidence against me that I had failed to do something I was not legally entitled to do. It was impossible for me to apply for and obtain an export licence under the circumstances. On the other hand, it was legally possible for me to purchase such an aircraft without one, as long as it remained within the borders of the continental United States.

I was still determined to go to trial and had no interest in 'copping a plea' (accepting a plea bargain, whereby the case is settled without going to trial, the defendant pleading guilty and receiving a sentence agreed between the defence and the prosecution). As far as I was concerned, I had nothing to lose by airing the dirty washing. The maximum sentence I could receive in any case was 44 months. While we were preparing for trial, I asked my attorneys to subpoena both Salcedo and Castro as witnesses for the defence, just to see what reaction this would get. The idea didn't seem to go down well with them, however, as at each subsequent visit they had done nothing about it. They advised me that the prosecution had no intention of calling Castro to give evidence. Any investigation into his background would reveal facts that would undermine his credibility as a confidential informer. He had been indicted in the past for the alleged smuggling of 425,000 lb of marijuana but the charge had been dropped when he set up a Contra training camp in the Florida Everglades. My attorneys believed that if we subpoenaed Castro, he would simply disappear into the Dominican Republic, not wanting his connections in Miami's Little Havana to know that he was a snitch.

The longer I spent in FDC Miami the more I learned about the American legal system. The prison was full of 'jailhouse lawyers'. US prisons tend to have very comprehensive law libraries and inmates research and file motions constantly. Many become very proficient in the law over the years and have a measure of success along the way. While the government dishes out ridiculously high sentences, the system allows any number of ways to appeal for a myriad of reasons that would never be permitted under British law. One of the most commonly used is 'ineffective assistance of counsel', or, in plain English, 'My attorney was a wanker.'

In the prison system, lawyers tended to be regarded as the lowest form of life on earth. From what I saw of some other inmates' cases, this was not always unjustified. American lawyers are generally driven by money to a greater degree than British ones are. There is a saying with respect to attorneys, 'You're innocent until proven broke.' The visiting room at

DIRTY COMBAT

FDC Miami was an interesting place. Unlike the staid solicitors and barristers in pinstripe suits I was used to, most of the attorneys would arrive in clothes that would not get them through the doors of a decent restaurant, turning up in denims and cowboy boots, or cargo pants and loafers. The more conservative dressers wore shiny suits and string ties. These outfits were often topped off with immaculate 'hair systems', as they preferred to call wigs. They greeted their clients with familiar hugs and backslapping, as if they were long-time friends. The more money you had, the bigger the greeting you got.

As time passed, nodding acquaintances developed into friendships. If you felt comfortable with someone, it was usually only after you had seen his rap sheet, which gave some indication of past offences or prior sentences. That way you could tell if he was straight or if he'd been a snitch in the past. I hooked up with some great characters whom I will always remember with a smile for all the laughs we had in that depressing place. Doc and Gary were two fraudsters who had cloned corporate identities using unshredded documents thrown out by banks. They had created driving licences, printed corporate cheques and bought expensive goods, which they then sold on eBay or to professional fences. 'Doc' was a nickname picked up in the various penitentiaries where he'd served a prior 20-year sentence. He was an unofficial surgeon who could proficiently stitch you up with dental floss or superglue you together if you had been cut or stabbed in a fight. This improvised treatment would keep you out of the hole or from being transferred to another prison.

'Griz' (as in grizzly bear – he could be a real handful if he didn't like you) was another great character, a very large, long-haired Virginian serving 25 years. He had come to FDC from Leavenworth Penitentiary, Kansas. Griz had spent years filing motions and appeals on behalf of the Outlaws motorcycle chapter of which he was a member, most of whom were serving life sentences in Leavenworth. He fought a 9-year legal battle arguing that his 25-year sentence was unconstitutional or illegal. After many appeals and rejections, a court had decided that he might be right and vacated his sentence. Now he was in Miami waiting to be resentenced. Griz was under no illusions; he knew freedom wasn't necessarily just around the corner. He went off for his hearing and we waited to see if he could beat the system.

When he returned to the cell block the following day, he did not look happy. The Probation Service had made an impassioned appeal that at his original trial he should have been sentenced as a 'habitual offender' or 'career criminal'. He had three prior felony convictions, which would have allowed an upward departure. In view of this error, the Probation Service was now asking the court to increase the sentence to 50 years! Griz reappeared to receive sentence and successfully argued that because the error had not been noticed until after the trial, this was a 'sentencing windfall' from which he was entitled to benefit. The new sentence was the same 25 years that he had originally been given. Griz was shipped back to Leavenworth and I wished him well.

Time passed slowly in FDC. The lack of fresh air was really getting to me. The library cart was changed only every couple of weeks and good books were at a premium. Life was a constant round of card games and reading. I would spend an hour a day in the small gym pedalling on the exercise bike, going nowhere. All the televisions transmitted sound on specific frequencies and the only way to hear them was to buy a Walkman radio with headphones. If you had no money, you had to learn to lip-read.

Almost a year went by as motions were filed and rejected. Flores and Smith were nice guys but I began to feel that we weren't going to produce a really spirited defence, no matter how much ammunition we had. I think, in fairness, that they both wanted me to win but that they knew what the system would do to ensure that I didn't.

A date was finally set for my plea appearance; if I pled not guilty, a trial date would be set. At the same time, a plea-bargain offer was made in a letter to my attorneys. It stated that the United States government had reason to believe that I might have information that would be of benefit to them and would like to speak to me. I would receive a 33-month sentence if I did not go to trial. If I would snitch on someone else, this might be reduced. I told my lawyers that I would offer no information to the government and refused to see anyone from any US agencies. After some cajoling, they convinced me that I should not refuse the meeting. Even if I gave no information, the prosecution could not state at sentencing that I had been uncooperative. I showed the letter to the guys I knew on the cell block and told them I was going to be interviewed by the feds. That way, I wasn't going in for a secret meeting, which usually meant someone was cutting a deal at someone else's expense.

The day of my plea arrived and the snitch agents had not yet been to see me. I still did not trust the 33-month offer and decided that I would plead not guilty. Flores and Smith told me that the federal agents would see me after my plea. I told my lawyers to go fuck themselves and walked out on them. Taken up to the court, I faced Alberto Jordan, the judge who would pass sentence on me. There were hurried conversations going on in hushed voices between the prosecution and defence attorneys. I was left standing at the podium, waiting to respond to the formal reading of the charges. The Assistant District Attorney asked permission for counsels to approach the bench. They gathered in a huddle, talking to the judge in lowered voices. When they had finished, the judge announced, in what the media reported as an unprecedented move, that the courtroom was to be cleared of all public and press. Perplexed spectators were ushered out and the judge retired to his chambers. I was introduced formally to the prosecutor, John Schlesinger (who is now a judge), and two federal agents, who apologised for not seeing me before. They told me that they would not renege on the 33-month offer if I accepted the plea bargain today. I had already crunched the numbers and it boiled down to a simple choice: I could accept the deal and serve the 13 months I had left to do; or I could plead not guilty, wait for a trial date, probably lose and cop the maximum 60 months for taking them on. For the first time in my life, I pled guilty.

The Probation Service completed their investigations and several weeks later, on 8 October 2004, I was in court again awaiting sentence. There was one last chance to reduce the sentence. The guidelines stated, with respect to my particular offence, that: 'In the unusual case where the offense conduct posed no such risk [to a security or foreign policy interest of the United States], a downward departure may be warranted.' My defence team made a strong case for a downward departure, pointing out that Escobar was at the top of the US most-wanted list, with a multimillion-dollar bounty on his head. It was strange listening to a professional talking about my exploits; by the time my attorney had finished, even I was convinced I was a cross between Robin Hood and the angel Gabriel.

The other side got their chance to rebut, another professional wading in on my life story. There was not a lot that could be said against me that was relevant. My past track record was inadmissible in law, as none of my offences had been committed in the USA and they were all more than ten years old. The prosecutor conceded that Escobar was a very bad man and that the offence was not against the interests of the US per se. But an American warplane armed with 500-lb bombs flying in Colombian airspace and dropping them on a prison would cause a rather large diplomatic incident. The prosecution summarised: 'Mr Tomkins travels the world like a one-man State Department and is a loose cannon.' I listened to all this and agreed with every word he said.

Then it was the turn of the Probation Service. The name might lead one to believe that they offered an alternative to prison if it was felt warranted. However, this body appeared to have only two objectives: to recommend as much prison time as the law would allow and to confiscate anything of value you might have and recommend the largest possible fine, which in my case was $250,000. The Probation Service could say little about me, although they advised the court that Washington's Interpol bureau had been advised by their counterparts in Bogotá that I was the subject of pending investigations into narcotics offences, explosives offences, terrorism offences and homicide. I knew the Colombian government was probably a bit pissed off about our escapades but I thought this little lot was slightly over the top.

The judge asked for clarification on the 'pending', as they'd had 14 years to bring charges. He ordered a new version of the probation report be written, omitting all pending investigations except the homicide. He also made it clear that there would be no consideration of upward or downward departure in my case. I was sentenced to 33 months in prison with no financial penalty.

Most South Florida prison transfers went via Atlanta, Georgia, where the average stay was six weeks, sometimes with four men to a cell, some sleeping on the floor. I had had enough crap, what with the time I'd spent in the hole, so I asked my attorney to ask the judge if I could be sent to the Federal Correctional Institution in Miami. This was only 30 miles away and in the sun. Whatever it was like, it would beat freezing my nuts off in a New York winter. While there was no guarantee, the judge recommended that I be sent to FCI Miami and wished me luck.

I spent another month in FDC before I received confirmation of my transfer to FCI Miami. I said goodbye to the friends I'd made and would never meet again. There were 18 of us on the bus but, after processing, I was the only one who would remain inside the wire; the others were going to the satellite camp close by. I was taken to cell block D, or Dolphin. The seven blocks, A to G, all had names such as Atlantic and Coral. Block H was, appropriately enough, the hole. FCI Miami was at that time rated medium/high security and some of the inmates had extremely long stretches to do. There were dozens of lifers and others who had been sentenced to 100 years plus. You might think this is not the sort of place you want to be if you've got jail time to do but you would be wrong. Overall, long-term cons are the best people you can do your time with. If you're not a snitch or otherwise looking to get killed quickly, they will take you in as one of them.

My cellmates were two very big black guys named Bud and Boogie. Bud ran the 'store', which was the illegal shop. If you ran out of something before commissary day, you could get it from Bud, as long as you were willing to pay a bit extra. Boogie was a Rastafarian, originally from Haiti. Both were gangbangers from the projects. They were a load of fun to be with, except for Boogie's snoring. At least I would never run out of cigarettes and I didn't have to pay extra, either.

FCI was quite nice to look at, for a prison. It had been built 20 or so years before, originally as a juvenile detention centre. While it had changed over the years, there were still no gun towers and the cell blocks were pastel-coloured with red shingle roofs. A limestone pit had been filled with water to form a small lake. The open areas were referred to as 'the compound' and were all rigged with anti-helicopter wire. The prison had a large recreation yard with a weight-training area. The weights were anchored to the ground by steel cables, allowing only the necessary movement for exercise. The yard had a covered basketball court, a football pitch, a softball diamond, racquetball courts and a running track. There were also courts for playing bocce, a game similar to bowls. After my previous prisons, the place was like a holiday camp.

It wasn't all fun and games, though. While there were no gun towers there were gun cars. Chevrolet pick-up trucks sat at fixed points outside the wire and watched our every move on the yard, while roving cars circled the perimeter. Some days, we could hear the crackle of gunfire coming from the shooting range close by. The prison was ringed by two layers of high chain-link fencing, fitted with fibre-optic vibration sensors and topped with coils of razor wire. Between the fences was more razor wire, three coils deep and three high. If you got over the first fence without getting shot, you would never make it over the next. Approaching the fence was forbidden. Everywhere but the yard, we were subject to 'controlled movement'. If you were leaving or returning to your cell block, you moved on a signal from the loudspeakers. This gave you ten minutes to move from point A to B. If you were still on the compound after that time, you were heading for the hole.

We ate in the 'chow hall', which took 480 at a sitting. Meal roster was determined each week by cell block inspection and the least amount of guys in the hole from your block. The food was OK: lots of rice, as there were many Latino inmates, soul food several times a week for the black guys and a salad bar. Considering where we were, I guess they did well with the $1.25 per day that was allocated to feed each of us.

For the next year, I would spend two hours a day sweeping the compound with a small brush and long-handled dustpan known as a 'Cadillac' with forty-five other guys. Two men could have dealt with the small amount of rubbish. Over the year, I don't think I picked up more than a handful. But everyone had to work, even though there were too few jobs to go round. The monthly salary I received for my efforts was the princely sum of $5.25. Twice a week, I went to the education block to attend typing and computer courses. I spent an hour a day doing weights in the yard and usually managed to fit in some sunbathing. Well, it was Florida, after all. On a working day, a headcount was taken at 4 p.m. and 9 p.m. During some counts, you were allowed to stay where you were, although you might be sitting or lying in your rack (bunk) but one count a day (usually the nine o'clock one) was a standing count. This was to ensure that everyone was actually alive. It had been known in the past for guards to count a man who had been killed by his cellmate.

The hole was always full, as a prison is full of tension, which usually results in fights. The buzzword in prison is 'respect'. If you disrespected someone, you could expect trouble and trouble came in many guises. Something as simple as 'cutting the line', what we would call pushing in to a queue, could be construed as disrespect. Debts must always be paid. The bookmakers were usually Italian American New Yorkers and mob-connected. Weed and booze were available to buy. The alcohol was home-made hooch called 'clear', a rot-gut brew created in innovative stills. We could be breath-tested at any time of the night or day, or woken up at 3 a.m. for a piss test by 'Deputy Dawg', as we called the guard responsible. The pot smokers and drinkers were easy to spot; they were the ones constantly drinking water, trying to flush out their systems after a Friday-night binge. Everyone in there had a hustle. We were frisked at random leaving the chow hall but an amazing assortment of food was stolen every day by kitchen workers and smuggled out by mules. Any serious infringement of the rules, such as a stabbing or gang fight, meant lockdown for everyone. This might last a few days or several weeks.

We may never meet again but I will always remember the characters I met at FCI Miami. Society had taken more than its pound of flesh from some of them, who will never see freedom again. Frank Bachner, my sunbathing pal, now transferred to Edgefield, South Carolina, was doing 100 years plus life without parole for smuggling cannabis. I made friends with Vinny 'Champagne' Sevick, who had evaded capture for more than 20 years and had so many aliases I don't think even he knew his real name. I met a British guy, Malcolm, who should never have been there. Another mate, Zane, had been given a $54,000,000 fine, which they were taking out of his prison salary! Then there was 'Bad Light', 'Tiny', 'Don Cappuccino', 'Drive-By' and many other faces too numerous to mention.

Doing time with us, funnily enough, was the ex-president of Panama, General Manuel Noriega. He was doing 30 years in solitary confinement, classed as a prisoner of war. Noriega's cell was a special unit attached to the medical block, adjacent to the guard captain's office. Every night at ten, Noriega was allowed to walk around the compound for an hour. The rest of us could see him from the smoking areas in each block, which had floor-to-ceiling bars referred to as 'the grille'. This pathetic little figure would shuffle around on his own, while the cons shouted out: 'Fuck George Bush and fuck America!' Noriega would acknowledge them by punching his fist into the air. I couldn't see how Noriega posed any threat; I figured he was kept in solitary confinement because he knew too much to be allowed to talk to anyone.

In October, nature added to the indignity of it all when Hurricane Wilma arrived with a bang. During the previous year's hurricane season, a military-style airlift had moved all FCI inmates to a brand-new prison in North Carolina, not yet officially open. For a few days, everyone had lived on takeaway food from outside. They would have moved us again but the forecast was for a relatively gentle Category 1 storm. When it descended, however, that nasty little bitch was Category 3 and fucked up South Florida big time. The lake flooded and the toilets backed up in the cells. Twenty-one Portaloos were shipped in for fifteen hundred of us and we could only use them at specific times. The power went out and, with no air conditioning, the cells were like sweatboxes. They brought in emergency generators and giant fans to circulate the humid air around the blocks. We lived on sandwiches and bottled water for several days as the rain lashed down and in through the smoking-area grilles, flooding the blocks. The wind sandblasted the paint off the grille bars. When it was finally over, we were taken a block at a time to the rec yard where we were hosed down. The damage was mainly cosmetic, although the ceilings had come down in the chow hall and parts of the education block. What trees and shrubs we had were pretty much shredded and dead birds littered the compound.

During my sentence, many of the long-term prisoners were moved out when the Bureau of Prisons decided to recategorise FCI Miami to a lower security level. Slowly, the faces I knew changed. Ten years was the maximum you could have left of your time to remain behind. I was serving the shortest term of anyone in the joint and was the subject of good-natured banter, as most had more 'good time' (time off for good behaviour) than I had sentence.

The Bureau of Prisons has some very wicked ways to make your life a living hell. One of these was known as 'diesel therapy'. Eventually, this could break even the hardest of men, psychologically and physically. The game is played like this. If you're considered a troublemaker, you can get transferred to another prison. If you're in South Florida, it's a long way to New York, especially by road. You get put in a van, hands and feet shackled, and start your journey north. The first leg of your journey will take you to a prison en route, a day's drive away. It could be a county jail somewhere that has been requested to house you until another van comes to take you onward. At this time, you have no phone privileges; these have not been revoked, as this would be classed as an unfair punishment. But, as you have no phone account at your temporary home, you can't make any calls. You will probably be housed in the hole for the first few days. Maybe you'll then get put into general population, perhaps write to your loved ones with your address. Then, after a week or two, all of a sudden in the early hours, you're on the move again. This process will continue and you will see the inside of more prisons and county jails than you can possibly imagine. You will have no commissary money, because that requires a permanent address to reach you. All contact with you will be lost. You might send letters but the replies won't reach you; they'll be making their way through the system, trying unsuccessfully to catch you up. Your journey will be mentally and physically arduous, and it won't necessarily go on for only a few weeks. A couple of years might pass before you reach your final destination.

A month or so before I was to leave FCI Miami, the unit cop instructed me to report to the guard captain. I pondered on what offence I might have committed to warrant this, as a visit to this office usually meant a trip to the hole. When I arrived, two others were also waiting and they had no idea why they were there, either. We were summoned in and told that a favour was required from all three of us.

'What kind of favour?' we asked suspiciously. He said that we could not be told what it was but that we were not in any kind of trouble and it would not cause us any problems with other inmates if we agreed. We looked at each other as if to say, 'What do you think?' As this was all very unusual, we were curious and said OK. We were told to say nothing to anyone, which would be easy enough, since we knew sod all about it anyway. We had to be outside the door adjacent to the visiting room and education block at 7.30 prompt the next morning.

The three of us met at the agreed time and place. This spot was one of the few that could not be seen from the compound. The door opened and we were led by a circuitous route to the offices of the maintenance workshops, close to the rear service gates. We still had no clue what we were doing or why. We were locked in the offices with one guard and a supply of cinnamon-flavoured coffee and biscuits. After a short while, there was a large explosion from somewhere near the rear gates, which made us jump and remark, 'What the fuck was that?' The cop then told us that we had just escaped!

The sirens and loudspeakers went into overdrive as the prison went to emergency lockdown. We could hear most of the communications on our guard's radio. We were the 'escapees' in a drill but the other cops had not been told that this was an exercise. Once lockdown was complete, the count procedure went into action in all cell blocks. We knew, of course, that the count was never going to be correct, as some of us were drinking coffee elsewhere. Once it was established that the count was wrong in three blocks they went to 'bed book' count. For each block, there was a folder called 'the bed book' that contained a photograph of each inmate in the unit and his bed number. This should have been kept up to date but cops get sloppy, too. Cons change cell or go to the hole and new faces take their places. We listened in amusement as the cops got more and more panicky about the count, not helped by the cons, who weren't particularly helpful towards them at the best of times. Eventually, the missing were identified. The search went on. The cops had to confirm that we had actually got out of the prison and were not hiding somewhere inside. Police cars were cruising around the perimeter, adding authenticity to the affair, as guards searched everywhere. Some thought had gone into the selection of the escapees. One of us was a pilot, one was a major Colombian drug runner and I was the explosives man who would blow our way out. It took three hours before someone eventually thought to look where we were.

In due course, my final day of federal time arrived. On 21 January 2006, I said my goodbyes and my friends and I wished each other luck. I was processed through R&D (reception and discharge) and signed for by Immigration and Customs Enforcement agents, who would be responsible for making sure I was deported. All my clothes had been given away to charity as the Bureau of Prisons had refused either to store them or send them to the UK. I was now dressed in a pair of prison jeans, my trainers and a sweatshirt, with no idea where I was going, as they tell you nothing.

A van took me to Miami International Airport. Any thoughts that I was about to be put on a plane home were swiftly dispelled when I was taken to the immigration offices. I spent that day and part of the next recreating my file. It would appear that it had been lost, along with my passport. Overnight, I slept on a chair in a storage cupboard. Finally, they took me to West Palm Beach county jail. I should have been sent to Krome Avenue Immigration Detention Center but it had been badly damaged in the hurricane. Nothing good can be said about the county jail and I was glad to get moved on after a month. Unfortunately, the next place, Hudson County Corrections Center in New Jersey, was even worse. That dump was the final indignity. It was like a Third World prison. The food was crap and breakfast was at 3.30 a.m.! All the inmates on my block were waiting to be deported; some had been there for years.

When my wife finally located me, through the British Embassy, I got money sent in to buy a phone card. I had no idea how long I would spend there, but Mary had been given a clue by the embassy. I was relieved to hear I'd be getting out soon. On 14 March, I was placed on a United Airlines flight from Newark to Heathrow. On arrival, I was politely questioned by two police officers who welcomed me home and wished me luck. My son Billy met me and took me home. It was finally over.